OXFORD READINGS I

Series Editor G. J.

THE PHILOSOPHY OF SOCIAL EXPLANATION

THE PHILOSOPHY OF SOCIAL EXPLANATION

Edited by

ALAN RYAN

OXFORD UNIVERSITY PRESS

Oxford University Press, Ely House, London W.1

OXFORD LONDON GLASGOW NEW YORK
TORONTO MELBOURNE WELLINGTON CAPE TOWN
IBADAN NAIROBI DAR ES SALAAM LUSAKA ADDIS ABABA
KUALA LUMPUR SINGAPORE JAKARTA HONG KONG TOKYO
DELHI BOMBAY CALCUTTA MADRAS KARACHI

ISBN 0 19 875025 0

First Published 1973
Reprinted 1976

PRINTED IN GREAT BRITAIN BY
J. W. ARROWSMITH LTD., BRISTOL, ENGLAND

CONTENTS

INTRODUCTION

IT IS all but definitive of a philosophical problem that its status should be uncertain, and that there should be considerable doubt about what would in principle count as a solution to it. On this criterion, the philosophy of science in recent years has done much to confirm its philosophical standing with widespread disagreement over the proper aims of the discipline. To put it crudely, the disagreement turns on whether the philosophy of science is a descriptive or a normative discipline. Is its proper task that of reporting on the tactics of discovery and the canons of explanation which scientists do employ, or that of laying down norms of scientific propriety to which they *ought* to conform, whether or not they do? The first step in making this account less crude is, of course, to recognize that no one is to be found occupying the extreme positions. It is as unattractive to claim that science is just the sum of the activities of self-professed 'scientists' as it is to pretend that it would do no damage to an account of scientific activity if no scientist could recognize in it even an approximate picture of his own practice. The history of science plainly contains a great deal of poor science; in retrospect, scientists are often moved to condemn their own performances as 'unscientific'. Yet, it would be difficult to understand as a philosophy of *science* one which did not recognize as scientific achievements at least most of what scientists and laymen accept as such.[1] Perhaps the second necessary step is to recognize that this dilemma characterizes other philosophical disciplines, too. The moral philosopher wishes neither to legitimate every moral position whatever nor to give an account of morality which makes what we ordinarily take to be moral positions simply unrecognizable as such.

The importance of this dilemma for the philosophy of the social sciences is that it is frequently felt that the normative or critical tendencies of the philosophy of science operate with a fierceness which is not apparent in discussions of the natural sciences. Philosophers, it might be said, justify the achievements of, say, physics with a model of scientific rectitude and a theory of explanation which they covertly derived from physics in the first place. But they criticize the achievements of psychology, sociology, or economics, not by reference to standards drawn from those disciplines but, once again, by the standards drawn from physical science. Philosophers

---

[1] I. Lakatos and A. Musgrave (eds.), *Criticism and the Growth of Knowledge* (Cambridge, 1970), *passim*.

who resent the accusation that they have alternated between toadying to the prestigious natural sciences and bullying the less prestigious social sciences have several quite adequate defences, however. In the first place, it is not true that all philosophers have elevated the physical sciences into models of epistemological and logical virtue. There has been a long tradition which has stressed that in some respects we know more about human behaviour already than we shall ever know about the natural world. On this view, the implied comparison between the developed state of the physical sciences and the primitive state of the social sciences rests on an illusion. Secondly, it is an adequate *ad hominem* retort to observe that social scientists themselves have for years tried to model their work on that of the physical scientist. Complaints that the social sciences have generated no triumphs of 'social engineering' to rival the feats of mechanical engineering made possible by physical science are heard as often from social scientists as from politicians or philosophers. Thirdly, it is certainly plausible to argue that present differences in methodology, rigour, and reliability are inessential and temporary differences between the social and physical sciences. Social science is the natural science of social life; and we naturally look to the most successful natural sciences as the standard of what we might achieve and as the guide to how we might achieve it.

It is manifestly inconsistent to rely on all of these defences simultaneously; but they all raise the one issue which has obsessed philosophers of the social sciences: are the social sciences a branch or branches of the natural sciences, and is the kind of knowledge they produce the same as that produced by the natural sciences? These are not clear questions. A short answer, say that both social and natural scientists look for causal explanations of empirically observed phenomena, can as well be dismissed as a miserable play on 'causal' and 'explanation' as accepted as the recognition of a genuine similarity. The frequent claim that an affirmative answer to the question depends on our eventually 'reducing' the social sciences to one or more branches of appropriate physical sciences presents, as we shall see, some difficulties created by the opacity of the concept of reduction involved. Yet, there is surely a common-sense assumption running through much of the literature on this subject that the social sciences simply must be, in principle, part of the complete science of nature. This feeling amounts to the claim that since men and their social dealings are part of the natural order, they must in principle be amenable to explanation in terms of the same sort of naturalistic principles that every aspect of nature conforms to. Historically, this has been the keynote of empiricism, and from Kant onwards it has been met by a variety of Idealist arguments intended to show that we are at any rate not *merely* part of the natural order. These historical origins of the argument go some way towards explaining the shocked tones in which contemporary empiricists confront the denial of the 'naturalness' of human behaviour—as if the denial was either wilfully obscure, or the first step in invoking the supernatural. Nonetheless, the claim that the social sciences are, or can be, part of the corpus of the natural sciences is itself obscure.

The defence of what is sometimes called 'unified science' is often ambiguous as between the claim that there is a unity of scientific method and the claim that ultimately all the disparate sciences ought to be 'reduced' to some single science. The success of Newtonian mechanics and its accompanying, if not wholly congruous, atomism has long been the symbol of the ambition to derive all the sciences from the science of matter in motion. On this analogy, it has been a frequent ambition to reduce sociology to psychology and psychology to physiology, thus paving the way for a complete reduction of the social sciences to the physical sciences. The propriety of this programme has been an extremely bloody battlefield in the philosophy of science. But one gain from the discussion has been the demonstration that since the terms belonging to the science which is to be 'reduced' are of a different logical category from those of the science to which it is proposed to 'reduce' it, the process of reduction cannot be straightforwardly deductive.[2] Rather, it requires what have been called 'bridge-statements', theoretical and therefore empirical linking propositions to the effect that one kind of phenomena—say changes in the colour of a light source—are also, or can properly be understood as, phenomena of a different kind—say changes in the rate of photon emission. The argument over the extent to which reduction can be assimilated to deduction need not concern us here, save to point out that on this reading there is no question of any of the 'reduced' sciences becoming merely branches, or special cases, of the science to which they are reduced. To reduce the social sciences to the natural sciences would therefore be the result of empirical discoveries which expanded the scope of the natural sciences, not of philosophical legislation. Chemistry is not a branch of physics in any straightforward sense, even though chemists take it for granted that there is some kind of physical explanation of chemical phenomena. Similarly, sociology will not become a mere branch of physiology even though it is surely likely that we shall eventually know more about how our social life depends upon the behavioural possibilities of organisms constructed like ourselves.

[2] E. Nagel, *The Structure of Science* (London, 1961), pp. 358–66.

If the claims of reduction are not clear, the claims of the unity of method are a good deal clearer. They are the claim that the logical properties of an adequate explanation are the same throughout science, and the attendant assumption that any methodological requirements valid in the natural sciences will be equally valid in the social sciences. The most famous defence of this claim is, perhaps, Mill's *System of Logic*, but it has been equally vigorously defended by Popper and Hempel in the past few years.[3] Briefly, the claim is that the essence of explanatory virtue lies in deductively relating the *explanandum*—what is to be explained—to its *explanans*—the laws and conditions explaining it. Hence the proper method of science is the constant testing of explanatory principles by matching derived predictions against observed results, whether these results are obtained experimentally or thrown up by nature. Of course, there will be many differences in the characteristic interests of particular sciences, both natural and social; but these neither fall into categories which coincide with the division between the social and the natural sciences nor do they require any substantial modification of this deductive account. Thus, for example, historians are often said to be interested in explaining single cases by *applying* laws, rather than in *finding* or *testing* them—but, it can fairly be said that a good deal of natural history is equally ideographic. Thus, much of the so-called 'theory of evolution' is a matter of applying laws to a single process, a sequence of unique events, and in this way its resemblance to the practice of historians is considerable. (And, on this view, Engels's claim that Marx was the Darwin of the social sciences would not be a surprising one.) The oft-asserted, if not quite accurate, claim that the social sciences are non-experimental sciences would mark at most a practical distinction concerning the ease with which we can obtain evidence, it obviously being simpler to manufacture most chemical reactions than to rerun the Russian Revolution for the sake of testing our understanding of it. Practical difficulties aside, then, what makes any discipline scientific is the seriousness with which it pursues the deductive explanation of its observations and the seriousness with which it tests its principles against its observations. There is no claim that the explanations of social scientists *look* like deductive arguments; but it is claimed that they can in principle be turned into deductive arguments, a move which both elucidates their explanatory force and renders their covering laws amenable to test. The extreme diffidence with which social scientists usually proceed when asked to formulate their explanations in this form

---

[3] e.g. J. S. Mill, *A System of Logic* (London, 1961), VI. i. 2; K. Popper, *The Poverty of Historicism* (London, 1957), sect. 29; C. G. Hempel, 'The Function of General Laws in History', *Journal of Philosophy*, xxxix (1942), 35–48.

stems, on this account, from three possible sources. The first is that the generalizations on which social science relies are usually imprecise, common-sensical, and rule of thumb ones which no one has thought out in the sort of detail which would render them amenable to rigorous testing. So, although the politician and the political scientist alike might agree that politicians who wish to be re-elected would be unwise to raise taxes just before an election, neither of them would want to commit himself to the generalization that, say, 'all voters vote against governments which raise taxes within two months prior to an election.' It takes no great wit to think of dozens of possible exceptions: some voters would vote out of party loyalty regardless, some might vote for the government because such seeming indifference to popularity struck them as admirable and honest, and, more importantly, very few people would resent the taxes if they were obviously required for universally approved purposes. It is not obvious that such open-ended imprecision is only to be found in the social sciences, but it is surely characteristic of explanation in at least many of them. The second reason why the deductiveness of explanations in social science is not apparent is that the backing laws are not drawn from the same subject-matter as the phenomena they explain. Thus it may be that the reason why there are so few generalizations defended by political scientists is that the general laws employed are psychological not political.[4] That is, the generalizations which explain how men behave in political situations are either commonplace or recondite psychological generalizations about the effects of, say, pride, anger, public spiritedness, self-interest, and so on. The political scientist would be interested in using these generalizations to make sense of political events, but he would not, *qua* political scientist, be interested in setting them out explicitly or trying to test them. So long as he supposed they held in the situations that concerned him, he would have no reason to bother with their truth in other situations. And this brings up the third possibility, which is that social scientists are commonly much more concerned about the situations within which they are applying their generalizations than with the generalizations themselves. That is, many of the underlying generalizations are so taken for granted that there is no real question of trying to falsify them. Rather, what we need to know is whether we have read the situation of their application correctly. Thus, when a starving populace fails to revolt against its government, we do not at once wonder whether people enjoy starving and are grateful to those who give them the chance to starve. What we wonder is whether they believe their hunger is the government's

---

[4] W. G. Runciman, *Sociology in Its Place* (Cambridge, 1971), pp. 10ff.

fault, whether they think there is any alternative to the present regime, and so on. In short, if the social scientist *is* producing deductively valid explanations, with some of the covering laws left implicit, he still seems to be much more critically concerned than are most natural scientists with the establishment of the 'initial conditions' element in his explanations. This would even be true of economics, on this reading, for there, too, the generalizations of the economist would be generalizations of applied psychology, vulnerable to any discovery which suggested that the conditions of application had been misrepresented.

Yet this third suggestion about the way in which we might defend the claims of the unity of science at once raises the point on which most of the critics of that case have insisted. In the above example, the 'initial conditions' were described in terms of the beliefs and wishes of the people whose actions we are explaining. This means that the important definition of the situation so far as the validity of the explanation is concerned turns out to be the definition accepted by the people concerned. It is not a matter of *our* believing that governments ought to secure the food supply of their subjects; it is a matter of what those subjects believe. There seems to be no parallel to this in most of the natural sciences—I say 'most' in order not to prejudge the study of animal behaviour where it is hard to believe that the animal's 'definition of the situation' is an irrelevant feature of the explanation of its behaviour. That is, the question is not whether the social scientist, conceived of as a quasi-experimental scientist, has correctly described the causal antecedents of a phenomenon, but whether he has understood how the persons involved would have described their situation. This does not straightforwardly rule out a belief in the unity of scientific method. Popper, for instance, insists on the applicability of the hypothetico-deductive model to historical explanation, while invoking it by way of what he terms 'the logic of the situation'. But it does mean we have to know what the agent thinks the situation is before it can begin to possess a logic for him, and therefore for us.

And discovering this seems both to permit and to demand methods for which there is no place in the natural sciences—animal behaviour here included without qualms. So far as our contemporaries go, we can *ask* them what they know, believe, or want; for our predecessors we can rely on written documents, or make plausible inferences from these. All this seems only possible with human beings, and where it is usable it seems to be the best possible way of finding out what we want to know—allowance being made for deception, the difficulties of translation, and so on. Where we cannot readily get such information, we are forced to rely on whatever contextual evidence we can find, or to put ourselves in the shoes of those whose behaviour we wish to understand. That such empathetic methods seem to be both possible and so generally necessary has frequently been taken as the great dividing line between the natural and the social sciences—or, to use the common German distinction, the *Naturwissenschaften* and the *Geisteswissenschaften*. Since the point of the empathetic recapturing of past situations is to supply us with an account of what those situations meant to those involved in them, it is not surprising that *Verstehen* has universally become the jargon term for that kind of understanding which tries to capture the meaning of actions and situations; nor is it surprising that there is continued controversy over the status of this kind of understanding. Some writers, Collingwood at one stage among them, have written as though *the* task of the historian or social scientist were to re-experience the situation to be explained, to re-enact it in thought.[5] Now this, even if a fair enough report on one kind of historical writing, is nothing like an adequate account of the whole intention of historical or sociological inquiry—nor, in fact, did Collingwood mean to suggest it was. One important point to notice is that at the level of adequately describing the concerns of social science, the extent to which social scientists try to recapture the situation as it appears to the agent, though essential, is often minimal. The entrepreneur of classical economic theory is defined by his intention to maximize profit, and we try to abstract from everything else in the real situation of the entrepreneur just the effects of this intention. We do not care whether he approaches the competitive struggle with the zest of a Rockefeller or the humility of Uriah Heep. But, this is not to deny *all* interest in his subjective appreciation of his situation; unless entrepreneurs see themselves in an appropriate way, none of our economic theory will make much sense of their behaviour. A man who sees himself as obliged to produce a traditional good at a 'just price' will not be easily understood if we try to picture his activities as an attempt to equate marginal cost and marginal revenue.

It is easy enough to picture *Verstehen* as simply a heuristic device, whereby we put ourselves in another man's shoes in order to inspire hypotheses about his behaviour, the scientific side of our activities then being confined to testing those hypotheses. It cannot be said that the original discussion by Weber is a model of lucidity on this point. But two points demand attention. The first is that even if the method of *Verstehen* is no more than a heuristic device, it is perfectly consistent with rigorous empirical checking at the level of what Weber called 'causal adequacy'. We may recreate as best as we can in our own minds the beliefs and values

<hr />

[5] R. G. Collingwood, *The Idea of History* (Oxford, 1943), pp. 282ff.

with which a sixteenth-century Calvinist approached the business of making a living. These beliefs must have certain behavioural consequences in terms of what sort of bargains he would make, whether and how determinedly he would save out of his profits, and so on. Unless we can find men behaving in this way, we must have failed to understand either their beliefs or their situation or some related phenomena. Just as in any other area of inquiry, it is impossible to be dogmatic about *which* of the indefinite number of conditions we have got wrong; the crucial point is that the social scientist is in principle exactly like any other natural scientist in his position. However, the second point is that it is not always the case that *Verstehen* can most plausibly be understood as a heuristic device. At some levels of sociological and anthropological analysis it seems to be an essential element in knowing what is going on. Thus S. F. Nadel, describing the anthropologist's efforts to uncover the social structure of an alien society, argues that he regards behavioural regularities as *evidence* for underlying norms and beliefs which together govern the behaviour of men in that society.[6] Here it seems that it is not a matter of *Verstehen* suggesting hypotheses about empirical regularities, but rather that the regularities are made intelligible by being related to the subjective meanings which agents attach to their behaviour. Professor Hart offers a similar example in *The Concept of Law*; one might observe the behavioural regularities of motorists at a traffic light, even if one knew nothing of traffic regulations, the purpose of traffic lights, and the rest. But it is plausible to argue that we make those regularities better understood by showing how they spring from the way in which motorists conform their behaviour to rules which give them reasons for behaving in one way rather than another.[7] Here the 'internal' aspect of the rules appears to be an essential element in their nature, and one which gives *Verstehen* a role strikingly greater than the heuristic. On any such account, the *Geisteswissenschaften* would certainly show some characteristic differences from the natural sciences both in terms of the content of their explanations and in the way in which they make their subject-matter intelligible to us. None of this, however, means either that we cannot put such explanations into the hypothetico-deductive pattern (though it strongly suggests that the effort is not worthwhile), or that there is no hope of explaining the findings of the social sciences in terms of those of the natural sciences. It ought, presumably, to be one of the ambitions of an adequate human biology to explain such typical human capacities as those for speech and rationality, and these are the basis of those subjective and intentional

---

[6] S. F. Nadel, *The Theory of Social Structure* (London, 1954), p. 25.
[7] H. L. A. Hart, *The Concept of Law* (Oxford, 1961), pp. 86–8.

aspects of social life to which the concept of *Verstehen* draws our attention.[8]

In the debate over the similarities and differences between the social and the natural sciences, a perennial issue has been that of prediction. It is one of the ironies of intellectual history that while it was the urge to emulate the predictive achievements of celestial mechanics which drove nineteenth-century philosophers to promote a social science modelled on the natural sciences, it has been just this urge which Popper has denounced as essentially unscientific.[9] It seems especially ironic, since it is an obvious consequence of the deductive model of explanation that prediction, retrodiction, and explanation are logically the same operation, save for the temporal standpoint of the scientist. Popper's argument is impossible to summarize, and can hardly be put more persuasively by anyone else. In part, it consists in a denial of determinism, for the notion of a 'complete' prediction of the future is ruled out as internally incoherent. Popper also distinguishes between predictions based on causal laws, which are essentially hypothetical and 'unconditional prophecy' based on extrapolating trends without regard to their dependence on particular initial conditions or the backing causal laws which would explain them. Whatever the justice of Popper's complaints against particular historical figures, the distinction between laws and trends is one well worth making in the social sciences. It is obviously true that a good deal of prediction in social matters does just amount to the extrapolation of trends, though it ought also to be said that social scientists at least keep a practised eye open for changes in the conditions and generalizations governing the trends they use. Most social science prediction is extremely tentative and short-range, and shows an exemplary adherence to Popper's warnings. Long-range forecasts necessarily seem vulnerable to two well-known difficulties, that they will either be self-refuting or else that they will be self-confirming. The former situation reflects the fact that the utterance of the prediction amounts to giving people reasons for making sure it does not come true—rather as telling a man he is getting drunk gives him a reason for stopping drinking, so telling a nation it is turning its rivers into cesspools gives governments a reason for improving the nation's sewage systems. The latter situation reflects the fact that the utterance of the prediction amounts to giving people reasons for making it come true—as when the prediction that town-centres will decay and life become impossible except in the suburbs gives everyone a reason to move out into the suburbs. The recent spate of futurology has exemplified just these points; what it

[8] N. Chomsky, *Language and Mind* (New York, 1968), Ch. 1.
[9] Popper, op. cit., sect. 15.

mostly consists of is elaborate warnings about what trends are visible together with some estimate of what we must do to alter them, and at what cost we can do this. Where prediction has been least plausible, it has been the result of its vulnerability to changes both in the conditions which are extrapolated into the future and the generalizations about our wants and knowledge which are taken for granted.

Several of the essays reprinted here either belong to, or touch on, the post-war debate over 'methodological individualism' and its rival 'methodological holism'. This is a debate in which the purely intellectual merits of the opposed positions have been entangled with their supposed political consequences. Holism was one of the intellectual positions which Popper's seminal *The Open Society and Its Enemies* seized on as the roots of twentieth-century totalitarianism. A calmer and more reflective understanding of such thinkers as Hegel has done something to weaken this association; more effective, perhaps, would be an equally careful consideration of how an obviously liberal thinker like Durkheim came to combine an adamant insistence on methodological holism with an equally adamant insistence on the moral value of the individual.[10] Political positions aside, the debate has centred on ambiguities in the concept of 'reduction', a concept whose importance and unclarity were mentioned above. Individualists have tended to insist that there are not both societies and their members, that when we say, for example, 'Britain modernized her economic structure during the late eighteenth century' we are talking about what Britons did. Conversely, holists tend to insist on the fact that what individuals do, they often do because of their place in social wholes. We cannot understand the behaviour of 'an entrepreneur' or 'a soldier', save by understanding the holistic phenomena of markets and armies. It has never been clear how damaging this claim is to the individualist case; Popper, for instance, has always insisted that individualism does not entail 'psychologism', by which he understands the belief that we can infer the dispositions of 'soldiers', 'entrepreneurs', and the other occupants of social roles from underlying psychological princpiles. But such a half-way house has never seemed an attractive resting place. If the 'individuals' we are talking of are only the typical occupants of roles, the explanation of their behaviour is non-psychological only because explanation in individualistic and holistic terms is the same thing. Explaining the behaviour of 'a soldier' is simply the same operation as explaining the function and organization of an army. And it is a painless enough truth that we can often explain the actions of concrete individuals non-psychologically by appealing to the

---

[10] Steven Lukes, *Emile Durkheim* (London, 1973)

roles they occupy; we make sense of what John Smith is up to by discovering that he is a soldier. All the same, it is highly implausible to suppose that we invoke no psychological assumptions when we explain how individuals or groups of individuals fulfil the requirements of the roles they occupy. It is easy enough—though pretty pointless—to think up ways in which perceptual, emotional, and cognitive capacities might constrain the possible forms of social life. But the discovery of such constraints in a serious form would still be the discovery of a contingent relationship, and would not amount to a logical reduction of social science into psychological science. But it does certainly seem that, so far from Durkheim having been right to claim that the autonomy of sociology entailed that psychological explanations of social phenomena were invariably fallacious, sociology must rely on psychological assumptions continuously. Durkheim's own practice certainly suggests as much.

The debate between holists and individualists has been bound up—as it very obviously is in the essays by Dore and Homans here—with the long running debate over the merits and demerits of functionalist explanations in sociology and anthropology. Ever since Plato, social theorists have been tempted to see societies as organisms writ large, and to ascribe to institutions, habits, and attitudes a role in maintaining a healthy social organism in much the same way that we ascribe to the activities of bodily organs a health-maintaining role. The weaknesses and limitations of the analogy have been apparent almost as long. In so far as functional explanations are a form of explanation by final causes, they fall under the general suspicion of teleological explanation which has characterized the philosophy of science for some three hundred years. So powerful is this suspicion that many functionalists have defended functionalism in terms which amount to an abdication—by claiming that all functionalism involves is the belief that there are connections between social phenomena. [11] But there have been bolder claims. The recent development of cybernetics and systems engineering has suggested ways in which teleological explanation may be made respectable. The overall behaviour of a self-regulating device exhibits teleologically explicable regularities, while the internal engineering of the system requires no more than the usual mechanical causal explanation. Simple self-regulating systems, such as central-heating systems with appropriate feedbacks between thermostats and pumps offer a model for the way in which a biologist, say, may properly employ functional terminology in characterizing various bodily homeostatic mechanisms, without in the least infringing on the assumption that step by step

[11] e.g. M. Levy, *International Encyclopedia of the Social Sciences* (London, 1968), vi. 22.

causal explanations can be given of the chemical and electrical processes involved. The question of how like any other self-regulating system a society is, seems practically unanswerable. There are, of course, innumerable examples of explicit regulation of social life, where we deliberately lay down rules whose point is to secure the performance of actions which we want performed for whatever reason. But the thrust of functionalism is towards explaining how actions not controlled in this deliberate fashion nonetheless contribute towards some socially useful goal. Thus, those unpublic-spirited characters, the old-fashioned political bosses, contributed to the integration of the immigrant into American society, without intending to do anything of the sort.[12] However, in this case there does not seem much temptation to explain the behaviour of bosses by reference to the beneficent effects they produce. The obvious answer to the question why Boss Tweed saw that the poor got coal at Christmas is that he wanted their votes. This indicates that where we are prepared to invoke final causes as explanations we want to be sure that the goal is not an *accidental* by-product of the behaviour we are explaining; it is, of course, feedback mechanisms which give us that assurance in the case of both organisms and self-regulating devices of the familiar kind. And it is their absence that makes such examples as the alleged 'latent functions' of bossism implausible.

But functionalism has recently been criticized more for its alleged ideological shortcomings than for its intellectual weaknesses. It is often claimed that functionalists have passed off conservative political views as if they were science. Thus, writing about the political functions of apathy may be condemned as an underhand way of justifying our continuing to make it more difficult for the poor or the ignorant to vote in proportion to their numbers by suggesting both that the social system generates such devices as lower-class abstention and that this is a good thing. It is true that many structural-functionalists have been conservative—*vis-à-vis* the American social and political order at least. But this is clearly an accidental connection. A radical might agree with the view that working-class apathy preserved the status quo, and then go on either to condemn both the status quo and apathy alike, or to claim that too much of the burden of maintaining the status quo was thereby placed on the working class whose apathy cost it its fair share of the benefits available from political activity. Since the 'function' of a form of behaviour in these contexts tends only to mean 'good consequences', it is open to anyone to ask 'good for whom?' as a first step, and to look for corresponding

---

[12] R. K. Merton, *Social Theory and Social Structure* (London, 1968), pp. 72ff.

bad consequences on his own behalf. The most that can be said for the connection between conservative political attitudes and functionalism is that it may be an inducement to conservatism to expect to find everywhere some sort of useful purpose served by every social phenomenon. It suggests a belief in the natural benignness of social processes which is unlikely to accompany a desire to remould them on a large scale.

Of course, social theory inevitably runs the risk of becoming special pleading for particular social and political arrangements. The indefinitely many ways in which social theory can and cannot be 'value-free' have preoccupied writers since Weber. It ought, however, to be noticed that not all writers have thought the value-laden nature of social theory was anything very alarming. Durkheim, for instance, appears to take it for granted that sociology is, like medicine, a science of the health and sickness of organisms. It is indeed hard to see how social theory could long remain value-irrelevant in at least two ways. The first is that it is inevitable that its 'problems' will often coincide with what people at large would agree to be social problems. The causation of economic depressions, crime, political violence—these are recognizably problems of social organization which are the starting-point for a great deal of social theory. Not that the interests of social theorists are always, or even often, those of policemen, politicians, and judges; social scientists, like all scientists, often become addicted to the technical puzzles involved in working out a given theory.[13] But it is implausible to suppose that this could for long dictate the choice of subject-matter about which to theorize. The second way in which value reference is necessarily secured is that— as Taylor argues below—much social and political science is concerned with how people do or do not satisfy their wants, and *this* is the raw material of moral and political argument. Moral and political argument necessarily rests on empirical assumptions about such matters, and the discovery of systematic empirical connections must impinge on this argument. None of this, however, is damaging to any claims for objectivity which social scientists may make, although it is possible that moral preconceptions may blind us to evidence, and it is also possible that disputes over the usefulness of particular forms of social theory may be indefinitely prolonged because they involve not only the assessment of evidence relevant to their support and falsification but also assessment of how important, in moral terms, the phenomena are. There are more general doubts about the extent to which incompatible theories can or cannot be

---

[13] D. Easton, 'The New Revolution in Political Science', *American Political Science Review*, lxiii (1969), 1051–61.

brought to decisive test, but such doubts are not peculiarly relevant to social theory in the way the traditional problem of value-freedom is.

The essays collected here cover in detail almost all the problems so lightly touched on above. Almost all of them have been reprinted before in the larger anthologies referred to in the bibliography. It ought to be said that many of the essays represent only one voice in a dialogue, and that they only become fully intelligible when the whole argument is heard. In particular, Professor Winch's *The Idea of a Social Science* and Professor Popper's *The Poverty of Historicism* as well as his *Open Society* are as much part of what is reprinted here as they well could be in their absence. A limited familiarity with some recent work in the social sciences is presupposed by several of the essays; Professor Nagel's essay ought to be read in conjunction with those of Professors Friedman and Koopmans to which he refers, while Mr. Taylor's essay and Professor Dore's make better sense to the reader who has read some recent work in comparative politics, for example. Such familiarity is hardly to stray far from philosophy, in view of the extreme concern with conceptual and logical problems which has dominated recent work in the social sciences. Indeed, the majority of the essays below originated in social science journals.

I

THE IDEA OF A SOCIAL SCIENCE

ALASDAIR MACINTYRE

MY AIM in this essay is to express dissent from the position taken in Mr. Peter Winch's book[1] whose title is also the title of this essay. Winch's book has been the subject of a good deal of misunderstanding, and he has been accused on the one hand of reviving familiar and long-refuted views[2] and on the other of holding views so eccentric in relation to social science as it actually is that they could not possibly have any practical effect on the conduct of that science.[3] In fact, however, Winch articulates a position which is at least partly implicit in a good deal of work already done, notably in anthropology, and he does so in an entirely original way. He writes in a genre recognizable to both sociologists and philosophers. Talcott Parsons and Alain Touraine have both found it necessary to preface their sociological work by discussions of norms and actions and have arrived at rather different conclusions from those of Winch; the importance of his work is therefore undeniable.

1

Wittgenstein says somewhere that when one gets into philosophical difficulties over the use of some of the concepts of our language, we are like savages confronted with something from an alien culture. I am simply indicating a corollary of this: that sociologists who misinterpret an alien culture are like philosophers getting into difficulty over the use of their own concepts.

This passage (p. 114) epitomizes a central part of Winch's thesis with its splendid successive characterizations of the figure baffled by an alien culture; a savage at one moment, he has become a sociologist at the next. And this is surely no slip of the pen. According to Winch, the successful sociologist has simply learned all that the ideal native informant could tell

From *Against the Self-Images of the Age* (London: Duckworth; New York: Schocken Books, 1971), pp. 211–29. First published in *Proceedings of the Aristotelian Society* Supplementary Volume xli (1967), 95–114. © 1967 The Aristotelian Society. Reprinted by courtesy of the Editor of the Aristotelian Society.

[1] *The Idea of a Social Science* (London: Routledge and Kegan Paul, 1958).

[2] See e.g. Richard Rudner, *The Philosophy of Social Science* (Englewood, N.J.: Prentice Hall, 1967), pp. 81–3.

[3] See A. R. Louch's review in *Inquiry*, vi (1963), 273.

him; sociological knowledge is the kind of knowledge possessed in implicit and partial form by the members of a society rendered explicit and complete (p. 88). It is not at first entirely clear just how far Winch is at odds in this contention with, for example, Malinowski, who insisted that the native Trobriander's account of Trobriand society must be inadequate, that the sociologists' account of institutions is a construction not available to the untutored awareness of the native informant.[4] For Winch of course is willing to allow into the sociologist's account concepts 'which are not taken from the forms of activity which he is investigating; but which are taken rather from the context of his own investigation', although he adds that 'these technical concepts will imply a prior understanding of those other concepts which belong to the activities under investigation.' Perhaps this might seem sufficient to remove the apparent disagreement of Winch and Malinowski, until we remember the conclusion of Malinowski's critique of the native informant's view. The sociologist who relies upon that view, he says,

obtains at best that lifeless body of laws, regulations, morals, and conventionalities which *ought* to be obeyed, but in reality are often only evaded. For in actual life rules are never entirely conformed to, and it remains, as the most difficult but indispensable part of the ethnographer's work, to ascertain the extent and mechanism of the deviations.[5]

This makes two points clear.

First, Malinowski makes a distinction between the rules acknowledged in a given society and the actual behaviour of individuals in that society, whereas Winch proclaims the proper object of sociological study to be that behaviour precisely as rule-governed. The second is that in the study of behaviour Malinowski is willing to use notions such as that of mechanism which are clearly causal; whereas Winch warns us against comparing sociological understanding with understanding in terms of 'statistics and causal laws' and says of the notion of function, so important to Malinowski, that it 'is a quasi-causal notion, which it is perilous to apply to social institutions' (p. 116).

It does appear, therefore, that, although Winch and Malinowski agree in seeing the ideal native informant's account of his own social life as incomplete by comparison with the ideal sociologist's account, they do disagree about the nature of that incompleteness and about how it is to be remedied. My purpose in this essay will be to defend Malinowski's point

---

[4] Bronislaw Malinowski, *The Sexual Life of Savages in North-Western Melanesia* (New York: Harcourt, Brace & Jovanovich; London: Routledge & Kegan Paul, 1932), pp. 425–9.

[5] Ibid., pp. 428–9.

of view on these matters against Winch's, but this purpose can only be understood if one reservation is immediately added. It is that in defending Malinowski's views on these points I must not be taken to be endorsing Malinowski's general theoretical position. I have in fact quoted Malinowski on these matters, but I might have quoted many other social scientists. For on these matters Malinowski speaks with the consensus.

2

A regularity or uniformity is the constant recurrence of the same kind of event on the same kind of occasion; hence statements of uniformities presuppose judgements of identity. But . . . criteria of identity are necessarily relative to some rule: with the corollary that two events which count as qualitatively similar from the point of view of one rule would count as different from the point of view of another. So to investigate the type of regularity studied in a given inquiry is to examine the nature of the rule according to which judgments of identity are made in that inquiry. Such judgments are intelligible only relatively to a given mode of human behavior, governed by its own rules (pp. 83–4).

This passage is the starting-point for Winch's argument that J. S. Mill was mistaken in supposing that to understand a social institution is to formulate empirical generalizations about regularities in human behaviour, generalizations which are causal and explanatory in precisely the same sense that generalizations in the natural sciences are. For the natural scientist makes the relevant judgements of identity according to *his* rules (that is, the rules incorporated in the practice of his science); whereas the social scientist must make his judgements of identity in accordance with the rules governing the behaviour of those whom he studies. *Their* rules, not *his*, define the object of his study.

So it is quite mistaken in principle to compare the activity of a student of a form of social behavior with that of, say, an engineer studying the working of a machine. If we are going to compare the social student to an engineer, we shall do better to compare him to an apprentice engineer who is studying what engineering—that is, the activity of engineering—is all about (p. 88).

What the type of understanding which Winch is commending consists in is made clearer in two other passages. He says that, although prediction is possible in the social sciences, it 'is quite different from predictions in the natural sciences, where a falsified prediction always implies some sort of mistake on the part of the predictor: false or inadequate data, faulty calculation, or defective theory' (pp. 91–2). This is because 'since understanding something involves understanding its contradictory, someone who, with understanding, performs X must be capable of envisaging the possibility of doing not-X" (p. 91). Where someone is following a rule, we cannot predict how he will interpret what is involved in following that rule in radically new circumstances; where decisions have to be made, the outcome 'cannot be *definitely* predicted', for otherwise 'we should not call them decisions.'

These points about prediction, if correct, reinforce Winch's argument about the difference between the natural sciences and the social sciences. For they amount to a denial of that symmetry between explanation and prediction which holds in the natural sciences. (It has been argued often enough that this symmetry does not hold in the natural sciences; Professor Adolf Grünbaum's arguments in Chapter 9 of the *Philosophy of Space and Time* seem a more than adequate rebuttal of these positions). But when we consider what Winch says here about decision, it is useful to take into account at the same time what he says about motives and reasons. Winch treats these as similar in this respect: that they are made intelligible by reference to the rules governing the form of social life in which the agent participates. So Winch points out that 'one can act "from considerations" only where there are accepted standards of what is appropriate to appeal to' (p. 82) and argues against Ryle that the 'law-like proposition' in terms of which someone's reasons must be understood concerns not the agent's disposition 'but the accepted standards of reasonable behavior current in his society' (p. 81).

From all this one can set out Winch's view of understanding and explanations in the social sciences in terms of a two-stage model. An action is *first* made intelligible as the outcome of motives, reasons, and decisions; and is then made *further* intelligible by those motives, reasons, and decisions being set in the context of the rules of a given form of social life. These rules logically determine the range of reasons and motives open to a given set of agents and hence also the range of decisions open to them. Thus Winch's contrast between explanation in terms of causal generalizations and explanations in terms of rules turns out to rest upon a version of the contrast between explanations in terms of causes and explanations in terms of reasons. This latter contrast must therefore be explored, and the most useful way of doing this will be to understand better what it is to act for a reason.

Many analyses of what it is to act for a reason have written into them an incompatibility between acting for a reason and behaving from a cause, just because they begin from the apparently simple and uncomplicated case where the action is actually performed, where the agent had one and only one reason for performing it, and where no doubt could arise for the agent as to why he had done what he had done. By concentrating attention upon this type of example, a basis is laid for making central to the analyses a contrast between the agent's knowledge of his own reasons for acting and his and others' knowledge of causes of his behaviour. For clearly in such a case the agent's claim that he did X for reason Y does not seem to stand in need of any warrant from a generalization founded upon observation; while equally clearly any claim that one particular event or state of affairs was the cause of another does stand in need of such a warrant. But this may be misleading. Consider two somewhat more complex cases that that outlined above. The first is that of a man who has several quite different reasons for performing a given action. He performs the action; how can he as agent know whether it was the conjoining of all the different reasons that was sufficient for him to perform the action or whether just one of the reasons was by itself alone sufficient or whether the action was overdetermined in the sense that there were two or more reasons, each of which would by itself alone have been sufficient? The problem arises partly because to know that one or other of these possibilities was indeed the case entails knowing the truth of certain unfulfilled conditionals.

A second case worth considering is that of two agents, each with the same reasons for performing a given action; one does not in fact perform it, the other does. Neither agent had what seemed to him a good reason or indeed had any reason for not performing the action in question. Here we can ask what made these reasons or some subset of them productive of action in the one case, but not in the other. In both these types of case we need to distinguish between the agent's having a reason for performing an action (not just in the sense of there being a reason for him to perform the action, but in the stronger sense of his being aware that he has such a reason) and the agent's being actually moved to action by his having such a reason. The importance of this point can be brought out by reconsidering a very familiar example, that of post-hypnotic suggestion.

Under the influence of post-hypnotic suggestion a subject will not only perform the action required by the hypnotist, but will offer apparently good reasons for performing it, while quite unaware of the true cause of the performance. So someone enjoined to walk out of the room might, on being asked why he was doing this, reply with all sincerity that he had felt in need of fresh air or decided to catch a train. In this type of case we would certainly not accept the agent's testimony as to the connection between reason and action, unless we are convinced of the untruth of the counter-factual. 'He would have walked out of the room, if no reason for doing so had occurred to him' and the truth of the counter-factual, 'he would not have walked out of the room, if he had not possessed some such reason for so doing.' The question of the truth or otherwise of the first of these is a matter of the experimentally established facts about post-hypnotic suggestion, and these facts are certainly expressed as causal generalizations. To establish the truth of the relevant generalization would entail establishing the untruth of the second counter-factual. But since to establish the truth of such causal generalizations entails consequences concerning the truth or untruth of generalizations about reasons, the question inevitably arises as to whether *the possession of a given reason* may not be the cause of an action in precisely the same sense in which hypnotic suggestion may be the cause of an action. The chief objection to this view has been that the relation of reason to action is internal and conceptual, not external and contingent, and cannot therefore be a causal relationship; but although nothing could count as a reason unless it stood in an internal relationship to an action, *the agent's possessing a reason* may be a state of affairs identifiable independently of the event which is *the agent's performance of the action*. Thus it does seem as if the possession of a reason by an agent is an item of a suitable type to figure as a cause, or an effect. But if this is so then to ask whether it was the agent's reason that roused him to act is to ask a causal question, the true answer to which depends upon what causal generalizations we have been able to establish. This puts in a different light the question of the agent's authority as to what roused him to act; for it follows from what has been said that this authority is at best prima facie. Far more of course needs to be said on this and related topics; but perhaps the argument so far entitles us to treat with scepticism Winch's claim that understanding in terms of rule-following and causal explanations have mutually exclusive subject-matters.

This has obvious implications for social science, and I wish to suggest some of these in order to provide direction for the rest of my argument. Clearly if the citing of reasons by an agent, with the concomitant appeal to rules, is not necessarily the citing of those reasons which are causally effective, a distinction may be made between those rules which agents in a given society sincerely profess to follow and to which their actions may in fact conform, but which do not in fact direct their actions, and those rules which, whether they profess to follow them or not, do in fact guide their acts by providing them with reasons and motives for acting in one way rather than another. The making of this distinction is essential to the notions of *ideology* and of *false consciousness*, notions which are extremely important to some non-Marxist as well as to Marxist social scientists.

But to allow that these notions could have application is to find oneself at odds with Winch's argument at yet another point. For it seems quite clear that the concept of ideology can find application in a society where the concept is not available to the members of the society, and furthermore that the application of this concept implies that criteria beyond those available in the society may be invoked to judge its rationality; and as such it would fall under Winch's ban as a concept unsuitable for social science. Hence there is a connection between Winch's view that social science is not appropriately concerned with causal generalizations and his view that only the concepts possessed by the members of a given society (or concepts logically tied to those concepts in some way) are to be used in the study of that society. Furthermore, it is important to note that Winch's views on those matters necessarily make his account of rules and their place in social behaviour defective.

3

The examples which Winch gives of rule-following behaviour are very multifarious: games, political thinking, musical composition, the monastic way of life, an anarchist's way of life, are all cited. His only example of non-rule-governed behaviour is 'the pointless behavior of a berserk lunatic' (p. 53), and he asserts roundly 'that all behavior which is meaningful (therefore all specifically human behavior) is *ipso facto* rule-governed'. Winch allows for different kinds of rules (p. 52); what he does not consider is whether the concept of a rule is perhaps being used so widely that quite different senses of *rule-governed* are being confused, let alone whether his account of meaningful behaviour can be plausibly applied to some actions at all.

If I go for a walk, or smoke a cigarette, are my actions rule-governed in the sense in which my actions in playing chess are rule-governed? Winch says that 'the test of whether a man's actions are the application of a rule is . . . whether it makes sense to distinguish between a right and a wrong way of doing things in connection with what he does.' What is the wrong way of going for a walk? And, if there is no wrong way, is my action in any sense rule-governed? To ask these questions is to begin to bring out the difference between those activities which form part of a coherent mode of behaviour and those which do not. It is to begin to see that although many actions must be rule-governed in the sense that the concept of some particular kinds of action may involve reference to a rule, the concept of an action as such does not involve such a reference. But even if we restrict our attention to activities which form part of some coherent larger whole, it is clear that rules may govern activity in quite different ways. This is easily seen if we consider the variety of uses to which social scientists have put the concept of a role and role concepts.

Role concepts are at first sight peculiarly well fitted to find a place in the type of analysis of which Winch would approve. S. F. Nadel wrote that 'the role concept is not an invention of anthropologists or sociologists but is employed by the very people they study', and added that 'it is the existence of names describing classes of people which make us think of roles.' It would therefore be significant for Winch's thesis if it were the case that role concepts had to be understood in relation to causes, if they were to discharge their analytic and explanatory function.

Consider first a use of the notion of role where causal questions do not arise. In a society such as ours there are a variety of roles which an individual may assume or not as he wills. Some occupational roles provide examples. To live out such a role is to make one's behaviour conform to certain norms. To speak of one's behaviour being governed by the norms is to use a sense of 'governed' close to that according to which the behaviour of a chess player is governed by the rules of chess. We are not disposed to say that the rules of chess or the norms which define the role of a head-waiter constrain the individual who conforms to them. The observation of the rules constitutes the behaviour and what it is; it is not a causal agency.

Contrast with this type of example the inquiry carried on by Erving Goffmann in his book *Asylums*. One of Goffman's concerns was to pose a question about mental patients: how far are the characteristic patterns of behaviour which they exhibit determined, not by the nature of the mental disorders from which they suffer, but by the nature of the institutions to which they have been consigned? Goffmann concludes that the behaviour of patients is determined to a considerable degree by institutional arrangements which provide a severely limited set of possible roles both for patients and for the doctors and orderlies with whom they have to deal. Thus the behaviour of individual patients of a given type might be explained as the effect of the role arrangements open to a person of his type. In case it is thought that the role structure of mental hospitals only has a causal effect upon the patients because they are *patients* (and the implication might be that they are not therefore rational agents but approach the condition of the exception Winch allows for, that of the berserk lunatic) it is worth nothing that Goffman's study of mental hospitals is part of a study of what he calls 'total institutions'. These include monasteries and armed services as well as mental hospitals. A successful terminus to his inquiry would therefore be the foundation of generalizations about the effects upon agents of different types of character of the role structure of such different types of institution.

If Winch were correct, and rule-governed behaviour were not to be understood as causal behaviour, then the contrast could not be drawn between those cases in which the relation of social structure to individuals may be correctly characterized in terms of control or constraint and those in which it may not. Winch's inability to make this contrast adequately in terms of his conceptual scheme is the counterpart to Durkheim's inability to make it adequately in terms of his; and the resemblance of Winch's failure to Durkheim's is illuminating in that Winch's position is, roughly speaking, that of Durkheim turned upside-down. Durkheim in a passage cited by Winch insisted, first, 'that social life should be explained, not by the notions of those who participate in it, but by more profound causes which are unperceived by consciousness' and, secondly, 'that these causes are to be sought mainly in the manner according to which the associated individuals are grouped'.[6] That is, Durkheim supposes, just as Winch does, that an investigation of social reality which uses the concepts available to the members of the society being studied, and an investigation of social reality which utilizes concepts not so available and invokes causal explanations of which the agents themselves are not aware, are mutually exclusive alternatives. But Durkheim supposes, as Winch does not, that the latter alternative is the one to be preferred. Yet his acceptance of the same dichotomy involves him in the same inability to understanp the different ways in which social structure may be related to individual action.

Durkheim's concept of *anomie* is the concept of a state in which the constraints and controls exercised by social structure have been loosened and the bonds which delimit and contain individual desire have therefore been at least partially removed. The picture embodied in the Durkheimian concept is thus one according to which the essential function of norms in social life is to restrain and inhibit psychological drives. For Durkheim, rules are an external imposition upon a human nature which can be defined independently of them; for Winch, they are the guidelines of behaviour which, did it not conform to them, could scarcely be human. What is equally odd in both is the way in which rules or norms are characterized as though they were all of a kind. Durkheim is unable to recognize social structure apart from the notions of constraint and control by the structure; Winch's concept of society has no room for these notions.

Just as Winch does not allow for the variety of relationships in which an agent may stand to a rule to which his behaviour conforms, so he does not allow also for the variety of types of deviance from rules which behaviour may exhibit. I quoted Malinowski earlier on the important gap between the rules professed in a society and the behaviour actually exhibited. On this Winch might well comment that his concern is with human behaviour as rule-following, not only with mere professions of

---

[6] Review of A. Labriola's *Essays on Historical Materialism*, Paris: Giard et Brière, n.d., in *Revue Philosophique*, xliv (1897), 645–51.

rule-following, except in so far as professing to follow rules is itself a human and (for him) *ipso facto* a rule-following activity. Moreover he explicitly allows that 'since understanding something involves understanding its contradictory, someone who, with understanding, performs X must be capable of envisaging the possibility of doing not-X.' He makes this remark in the context of his discussion of predictability; and what he does not allow for in this discussion is that in fact the behaviour of agents may exhibit regularities of a Humean kind and be predictable just as natural events are predictable, even though it can also be characterized and in some cases must also be characterized in terms of following and deviating from certain rules. That this is so makes it possible to speak not only, as Malinowski does in the passage quoted earlier, of mechanisms of deviation, but also of mechanisms of conformity. Of course those who deviate from the accepted rules may have a variety of reasons for so doing, and in so far as they share the same reasons their behaviour will exhibit rule-following regularities. But it may well be that agents have a variety of reasons for their deviance and yet deviate uniformly in certain circumstances, this uniformity being independent of their reasons. Whether in a particular case this is so or not seems to me to be an empirical question and one which it would be well not to attempt to settle *a priori*.

I can put my general point as follows. We can in a given society discover a variety of systematic regularities. There are the systems of rules which agents professedly follow; there are the systems of rules which they actually follow; there are causal regularities exhibited in the correlation of statuses and forms of behaviour, and of one form of behaviour and another, which are not rule-governed at all; there are regularities which are in themselves neither causal nor rule-governed, although dependent for their existence perhaps on regularities of both types, such as the cyclical patterns of development exhibited in some societies; and there are the interrelationships which exist between all these. Winch concentrates on some of these at the expense of the others. In doing so he is perhaps influenced by a peculiarly British tradition in social anthropology and by a focus of attention in recent philosophy.

The anthropological tradition is that centred on the work of Professor E. E. Evans-Pritchard, work which exemplifies the rewards to be gained from understanding a people first of all in their own terms. Winch rightly treats Evans-Pritchard's writing as a paradigm case of a social scientist knowing his own business,[7] but neglects the existence of alternative paradigms. Edmund Leach, for example, in his *Pul Eliya, a Village in*

[7] In 'Understanding a Primitive Society', *American Philosophical Quarterly*, Vol. i, No. 4 (1964), 307–24.

Ceylon has remarked how ecological factors do not in fact genuinely figure in the explanatory framework of Evans-Pritchard's *The Nuer*. Now it is clear that such factors may affect the form of social life either in ways of which the agents are conscious (by posing problems to which they have to formulate solutions) or in ways of which they are unaware. This elementary distinction is perhaps not given its full weight in a recent discussion by Walter Goldschmidt[8] in which the very problems discussed by Winch are faced from the standpoint of an anthropologist especially concerned with ecological factors. Goldschmidt offers the example of the high correlation between agnatic segmentary kinship systems and nomadic pastoralism as a form of economy. He argues that nomadic pastoralism, to be a viable form of economy, has to satisfy requirements which are met most usually by segmentary lineages, but 'age-sets can perform some of the same functions—especially those associated with the military—with equal effectiveness . . . .' Goldschmidt's claim is at least superficially ambiguous. He might be read (at least by a critic determined to be captious) as asserting that first there are economic forms, these pose problems of which the agents become aware, and segmentary or age-set patterns are constructed as solutions by the agents. Or he might be read (more profitably, I imagine) as moving toward a theory in which social patterns (including kinship patterns) represent adaptations (of which the agents themselves are not aware) to the environment and to the level of technology prevailing. It would then in principle be possible to formulate causal laws governing such adaptations, and work like Leach's on Pul Eliya or Goldschmidt's on East Africa could be placed in a more general explanatory framework. This type of project is at the opposite extreme from Evans-Pritchard's concern with conceptual particularity.

Secondly, in Winch's account the social sciences characterize what they characterize by using action descriptions. In his stress upon these, Winch follows much recent philosophical writing. It is on what people *do* and not what they *are* or *suffer* that he dwells. But social scientists are concerned with the causes and effects of *being unemployed, having kin relations of a particular kind, rates of population change*, and a myriad of conditions of individuals and societies, the descriptions of which have a logical character other than that of action descriptions. None of this appears in Winch's account.

4

The positive value of Winch's book is partly as a corrective to the Durkheimian position which he rightly castigates. But it is more than a

[8] *Comparative Functionalism* (Berkeley: University of California Press, 1966), pp. 122–4.

corrective because what Winch characterizes as the whole task of the social sciences is in fact their true starting-point. Unless we begin by a characterization of a society in its own terms, we shall be unable to identify the matter that requires explanation. Attention to intentions, motives, and reasons must precede attention to causes; description in terms of the agent's concepts and beliefs must precede description in terms of our concepts and beliefs. The force of this contention can be brought out by considering and expanding what Winch says about Durkheim's *Suicide* (p. 110). Winch invites us to notice the connection between Durkheim's conclusion that the true explanation of suicide is in terms of factors outside the consciousness of the agents themselves such that the reasons of the agents themselves are effectively irrelevant and his initial decision to give the term 'suicide' a meaning quite other than that which it had for those agents. What is he inviting us to notice?

A number of points, I suspect, of which one is a central insight, the others in error. The insight is that Durkheim's particular procedure of giving to 'suicide' a meaning of his own *entails* the irrelevance of the agent's reasons in the explanation of suicide. Durkheim does in fact bring forward independent arguments designed to show that reasons are either irrelevant or inaccessible, and very bad arguments they are. But even if he had not believed himself to have grounds drawn from these arguments, he would have been unable to take reasons into account, given his decision about meaning. Durkheim arbitrarily equates the concept of *suicide* with that of *doing anything that the agent knows will bring about his own death* and thus classifies as suicide both the intended self-destruction of the Prussian or English officer who shoots himself to save the regiment the disgrace of a court martial and the death in battle of such an officer who has courageously headed a charge in such a way that he knows that he will not survive. (I choose these two examples because they both belong to the same category in Durkheim's classification.) Thus he ignores the distinction between *doing X intending that Y shall result* and *doing X knowing that Y will result*. Now clearly if these two are to be assimilated, the roles of deliberation and the relevance of the agent's reasons will disappear from view. For clearly in the former case the character of Y must be central to the reasons the agent has for doing X, but in the latter case the agent may well be doing X either in spite of the character of Y, or not caring one way or the other about the character of Y, or again finding the character of Y desirable, but not desirable enough for him for it to constitute a reason or a motive for doing X. Thus the nature of the reasons *must* differ in the two cases, and if the two cases are to have the same explanation the agent's reasons can scarcely figure in that explanation. That is, Durkheim is forced by his initial semantic decision to the conclusion that the agent's reasons are in cases of what agents in the society which he studies would have called suicide (which are included as a subclass of what he calls suicide) *never* causally effective.

But there are two further conclusions which might be thought to, but do not in fact, follow. It does not follow that all such decisions to bring actions under descriptions other than those used by the agents themselves are bound to lead to the same *a priori* obliteration of the explanatory role of reasons; for this obliteration was in Durkheim's case, as I have just shown, a consequence of certain special features of his treatment of the concept of suicide, and not a consequence of any general feature of the procedure of inventing new descriptive terms in social sciences. Secondly, from the fact that explanation in terms of reason ought not to be excluded by any initial decision of the social scientist, it does not follow that such explanation is incompatible with causal explanation. Here my argument in the second section of this essay bears on what Winch says about Weber. Winch says that Weber was confused because he did not realize that 'a context of humanly followed rules . . . cannot be combined with a context of causal laws' without creating logical difficulties, and he is referring specifically to Weber's contention that the manipulation of machinery and the manipulation of his employees by a manufacturer may be understood in the same way, so far as the logic of the explanation is concerned. So Weber wrote, 'that in the one case "events of consciousness" do enter into the causal chain and in the other case do not, makes "logically" not the slightest difference.' I also have an objection to Weber's argument, but it is in effect that Weber's position is too close to Winch's. For Weber supposes that in order to introduce causal explanation he must abandon description of the social situation in terms of actions, roles, and the like. So he proposes speaking not of the workers being paid, but of their being handed pieces of metal. In so doing Weber concedes Winch's point that descriptions in terms of actions, reasons, and all that falls under his term 'events of consciousness' cannot figure in causal explanations without a conceptual mistake being committed. But in this surely he is wrong.

Compare two situations: first, one in which managers minimize shop-floor trade-union activity in a factory by concentrating opportunities of extra overtime and of earning bonuses in those parts of the factory where such activity shows signs of flourishing; and then one in which managers similarly minimize trade-union activity by a process of continual transfers between one part of the factory and another or between different factories. In both cases it may be possible to explain the low level of trade-union activity causally by reference to the managers' policies; but in the former case the reasons which the workers have for pursuing overtime and bonuses can find a place in the explanation without it losing its causal character and in both cases a necessary condition of the managers' actions being causally effective may well be that the workers in question remain ignorant of the policy behind the actions. The causal character of the explanations can be brought out by considering how generalizations might be formulated in which certain behaviour of the managers can supply either the necessary or the sufficient condition or both for the behaviour of the workers. But in such a formulation one important fact will emerge; namely, that true causal explanations cannot be formulated—where actions are concerned—unless intentions, motives, and reasons are taken into account. That is, it is not only the case as I have argued in the second section of this essay that a true explanation in terms of reasons must entail some account of the causal background; it is also true that a causal account of action will require a corresponding account of the intentions, motives, and reasons involved. It is this latter point that Durkheim misses and Winch stresses. In the light of this it is worth returning to one aspect of the explanation of suicide.

In modern cities more than one study has shown a correlation between the suicide rate for different parts of the city and the proportion of the population living an isolated, single-room apartment existence. What are the conditions which must be satisfied if such a correlation is to begin to play a part in explaining why suicide is committed? First it must be shown that at least a certain proportion of the individuals who commit suicide live in such isolated conditions; otherwise (unless, for example, it was the landlord of such apartments who committed suicide) we should find the correlation of explanatory assistance only in so far as it pointed us toward a common explanation of the two rates. But suppose that we do find that it is the individuals who live in such isolated conditions who are more likely to commit suicide. We still have to ask whether it is the pressure on the emotions of the isolation itself, or whether it is the insolubility of certain other problems in conditions of isolation which leads to suicide. Unless such questions about motives and reasons are answered, the causal generalization 'isolated living of a certain kind tends to lead to acts of suicide' is not so much an explanation in itself as an additional fact to be explained, even though it is a perfectly sound generalization and even though to learn its truth might be to learn how the suicide rate could be increased or decreased in large cities by changing our housing policies.

Now we cannot raise the questions about motives and reasons, the answers to which would explain why isolation has the effect which it has, unless we first of all understand the acts of suicide in terms of the intentions of the agents and therefore in terms of their own action descriptions. Thus Winch's starting-point proves to be the correct one, provided it is a starting-point. We could not even formulate our initial causal generalization about isolation and suicide, in such a way that the necessary question about motives and reasons could be raised later, unless the expression 'suicide' and kindred expressions which figured in our causal generalizations possessed the same meaning as they did for the agents who committed the acts. We can understand very clearly why Winch's starting-point must be substantially correct if we remember how he compares sociological understanding with understanding a language (p. 115). The crude notion that one can first learn a language and then secondly and separately go on to understand the social life of those who speak it can only flourish where the languages studied are those of peoples whose social life is so largely the same as our own that we do not notice the understanding of social life embodied in our grasp of the language; but attempts to learn the alien language of an alien culture soon dispose of it. Yet the understanding that we thus acquire, although a necessary preliminary, is only a preliminary. It would be equally harmful if Winch's attempt to make of this preliminary the substance of social science were to convince, or if a proper understanding of the need to go further were not to allow for the truth in his arguments.

5

These dangers are likely to be especially inhibiting in the present state of parts of social science. Two important essays by anthropologists, Leach's *Rethinking Anthropology* and Goldschmidt's *Comparative Functionalism* (to which I have referred earlier), focus upon problems to which adherence to Winch's conclusions would preclude any solution. At the outset I contrasted Winch with Malinowski, but this was in respects in which most contemporary social scientists would take the standpoint quoted from Malinowski for granted. We owe also to Malinowski, however, the tradition of what Goldschmidt calls 'the detailed internal analysis of individual cultures' with the further comparison of institutional arrangements in different societies resting on such analyses. This tradition has been criticized by both Leach and Goldschmidt; the latter believes that because institutions are defined by each culture in its own terms, it is not at the level of institutions that cross-cultural analyses will be fruitful. The former has recommended us to search for recurrent topological patterns in, for example, kinship arrangements, with the same aim of breaking free from institutional ethnocentrism. I think that both Leach and Goldschmidt are going to prove to be seminal writers on this point and it is clear that their arguments are incompatible with Winch's. It would therefore be an important lacuna in this essay if I did not open up directly the question of the bearing of Winch's arguments on this topic.

Winch argues, consistently with his rejection of any place for causal laws in social science, that comparison between different cases is not dependent on any grasp of theoretical generalizations (pp. 134–6), and he sets limits to any possible comparison by his insistence that each set of activities must be understood solely in its own terms. In so doing he must necessarily reject for example all those various theories which insist that religions of quite different kinds express unacknowledged needs of the same kind. (No such theory needs to be committed to the view that religions are and do no more than this.) Indeed in his discussion of Pareto (pp. 104–11) he appears to make such a rejection explicit by the generality of the grounds on which he rejects Pareto's comparison of Christian baptism with pagan rites. I hold no brief for the theory of residues and derivations. But when Winch insists that each religious rite must be understood in its own terms to the exclusion of any generalization about religion or that each social system must be so understood to the exclusion of any generalization about status and prestige, he must be pressed to make his grounds precise. In his later discussion of Evans-Pritchard, one aspect of Winch's views becomes clear; namely, the implication of his remark that 'criteria of logic are not a direct gift of God, but arise out of, and are only intelligible in the context of, ways of living or modes of social life' (p. 100). Winch's one substantial point of difference with Evans-Pritchard in his treatment of witchcraft among the Azande is that he thinks it impossible to ask whether the Zande beliefs about witches are true.[9] We can ask from within the Zande system of beliefs if there are witches and will receive the answer 'Yes'. We can ask from within the system of beliefs of modern science if there are witches and will receive the answer 'No.' But we cannot ask which system of beliefs is the superior in respect of rationality and truth; for this would be to invoke criteria which can be understood independently of any particular way of life, and in Winch's view there are no such criteria.

This represents a far more extreme view of the difficulties of cultural comparison than Goldschmidt, for example, advances. Both its extreme character and its error can be understood by considering two arguments against it. The first is to the effect that in Winch's view certain actual historical transitions are made unintelligible; I refer to those transitions from one system of beliefs to another which are necessarily characterized

[9] *American Philosophical Quarterly*, Vol. i, No. 4 (1964), 309.

by raising questions of the kind that Winch rejects. In seventeenth-century Scotland, for example, the question could not but be raised, 'but are there witches?' If Winch asks, from within what way of social life, under what system of belief was this question asked, the only answer is that it was asked by men who confronted alternative systems and were able to draw out of what confronted them independent criteria of judgement. Many Africans today are in the same situation.

This type of argument is of course necessarily inconclusive; any historical counter-example to Winch's thesis will be open to questions of interpretation that will make it less than decisive. But there is another important argument. Consider the statement made by some Zande theorist or by King James VI and I, 'there are witches' and the statement made by some modern sceptic, 'there are no witches.' Unless one of these statements denies what the other asserts, the negation of the sentence expressing the former could not be a correct translation of the sentence expressing the latter. Thus if we could not deny from our own standpoint and in our own language what the Azande or King James assert in theirs, we should be unable to translate their expression into our langauge. Cultural idiosyncracy would have entailed linguistic idiosyncrasy and cross-cultural comparison would have been rendered logically impossible. But of course translation is not impossible.

Yet if we treat seriously, not what I take to be Winch's mistaken thesis that we cannot go beyond a society's own self-description, but what I take to be his true thesis that we must not do this except and until we have grasped the criteria embodied in that self-description, then we shall have to conclude that the contingently different conceptual schemes and institutional arrangements of different societies make translation difficult to the point at which attempts at cross-cultural generalization too often become little more than a construction of lists. Goldschmidt and Leach have both pointed out how the building up of typologies and classificatory schemes becomes empty and purposeless unless we have a theory which gives point and criteria to our classificatory activities. Both have also pointed out how, if we compare for example marital institutions in different cultures, our definition of 'marriage' will either be drawn from one culture in terms of whose concepts other cultures will be described or rather misdescribed, or else will be so neutral, bare, and empty as to be valueless.[10] That is, the understanding of a people in terms of their own

[10] See Kathleen Gough, 'The Nayars and the Definition of Marriage', in P. B. Hammond (ed.), *Cultural and Social Anthropology*, New York: Macmillan, 1964; E. R. Leach, 'Polyandry, Inheritance and the Definition of Marriage with Particular Reference to Sinhalese Customary Law', in *Rethinking Anthropology*, London: Athlone Press, 1966; and Goldschmidt, op. cit., pp. 17–26.

concepts and beliefs does in fact tend to preclude understanding them in any other term. To this extent Winch is vindicated. But an opposite moral to his can be drawn. We may conclude not that we ought not to generalize but that such generalization must move at another level. Goldschmidt argues for the recommendation: do not ask what an institution means for the agents themselves, ask what necessary needs and purposes it serves. He argues for this not because he looks for functionalist explanations of a Malinowskian kind, but because he believes that different institutions, embodying different conceptual schemes, may be illuminatingly seen as serving the same social necessities. To carry the argument further would be to raise questions that are not and cannot be raised within the framework of Winch's book. It is because I believe writers such as Goldschmidt are correct in saying that one must transcend such a framework that I believe also that Winch's book deserves close critical attention.

II

REASON AND RITUAL

MARTIN HOLLIS

CERTAIN primitive Yoruba carry about with them boxes covered with cowrie shells, which they treat with special regard. When asked what they are doing, they apparently reply that the boxes are their heads or souls and that they are protecting them against witchcraft. Is that an interesting fact or a bad translation? The question is, I believe, partly philosophical. In what follows, I shall propound and try to solve the philosopher's question, arguing that it has large implications for the theory of Social Anthropology.[1]

An anthropologist sets himself to understand a culture which is not his own. He has succeeded when he understands everything the natives say, do, and believe. But does he always know that he has understood? What, for instance, would give him the right to be sure that the Yoruba believe boxes covered with cowrie shells to be their heads or souls? It is a curious belief to find among people who are often as rational as we. Yet we claim to know that rational men do sometimes hold curious metaphysical beliefs; so presumably we have some way of identifying such beliefs. On the other hand we sometimes reject proffered accounts of beliefs on the ground that the beliefs are unintelligible. How, then, do we decide when it is more plausible to reject a translation than to accept that a society believes what the translator claims they believe? I shall call those metaphysical beliefs which inform ritual actions 'ritual beliefs'. Our problem is how we know when we have identified a ritual belief.

This looks like an empirical question. For, it might be said, the problem is that of knowing when a language has been correctly translated and it is surely an empirical matter what native utterances mean. The anthropologist can learn Yoruba and ask the natives what they believe. Provided that his attempts to speak Yoruba have met with success in everyday contexts, and he has no reason to suppose that the Yoruba are lying about

From *Philosophy*, xliii (1967), 165, 231–47. Reprinted by permission of the author and the Editor of *Philosophy*.

[1] I am grateful to Prof. F. Willett of Northwestern University for the Yoruba example and the possible explanation of it given later; and to Messrs. S. Lukes, P. M. Hacker, and A. Kenny for many helpful discussions of the matters raised.

their ritual beliefs, then there is no reason to doubt the resulting translations. Besides, he can always recruit an intelligent bilingual to settle
any doubtful points. Admittedly ritual beliefs, like Yoruba boxes, may
seem unintelligible in isolation. But this shows only that they should not
be taken in isolation. They belong to a ritual context and will be found to
make sense when the whole context is grasped. Moreover, ritual is of its
essence expressive rather than informative and mystical rather than
rational. Consequently a literal translation need not produce a statement
which the natives believe literally. Metaphor is to the temple what literal
sense is to the market-place. There are, in short, no *a priori* limits on what
a society may believe and it is thus an empirical matter whether an anthropologist's account is correct.

If this line of thought is right, there is nothing for a philosopher to
discuss. But, I shall argue, far from making anthropology an empirical
matter, it makes it instead impossible. If a ritual belief is to be identified
after the manner of an everyday belief, then it cannot be identified at all.

The identification of everyday beliefs is indeed (within limits to be
discussed later) an empirical matter. The anthropologist learns the native
language by discovering the native signs for assent and dissent and the
native names for common objects. He then composes statements about
objects and elicits assent or dissent from the natives. He thus frames
hypotheses by assuming that the natives assent to true statements and
dissent from false ones. The exact history of his progress does not concern
us but the last assumption is important. For unless the native utterances
make sense in simple everyday situations, the anthropologists will not
even begin. If the natives made no statements about the cat on the mat
and the cow in the corn which can be translated to yield truths, then the
anthropologist has no way into the maze. In general identifying an
everyday belief involves knowing the truth-conditions of the statements
which express it. This does not imply that every native belief must, when
translated, yield a true statement but it does imply that most of them must.
Equally any claim that the natives say something false must be backed by
an explanation of why they fail to see that the belief is false. Otherwise
the falsity of the belief, as translated, will be sufficient reason for rejecting
the translation. Thus Caesar tells us that some German tribes believe
that the elk has no joints in its knees and therefore sleeps leaning against
a tree, since, if it lies down, it cannot get up again. Without some explanation of how they manage to believe this taradiddle, we shall have sufficient
reason to suppose either that the Germans did not believe it (Caesar's
informant was perhaps pulling his leg) or that there had been a mistransla-
tion. In neither case will Caesar have identified a belief which the Germans

held. The point is that everyday beliefs have objectively specifiable truth-conditions. That the truth-conditions are objective both gives the anthropologist his lead in and, in the absence of a special explanation, provides the tests of his hypotheses.

Ritual beliefs, by contrast, do not have objectively specifiable truth-conditions. To be sure, a Yoruba, who believed a box covered with cowrie shells to be his head or soul, might take that belief to be true. But this is not to say that any fact referred to is objectively specifiable. Consequently the anthropologist cannot use the facts to get at the beliefs: he can, at best, use the beliefs to get at the facts. Here, then, is a first difference between ritual and everyday beliefs.

But this does not dispose of the claim that we are dealing with a wholly empirical question. Is it not an empirical matter what words mean, even in a ritual context? May we not translate ritual literally, marking the fact that we are translating ritual utterances by noting that the statements may be taken metaphorically? Thus we know that some Australian aborigines believe the sun is a white cockatoo, because we have firm everyday translations for 'sun', 'is', 'white', and 'cockatoo' and aboriginal assent to the resulting utterance. Of course the claim would be absurd, if the aborigines were expected to take the belief literally, but it is a ritual belief and they take it metaphorically.

As it stands, this move is useless, since it rests on using the notion of metaphor, without giving it any independent leverage. The notion of metaphor, like that of ritual, must do more than signal a failure to produce sense. If we take a ritual utterance, translate it literally, and dub the result 'metaphorical', how do we know that what we now have is equivalent to the original? To put it another way, how do we know what the metaphorical sense of an utterance is, seeing that any utterance might have many metaphorical senses? To put it yet another way, how do we know what words are not used equivocally in ritual contexts? If any piece of literal nonsense can be taken metaphorically, then anthropology rapidly becomes impossible. For there is no way of telling which of rival accounts of ritual beliefs is the right one—the literal nonsense which one anthropologist interprets in one way can always be given a different metaphorical sense by another anthropologist. We need, then, a better test of success than the accuracy of a literal translation.

Let us try next to give the notion of ritual some independent leverage. What is the force of calling something a ritual belief? We have said that ritual beliefs are metaphysical and inform ritual actions (in the sense that ritual actions are identified as the actions which express ritual beliefs). But, so far, this serves merely to sweep them under the rug as beliefs which we have failed to identify by making literal sense of the utterances used to express them. What then is the category of ritual more than a waste bin for unidentified beliefs?

This question has been given an interesting answer by Suzanne Langer in her *Philosophy in a New Key*.[2] Man, she says, is a symbolizing animal and his symbolizing takes two main forms. First there is practical symbolism of the kind used in everyday discourse and in science. Practical symbolism is experience transformed into a form in which it can be talked about, as a means to some practical end. Practical symbolism in effect comprises all and only those utterances which a Logical Positivist would allow to be literally meaningful. Secondly there is expressive or presentational symbolism of the kind found in music or religion. Expressive symbolism is an end in itself and any example of it (like a piece of music) forms a whole, in the sense that its meaning is not a compound of the discrete units which constitute it. Thus language is the best example of practical symbolism, because it is analysable and instrumental; whereas music is the best example of expressive symbolism, because its meaning is total and it is an end in itself. Miss Langer puts the distinction thus:

It appears then that although the different media of non-verbal representation are often referred to as distinct 'languages' [e.g. the 'language' of painting], this is really a loose terminology. Language in the strict sense is essentially discursive; it has permanent units of meaning which are combinable into larger units; it has fixed equivalences which make definition and translation possible; its connotations are general so that it requires non-verbal acts like pointing, looking or emphatic voice inflections to assign specific denotations to its terms. In all these salient characters it differs from wordless symbolism, which is non-discursive and untranslatable, does not allow of definitions within its own system, and cannot directly convey generalisations.[3]

Ritual beliefs, then, if we follow Miss Langer, are the significance of acts of expressive or presentational symbolism. Thus the behaviour of Yoruba towards their boxes covered with cowrie shells may perhaps express a total view of the nature of man, rather as Beethoven's music is sometimes alleged to express a total view about the order of the universe. The reason that Yoruba statements do not make literal sense is that they are, if used to express ritual beliefs, not statements at all and, if used to describe ritual beliefs, not so much statements as clues. Equally if Beethoven was expressing any total belief in his music, then that belief cannot be more than hinted at in words. For, according to Miss Langer, the vehicle of expression is not a means to an end but an unanalysable end in itself.

---

[2] S. Langer, *Philosophy in a New Key*, 3rd edn., Cambridge, Mass.: Harvard University Press, 1963.

[3] Ibid., pp. 96f.

If so, then the reason that ritual statements cannot be taken out of context is that they do not mean anything out of context. Ritual beliefs are the beliefs they are because of their place in a whole. Identification of each depends on the identification of all.

In distinguishing practical and expressive symbolism as she does, Miss Langer is following Carnap, from whom she quotes these remarks:

Metaphysical propositions—like lyrical verses—have only an expressive function, but no representative function. Metaphysical propositions are neither true nor false, because they assert nothing. . . . . But they are, like laughing, lyrics and music, expressive. They express not so much temporary feelings as permanent emotional and volitional dispositions.[4]

When Miss Langer's view of symbolism is added to Carnap's view of metaphysical propositions, the result is a close analogy between ritual and music. This may seem a promising start at characterizing ritual beliefs. But it would be defeat to accept it, as it makes impossible to identify the ritual beliefs we are characterizing. A ritual belief, on this view, not only lacks a truth-value but also is unanalysable and untranslatable. If this is right, then all we can ever say about two rival anthropologists' accounts of a ritual belief is that they are both wrong. An anthropologist's account of ritual would be limited to what his camera (equipped for sound) could record: as soon as he told us that the Yoruba believed that their boxes were their souls, he would have tried to translate the untranslatable. His and any rival account, then, would be bound to break down, as soon as they tried to put the significance of the ritual into words.

So far, then, we do not see how to exploit either the fact that natives take their ritual beliefs to be true, or the fact that ritual beliefs can be expressed in words or the fact that ritual has affinities with art, in order to identify these elusive beliefs. But before offering a denouement, I would like to glance at a way of trying to by-pass the problem. We have been assuming that the significance of ritual must lie in the beliefs which it expresses, and this has left us trying to grapple with seemingly untranslatable alien metaphysics. Perhaps, then, the significance of ritual is to be sought strictly in its social effects. Thus Evans-Pritchard found in his studies of the Azande that Zande beliefs in witchcraft, oracles, and magic served, *inter alia*, to maintain the power structure of Zande society.[5] It is tempting to argue from this that Zande ritual statements simply are statements 'about' social relations among the Azande. The attraction of such a move is that it gives us something objective for ritual statements to be

[4] R. Carnap, *Philosophy and Logical Syntax*, London: K. Paul, Trench, Trubner and Co., 1935, p. 28, quoted by Miss Langer in Ch. IV, p. 84.

[5] E. E. Evans-Pritchard, *Witchcraft, Oracles and Magic Among the Azande*, Oxford, 1937. I am not implying that Evans-Pritchard thinks this line to be correct.

'about' and so restores to us objective truth conditions to back our identifications. But in referring ritual beliefs to the social structure, would we be
identifying them or would we be, at most, explaining how they come to be
held? The latter, I suggest. A Zande, who believes he has been bewitched,
surely does not believe that he has offended some social authority or other.
If he did, he could perfectly well say so. He surely believes, rather, that
he is the victim of supernatural interference. If so, facts about the Zande
social structure serve at most to explain why he believes this and perhaps
why such a belief is common among the Azande or takes the form it does.
But they will not serve to identify the belief, as they do not constitute it.
Equally, Catholic beliefs evidenced in the Eucharist might be found to be
causally connected with some fact of human social history. But no convinced Catholic would agree that the beliefs were about social facts, if
this meant denying them the status of metaphysical truths. Admittedly it
might be possible to argue in reply that Azande and Catholics simply did
not know what their beliefs were about or even that their beliefs did not
exist, being fictions inferred from social behaviour.[6] But this takes us
outside the scope of the present paper. I shall continue to assume that
there are ritual beliefs and that our problem is to show how they can be
identified. If this is the problem, then social explanations are not identifications.

So our problem is not to be solved by looking for empirical truth conditions nor by sanctifying a literal translation with the name of Metaphor.
Nor is it removed by saying metaphorical propositions are non-assertive
and untranslatable. Nor is it by-passed by concentrating on social facts.
So how is it possible to identify a ritual belief? The answer is, I believe, to
appeal to our own criteria of rationality.

Miss Langer claims that her account of presentational or expressive
symbolism has the merit of making it rational. She writes:

The recognition of presentational symbolism as a normal and prevalent vehicle
of meaning widens our conception of rationality far beyond the traditional
boundaries, yet never breaks faith with logic in the strict sense.[7]
Rationality is the essence of mind and symbolic transformation its elementary
process. It is a fundamental error, therefore, to recognize it only in the phenomenon of systematic explicit reasoning. That is a mature and precarious product.[8]

This will hardly do as it stands. Presentational symbolism, she has just
finished saying, 'is non-discursive, untranslatable, does not allow of defini-

---

[6] Cf. E. R. Leach, *Political Systems of Highland Burma*, London: Bell and Sons, 1954,
p. 14: 'In sum then, my view here is that ritual action and belief are alike to be understood as forms of symbolic statements about the social order.'
[7] S. Langer, op. cit., p. 97.
[8] Ibid., p. 99.

tions within its own system and cannot directly convey generalizations'. Its best example is music. Very well then—how can it possibly fail to 'break faith with logic in the strict sense'? Logic in the 'strict sense' (whatever that may be) requires the notions of well-formed formula, truth and falsehood, contradiction, and so forth which are notably absent in music. Above all it has criteria of identity for formulae and decision procedures for checking inferences. These notions are, I agree with Miss Langer, what we are looking for. They are not to be found, however, in her presentational symbolism.

It is my thesis that we can identify a ritual belief only if it is rational by our standards of rationality. This will seem parochial: why should the natives share our standards of rationality? In answer I shall try to show that some assumption about rationality has to be made *a priori* if anthropology is to be possible; and that we have no choice about what assumption to make. I begin by arguing that the anthropologist works with a number of *a priori* assumptions, of which rationality is only one.[9]

Let us start with those simple everyday beliefs which the anthropologist shares with the natives. The natives believe that the cat is on the mat and the cow is in the corn. That they hold these particular beliefs is a matter of empirical discovery but the discovery can only be made if some *a priori* assumptions work. The anthropologist begins in earnest by eliciting from a native a true utterance about a common perceived object, or perhaps by eliciting assent to such an utterance. The assumptions here are that the object has properties which they both perceive it to have, that the utterance refers to the object; and that the native believes the utterance to be true. Only if these assumptions are correct, may the native be taken to have said in his language what the anthropologist would have said in his own. I want to insist first that they are *assumptions* and secondly that the anthropologist has no option about making them.

Since the anthropologist knew nothing about the natives when he started, it seems that he discovers everything he knows in the end. Very well; how does he *discover* that the natives sometimes perceive what he perceives? Two possible answers are that he observes their behaviour and that he translates their utterances. But if there is anything to be in doubt about, then observing their behaviour will not help. For he needs to discover that the natives discriminate among phenomena as he does, and this is not guaranteed by outward similarity of reactions to the

---

[9] It will be seen that I am much indebted to W. V. O. Quine (especially to the second chapter of *Word and Object*) for several ideas in this paper. But, in virtue of his doctrine that all beliefs are revisable, he is, I think, an empiricist (what C. I. Lewis calls a Conceptual Pragmatist), and I have tried to show that no empiricist can sail so close to the rationalist wind.

phenomena. For, until he knows how the natives discriminate, he is imposing his own classification of reactions on their behaviour. And this implies that he is also identifying the phenomena according to his own perceptions, or else simply assuming that the phenomena are common to both parties, which is what he is purporting to discover. To show that he had discovered how they perceived the world, and not merely credited them with his own perceptions, he would have to translate their judgements of perception.

He cannot translate these judgements, however, until he has made some assumption about what the natives perceive. In translating a native word as 'cat', for instance, he is bound to be guided by the fact that it applies only to cats. But now it is too late to discover that they do not perceive what he does when he perceives a cat. He can, of course, be so open-minded that he fails to translate any native word at all. But he cannot first translate the word for 'cat' and then discover that the natives perceive cats. That 'discovery' must come first and the later translation does not confirm it, since the translation depends on it.

The *a priori* element in the process is obscured by some seductive empirical facts. Thus it is an empirical fact that the natives have a word for 'cat', and, indeed, that they have a word for anything. It is also an empirical fact that they react to phenomena and that they make perceptual judgements. All these facts might not have been so; and the anthropologist has *discovered* that they are so. He has not discovered, however, that they perceive phenomena one way and not another way, that they make judgements about phenomena instead of making them only about something else, that they take blue objects to be blue and not pink. Equally, to advance a little further, he has not discovered that when they assent they mean 'yes' or that when they sincerely assent to something they believe it to be true. For he needed this information in order to translate any utterances at all, and it is then too late to discover it false.

This contention floats uneasily between the Scylla of the Whorf hypothesis and the Charybdis of the doctrine of analyticity. I shall next try to avoid both dangers.

The idea common to the many variants of the Whorf hypothesis is that what a man perceives is a function of his language, in the sense that he discriminates among phenomena according to the linguistic categories he has been trained to use. So long as this is a thesis about limited differences in perception embedded in a general agreement in perception, it is an empirical hypothesis, which a philosopher has no business to dispute. But it ceases to be an empirical hypothesis, if it is suggested that two people or societies might have no perceptions in common at all. Such a claim could not be shown empirically false, since there will always be cases uninvestigated. Nor, and this is what counts, can it be shown empirically true. For this would require that the totally different perceptions be the product of a translatable language and translation depends on some apparent agreement of perceptions.

I say 'apparent agreement' advisedly. Let us in a flight of philosophic fancy suppose that a tribe with only the sense of sight meets a tribe with only the sense of touch. Each tribe has a language for describing the world, one without tactual terms, the other without visual. Communication seems impossible, since, without any overlap in perceptions, neither tribe can establish any bridgehead. But now suppose that the tribes inhabit a world where every visual property of objects is, in fact, correlated with just one tactual property, where, for instance, all and only red objects feel square, or, more disingenuously, all and only objects which look square feel square. In these special conditions each tribe could successfully assume that there was overlap in perceptions. While restricted to its peculiar sense, neither could detect or correct the mistake. And so each could chart the other's language to its own satisfaction, provided the languages had the same structure. Now, if this flight of fancy is coherent, it is logically possible for one man to be totally, though systematically, mistaken about the content of another's experience. If the flight of fancy is incoherent, then it is so on *a priori* grounds. In neither case is it an empirical hypothesis that perception is a function of language. Apparent success in translation guarantees identity of the conceptual structure given to experience but not of the experience itself. Identity of content remains, however, a necessary condition of correct translation.

So is it not then analytic that languages are genuinely intertranslatable, only if speakers share experiences and conceptualize them in broadly the same way? That depends, I think, on the sense given to 'analytic'. If 'analytic' is defined broadly and neutrally as *a priori* there is no Charybdis of analyticity to avoid. Indeed, I shall argue later that what is here true of two languages applies equally to one and that we are seeking *a priori* conditions of the possibility of language in general. But 'analytic' is usually given an empiricist definition, whose key idea is that of revisable options. (This may or may not be attached to a sharp analytic-synthetic distinction or one between uninformative and factual.) If the anthropologist's assumptions are *a priori* without being optional, then I suggest that we are committed to some rationalist doctrine about the place of necessary truths in knowledge. With this in mind, I shall first extend the list of assumptions and then continue to argue that we have no option about what to assume.

The assumptions required for identifying everyday empirical beliefs are common perceptions, common ways of referring to things perceived and a common notion of empirical truth.[10] Unless these assumptions work, the anthropologist cannot get his bridgehead—the set of utterances taken as definitive of the meanings of everyday words. Thus to identify the native signs of assent and dissent, he must assume that the natives in the main assent to what is true and dissent from what is false. If his translation has them doing the opposite, that is sufficient reason for rejecting it. If it has them doing something quite different, for example expressing aesthetic reactions to the sound-pattern of the words, then he cannot claim to know what the words mean. Translation is possible only if the natives speak sooth about everyday objects as the anthropologist does and no translation can either verify or falsify this assumption.

The notions of truth and falsehood cannot be separated from the notion of logical reasoning. For they form a pair whose identity depends on the law of contradiction. An anthropologist does not know what he can say in the native language, unless he also knows what he cannot say. (This is why it is much easier to work with a native informant who can say 'No' to a question, than with a set of texts, which cannot.) A language has a word for negation only if its speakers take the truth of a proposition to entail the falsity of a denial of that proposition. A language without a word for negation is translatable only if it is embedded in one which distinguishes what can and cannot be said. The anthropologist must find the word for 'no', and to do so must assume that the natives share (at least partly) his concepts of identity, contradiction, and inference.

The case for this needs to be made out with care. The idea of an alternative logic to our own is not obviously absurd and, indeed, it has been claimed that pre-logical peoples actually exist.[11] The right of the law of the Excluded Middle to feature in the corpus of indubitable axioms can certainly be disputed. What, then, is special about Identity, Contradiction, and Inference?

The answer is, I believe, that these notions set the conditions for the existence not only of a particular kind of logical reasoning but also of any kind whatever. Let us try to suppose that our natives reason logically but not according to the scheme 'If p and if p implies q, then q.' They

<hr />

[10] This might be denied by supposing a tribe which dealt exclusively in imperatives. Here an analogous assumption needs to be made about when an imperative has been put into effect. But, if we stick to imperatives, we shall never get to beliefs at all, much less to ritual beliefs. I shall therefore ignore this enticing alley.

[11] e.g. L. L. Lévy-Bruhl, *La Mentalité primitive* (Herbert Spencer Memorial Lecture), Oxford, 1931, p. 21. But see also his *Les Carnets*, Paris: Presses Universitaires, 1949, pp. 130f.

must reason somehow, however, so let us suppose them to infer something like this:

$$p \star q$$
$$p$$
$$\overline{}$$
$$!q$$

How might we translate this? Well not by 'If p and if p implies q, then q' as that would give us *modus ponens* again. Nor by 'If p and if p implies q, then not q' as that would involve a self-refuting claim that 'p', 'q', '$\star$' '!' '—' have the meanings or functions in the native language which 'p', 'q', 'if . . . then', and 'implies' have in English. In general we cannot first identify a native constant as 'if . . . then' and then go on to show that *modus ponens* does not hold, since, if *modus ponens* does not hold, then the constant has been wrongly identified. Nor can we identify a native constant without saying what constant it is, since that gives us no ground for believing it is a constant. Native logic must either turn out to be a version of our own or remain untranslatable.

If this is right, 'p → p', '—(p . p̄)', and '(p . (p → q)) → q' express more than axioms in a particular system or rules in a particular game. They express, rather, requirements for something's being a system of logical reasoning at all. To look for alternatives is like looking for a novel means of transport which is novel not only in that it has no engine but also in that it does not convey bodies from one place to another. Anything which satisfies the latter condition could not be a means of transport at all. If the natives reason logically at all, then they reason as we do.

I suggest, then, that what sentences mean depends on how the beliefs which they express are connected, and that to justify a claim to have identified a belief one must show the belief is connected to others. Logical connection is not the only kind and to identify ritual beliefs we need to introduce the notion of rational connection. I shall try to show that a ritual belief p can be identified only if there is a belief q which supplies the holder of p and q with a reason for believing p.

Let us return for a moment to the Yoruba and their boxes. One possible explanation which has been put forward is that these Yoruba believe each man to have a spiritual counterpart in heaven, who is susceptible to witchcraft. Witchcraft can be fended off by ritual treatment of the box, which represents the spiritual counterpart of the owner. Thus, when the Yoruba say the boxes are their heads or souls, they are using 'are' of symbolization and not of identity. In this explanation a pattern of behaviour is referred to a set of ritual beliefs and some of the beliefs are used to determine the translation of sentences expressing others. In seeing why the explanation has any force, we may perhaps answer our original question about the identification of ritual beliefs.

Are we to test Yoruba beliefs for rationality at all and, if we do, are we to pronounce them rational or irrational? As ritual beliefs rarely entail each other and are sometimes contradictory and as they do not correspond to objective facts, they will be unidentifiable, unless connected according to some notion of rationality. Besides we must surely allow for the fact that the Yoruba think their beliefs (whatever they are) true; and whatever the Yoruba take to make them true will make them *pro tanto* rational, from a Yoruba point of view. But this is not yet to say that we and they must have our concept of rationality and we may be reluctant to do so, as that might oblige us to believe in witchcraft too. So I shall consider next whether Yoruba beliefs may be rational by their standards but irrational by ours.

It may seem irrational to hold as true a belief which corresponds to no empirical reality. Ritual beliefs, as defined in this paper, are certainly of this sort. Equally ritual beliefs can be incoherent, and this might also seem to make them irrational. But this is not to say that we can accept identifications which make the empirical falsity and logical incoherence explicit, general, and recognized. For that would give us sufficient reason to reject the identification on the grounds that, given this degree of laxity, we no longer have any way of deciding between rival translations. A man may believe a contradiction but, if he were also to believe that it was a contradiction, he might believe anything and neither we nor he could identify what he did believe. The only relevant fact about someone's ritual beliefs cannot be that we find them irrational.

Perhaps, however, the natives find rational what we find irrational, in the sense that they have a different notion of 'being a reason for'. We could discover this only if we could first identify the beliefs and then see how they were connected. In other words, we must be able to reach a partial translation of the form 'I believe p * I believe q' without translating '*' and then go on to translate '*' without making it our own (rational) 'because'. But now we are stuck. We could take '*' as 'although'; but this would leave us with our concept of rational connection. There is no English word, however, for an alternative to our (rational) 'because'; and, if there were, the native language would again turn out to be a version of ours. Moreover, without a translation of '*', how do we know that we have identified p and q? If p is 'this box is my soul', what makes that a correct translation? Why not 'this box is my spiritual identity card'? I contend that, without a translation of '*', the only answers are those mentioned at the beginning of this paper, and I would hope that the argument has by now advanced beyond them.

It may be well to disentangle the *a priori* and empirical elements here. It is an empirical matter what ritual beliefs the natives hold, what sentences they express them in, and how they express the connection between them. It is *a priori*, however, that any ritual beliefs which we can identify form a related set whose members supply reasons for each other. This is *a priori* in the sense that it is an assumption which determines the translation of native sentences and so cannot be shown to be false. It is not optional, in the sense that, if we try to make any other assumption, we cannot identify any native ritual beliefs at all.

An anthropologist is thus obliged, I suggest, to remove obvious incoherences, if he is to give his readers better reason to accept his account than to reject it. It may be of interest to note how Evans-Pritchard does so in his *Witchcraft, Oracles and Magic among the Azande*. He writes:

Azande see as well as we that the failure of their oracle to prophesy truly calls for explanation, but so entangled are they in mystical notions that they must make use of them to account for the failure. The contradition between experience and one mystical notion is explained by reference to other mystical notions.[12]

Thus, for instance, an oracle can be bewitched and so its failure will reinforce beliefs about witchcraft. The connectedness of Zande thought is crucial to Evans-Pritchard's account. He finds that:

Witchcraft, oracles and magic form an intellectually coherent system. Each explains and proves the others. Death is a proof of witchcraft. It is avenged by magic. The achievement of vengeance-magic is proved by the poison-oracle. The accuracy of the poison-oracle is determined by the king's oracle, which is above suspicion.[13]

Elsewhere in the book he says:

In this web of belief every strand depends on every other strand and a Zande cannot get out of its meshes because it is the only world he knows. The web is not an external structure in which he is enclosed. It is the texture of his thought and he cannot think that his thought is wrong.[14]

Although Evans-Pritchard may have changed his philosophical ground in later works, here he takes the line that Zande beliefs are empirically false but rational both for them and for us. If my argument is sound, this approach is the only one which allows the identification of ritual beliefs. Recently a belief in 'Interpretative Charity' has found general

---

[12] E. E. Evans-Pritchard, op. cit., p. 338 (Pt. 3, Ch. IV, section viii).
[13] Ibid., p. 476. This is one of 22 reasons cited to account for the failure of the Azande to perceive the futility of their magic.
[14] Ibid., p. 195.

favour.[15] If interpretative Charity means merely making the native society as rational as possible, I have no objection. But if it means making the notions of reality and rationality relative to the native conceptual scheme, in the belief that we should not claim the monopoly of these notions, then I maintain that anthropology is in consequence impossible. Without assumptions about reality and rationality we cannot translate anything and no translation could show the assumptions to be wrong.

In agreeing with Miss Langer that ritual beliefs are to be identified by treating ritual utterances as acts of expressive, rather than presentational symbolism, I am taking rationality as a relation between beliefs. A ritual belief p is rational if and only if there is a belief q such that q supplies a reason for holding p and p does not entail the falsity of q. This, I hope will 'extend the concept of rationality without breaking faith with logic in the strict sense'. In other words, since the Correspondence Theory of Truth is beside the point, we must make use of the Coherence Theory. To explain this, I shall next draw an analogy between an anthropologist and an unbelieving theologian.

Most theologians are believers and hold their own religions to be internally rational. They may take religion to begin with faith and end with mystery but they also hold that every belief which can be made explicit either makes rational another belief or is made rational by another belief or both. An unbelieving theologian can take the same line. He can certainly judge that the system is in sum irrational but he may (and, I contend, must) hold that most individual beliefs are connected rationally. In short, he may disagree totally with a believing theologian, but he must also agree with him in most particulars. Otherwise the believer will be entitled to claim that the unbeliever does not understand what he is disagreeing about. Mystery is divine truth to the believer and human nonsense to the unbeliever. But both can agree where it sets in. A mysterious belief is presumably one for which some other (non-mysterious) beliefs supply reasons but which does not in turn supply reasons for other beliefs. This is, at least, as far into the unknown as I can stretch the notion of identifying a ritual belief. Here, however, both theology and my analogy stop: a complete mystery is unintelligible to all.

The analogy between anthropologist and unbelieving theologian may be missed, because it is easy simply to credit the theologian with an understanding of the language of the faithful. The theologian, in other words, is his own bilingual. If so, the price of drawing the analogy seems to be the collapse of my thesis, since, as remarked at the beginning, an

[15] e.g. Peter Winch, 'Understanding a Primitive Society', *American Philosophical Quarterly*, i (1964), 307–24, and the references cited in that article.

articulate and intelligent bilingual can apparently make the anthropologist a gift of all the natives' ritual beliefs. But this presupposes that the bilingual has already identified the ritual beliefs and can present them in English sentences intelligible to the anthropologist. The conceptual problem, however, remains the same whether it is stated for two men and two languages or for one man and one language. It is that of putting ritual beliefs into a form in which they can be classed as rational without ceasing to be the beliefs in question. This is one task of theology.

As proof of the pudding, let me offer as a model piece of anthropology a quotation from the Greek Cardinal Bessarion:

> In the sacrament of the Eucharist there is one thing which is merely a sign, namely, the visible species of bread and wine; and another thing which is the reality signified, namely, the true body and blood of Our Lord, which he took from the pure flesh of the Blessed Virgin. But the body and blood of Christ, while it is a reality pointed to by the sign of the bread and wine, as we shall shortly show, nevertheless is, itself, the sign of another reality, since it points to the Mystical Body of Christ, and the Unity of the Church in the Holy Ghost. This Mystical Body, however, and this unity do not point beyond themselves to any other reality, but are only themselves pointed to.[16]

Bessarion is a believing theologian. How is the unbeliever to understand his account, without becoming a convert? He should, I suggest, take it literally and test it for rationality, in order to understand it, and then deny that it corresponds to anything, in order to disagree with it. For, if it is taken as simply metaphorical or false or without truth-value or irrational, then it is unintelligible, and, if it is taken not to make any empirical claims, then there is nothing to disagree with.

Unless we take the expression of some ritual beliefs literally, we shall again make anthropology impossible. I said earlier that a ritual belief p could be identified only if it was rational and that it was rational if and only if there was a belief q which supplied a reason for holding it. If q is itself a ritual belief then we need a further belief r which supplies a reason for holding q. In other words, if ritual beliefs form an autonomous system, we cannot understand one without understanding many or many without understanding one. We need, then, a belief Z which is expressed in practical, and not in expressive, symbolism and which supplies a reason for holding some ritual beliefs. Moreover Z must itself be identified and so must either be true or be traceable in the same way to some further empirical belief which is true.[17] For, as has been argued all along, understanding

---

[16] *De Sacramento Eucharistiae*, P. G. 161, 496. The passage is quoted and discussed by Fr. Bernard Leeming, S.J., in his *Principles of Sacramental Theology*, London: Longmans Green and Co., 1956, p. 256.

[17] Mr. Hacker has pointed out that the argument, if sound, should hold against Intuitionist Theories of Ethics.

is only possible if it advances from a bridgehead of true and rational empirical statements. Literal sense is as important to the temple as it is to the market-place.

But, it will be objected, people speak in metaphors, especially in ritual. The objects used in sacraments may be everyday things, like bread, blood, and water, but they are used symbolically. If the upshot of this paper is that metaphor is impossible or unintelligible, so much the worse for the paper. My answer is that some metaphors are unintelligible, in the way that some mysteries are.

> Life like a dome of many-coloured glass
> Stains the white radiance of eternity.

This is what Carnap would call a Metaphysical Proposition and only a rash man would claim to know what it means. At any rate, since the claim is undemonstrable, we are free to reject it. Here, I think, we can at last settle for Miss Langer's analogy between ritual and music. Shelley's metaphors cannot be rendered discursive.

Not all metaphors are so resistant. Some can be cashed (only indirectly, perhaps) in terms which can be u derstood literally. Thus the metaphor in 'He makes my blood boil', like the symbolism in the Statue of Liberty, is easily dissected. Metaphor, while it is still alive and not dead, is a new and self-conscious way of conceptualizing experience and, although not purely descriptive, can be traced to descriptive statements. But this makes it a civilized phenomenon; a savage who says 'He makes my blood boil', is likely to mean exactly what he says.[18] I am not saying here that there is no difficulty about metaphor. Indeed, I would agree that many metaphors have to be construed by analogy with music, and this requires a sense of 'understanding' which I do not pretend to grasp. I am saying only that claims to have identified the metaphorical uses of words and gestures must be rationally justified. This involves cashing the metaphors and therefore the notion of 'metaphorical use' never has any explanatory force.

---

[18] It is important also that a similar 'civilized' distinction between instrumental and symbolic behaviour does not always hold in primitive thought. Thus Evans-Pritchard remarks of the Azande: 'When a man chooses a suitable tree and fells it and hollows its wood into a gong his actions are empirical, but when he abstains from sexual intercourse during his labour we speak of his abstinence as ritual, since it has no objective relation to the making of gongs and since it involves ideas of taboo. We thus classify Zande behaviour into empirical and ritual, and Zande notions into common sense and mystical, according to our knowledge of natural processes and not according to theirs. For we raise quite a different question when we ask whether the Zande himself distinguishes between those techniques we call empirical and those techniques we call magical', (op. cit., p. 492). The passage does not imply relativism.

This paper stands or falls with the claim that a theorist of social anthropology must budget for *a priori* elements which are not optional. It may be as well to finish by rehearsing the claim. The *a priori* elements are those notions which the natives must be assumed to have, if any identification of their ritual beliefs is to be known to be correct. To get at ritual beliefs, the anthropologist works from an understanding of the native language in everyday contexts. To establish a bridgehead, by which I mean a set of utterances definitive of the standard meanings of words, he has to assume at least that he and the native share the same perceptions and make the same empirical judgements in simple situations. This involves assumptions about empirical truth and reference, which in turn involve crediting the natives with his own skeletal notion of logical reasoning. To identify their ritual beliefs he has to assume that they share his concept of 'being a reason for'. There will be better reason to accept his account than to reject it, only if he makes most native beliefs coherent and rational and most empirical beliefs in addition true. These notions are *a priori* in the sense that they belong to his tools and not to his discoveries, providing the yardsticks by which he accepts or rejects possible interpretations. They are not optional, in that they are the only conditions upon which his account will be even intelligible. In short, although it is an empirical fact that the natives hold any beliefs and have any language at all, and although it is a matter of hard work and huge expertise to discover what forms they take, the anthropologist needs conceptual tools before he can even begin. When packing his tool box, he is a philosopher.

Evans-Pritchard ends his book on Nuer Religion with these words:

Though prayer and sacrifice are exterior actions, Nuer religion is ultimately an interior state. This state is externalized in rites which we can observe, but their meaning depends finally on an awareness of God and that men are dependent on him and must be resigned to his will. At this point the theologian takes over from the anthropologist.[19]

The theologian seems already to have taken over from the anthropologist. But why not? Sacred anthropology is sceptical theology.

[19] E. E. Evans-Pritchard, *Nuer Religion*, Oxford, 1956, Ch. XII, p. 322.

III

BRINGING MEN BACK IN

GEORGE C. HOMANS

A theory of a phenomenon is an explanation of it, showing how it follows as a conclusion from general propositions in a deductive system. With all its empirical achievements, the functional school never produced a theory that was also an explanation, since from its general propositions about the conditions of social equilibrium no definite conclusions could be drawn. When a serious effort is made, even by functionalists, to construct an explanatory theory, its general propositions turn out to be psychological—propositions about the behavior of men, not the equilibrium of societies.

I AM GOING to talk about an issue we have worried over many times. I have worried over it myself. But I make no excuses for taking it up again. Although it is an old issue, it is still not a settled one, and I think it is the most general intellectual issue in sociology. If I have only one chance to speak *ex cathedra*, I cannot afford to say something innocuous. On the contrary, now if ever is the time to be nocuous.

In the early 1930s a distinct school of sociological thought was beginning to form. Its chief, though certainly not its only, intellectual parents were Durkheim and Radcliffe-Brown. I call it a school, though not all its adherents accepted just the same tenets; and many sociologists went ahead and made great progress without giving a thought to it. The school is usually called that of structural-functionalism, or functionalism for short. For a whole generation it has been the dominant, indeed the only distinct, school of sociological thought. I think it has run its course, done its work, and now positively gets in the way of our understanding social phenomena. And I propose to ask, Why?

THE INTERESTS OF FUNCTIONALISM

I begin by reminding you of the chief interests and assumptions of functionalism, especially as contrasted with what it was not interested in and took for granted, for the questions it did not ask have returned to plague it. If what I say seems a caricature, remember that a caricature emphasizes a person's most characteristic features.

From the *American Sociological Review*, xxix, No. 5 (Dec. 1964), 809–18. Reprinted by permission of the author and the American Sociological Association.

First, the school took its start from the study of norms, the statements the members of a group make about how they ought to behave, and indeed often do behave, in various circumstances. It was especially interested in the cluster of norms called a role and in the cluster of roles called an institution. It never tired of asserting that its concern was with institutionalized behaviour, and that the unit of social analysis was not the acting individual but the role. The school did not ask why there should be roles at all.

Second, the school was empirically interested in the interrelations of roles, the interrelations of institutions: this was the structural side of its work. It was the sort of thing the social anthropologists had been doing, showing how the institutions of a primitive society fitted together; and the sociologists extended the effort to advanced societies. They would point out, for instance, that the nuclear family rather than some form of extended kinship was characteristic of industrialized societies. But they were more interested in establishing *what* the interrelations of institutions were than in *why* they were so. In the beginning the analyses tended to be static, as it is more convincing to speak of a social structure in a society conceived to be stable than in one undergoing rapid change. Recently the school has turned to the study of social change, but in so doing it has had to take up the question it disregarded earlier. If an institution is changing, one can hardly avoid asking why it is changing in one direction rather than another.

Third, the school was, to put it crudely, more interested in the consequences than in the causes of an institution, particularly in the consequences for a social system considered as a whole. These consequences were the *functions* of the institution. Thus the members of the school never tired of pointing out the functions and dysfunctions of a status system, without asking why a status system should exist in the first place, why it was there to have functions. They were especially interested in showing how its institutions helped maintain a society in equilibrium, as a going concern. The model for research was Durkheim's effort to show, in *The Elementary Forms of the Religious Life*, how the religion of a primitive tribe helped hold the tribe together.

Such were the empirical interests of functionalism. As empirically I have been a functionalist myself, I shall be the last to quarrel with them. It is certainly one of the jobs of a sociologist to discover what the norms of a society are. Though a role is not actual behaviour, it is for some purposes a useful simplification. Institutions *are* interrelated, and it is certainly one of the jobs of a sociologist to show what the interrelations are. Institutions do have consequences, in the sense that, if one institution may be taken as given, the other kinds of institution that may exist in the society are probably not infinite in number. It is certainly one of the jobs of a sociologist to search out these consequences and even, though this is more difficult, to determine whether their consequences are good or bad for the society as a whole. At any rate, the empirical interests of functionalism have led to an enormous amount of good work. Think only of the studies made by Murdock[1] and others on the cross-cultural interrelations of institutions.

As it began to crystallize, the functional school developed theoretical interests as well as empirical ones. There was no necessity for the two to go together, and the British social anthropologists remained relatively untheoretical. Not so the American sociologists, particularly Talcott Parsons, who claimed that they were not only theorists but something called general theorists, and strongly emphasized the importance of theory.

Theirs was to be, moreover, a certain kind of theory. They were students of Durkheim and took seriously his famous definition of *social facts*: 'Since their essential characteristic consists in the power they possess of exerting, from outside, a pressure on individual consciousnesses, they do not derive from individual consciousnesses, and in consequence sociology is not a corollary of psychology.'[2] Since Durkheim was a great man, one can find statements in his writings that have quite other implications, but this caricature of himself was the one that made the difference. If not in what they said, then surely in what they did, the functionalists took Durkheim seriously. Their fundamental unit, the role, was a social fact in Durkheim's sense. And their theoretical programme assumed, as he did, that sociology should be an independent science, in the sense that its propositions should not be derivable from some other social science, such as psychology. This meant, in effect, that the general propositions of sociology were not to be propositions about the behaviour of 'individual consciousnesses'—or, as I should say, about men—but propositions about the characteristics of societies or other social groups as such.

Where functionalism failed was not in its empirical interests but, curiously, in what it most prided itself on, its general theory. Let me be very careful here. In a recent Presidential Address, Kingsley Davis asserted that we are all functionalists now,[3] and there is a sense in which he was quite right. But note that he was talking about functional *analysis*. One carries out functional analysis when, starting from the existence of a

[1] George P. Murdock, *Social Structure*, New York: Macmillan, 1949.

[2] Emile Durkheim, *Les Regles de la méthode sociologique* (8th edn.), Paris: Alcan, 1927, pp. 124–5.

[3] 'The Myth of Functional Analysis as a Special Method in Sociology and Anthropology', *American Sociological Review*, xxiv (Dec. 1959), 757–73.

particular institution, one tries to find out what difference the institution makes to the other aspects of social structure. That is, one carries out the empirical programme of functionalism. Since we have all learned to carry out functional analyses, we are in this sense all functionalists now. But functional analysis, as a method, is not the same thing as functional theory. And if we are all functional analysts, we are certainly not all functional theorists. Count me out, for one.

The only inescapable office of theory is to explain. The theory of evolution is an explanation why and how evolution occurs. To look for the consequences of institutions, to show the interrelationships of institutions is not the same thing as explaining why the interrelationships are what they are. The question is a practical and not a philosophical one—not whether it is legitimate to take the role as the fundamental unit, nor whether institutions are really real, but whether the theoretical programme of functionalism has in fact led to explanations of social phenomena, including the findings of functional analysis itself. Nor is the question whether functionalism might not do so, but whether it has done as of today. I think it has not.

2. THE NATURE OF THEORY

With all their talk about theory, the functionalists never—and I speak advisedly—succeeded in making clear what a theory was. It must be allowed in their excuse that, in the early days, the philosophers of science had not given as clear an answer to the question as they have now.[4] But even then, the functionalists could have done better than they did, and certainly the excuse is valid no longer. Today we should stop talking to our students about sociological theory until we have taught them what a theory is.

A theory of a phenomenon consists of a series of propositions, each stating a relationship between properties of nature. But not every kind of sentence qualifies as such a proposition. The propositions do not consist of definitions of the properties: the construction of a conceptual scheme is an indispensable part of theoretical work but is not itself theory. Nor may a proposition simply say that there is some relationship between the properties. Instead, if there is some change in one of the properties, it must at least begin to specify what the change in the other property will be. If one of the properties is absent, the other will also be absent, or if one of the properties increases in value, the other will too. The properties, the variables, may be probabilities.

[4] See especially R. B. Braithwaite, *Scientific Explanation*, Cambridge: Cambridge University Press, 1953.

Accordingly, to take a famous example, Marx's statement that the economic organization of a society determines the nature of its other institutions is an immensely useful guide to research. For it says: "Look for the social consequences of economic change, and if you look, you will surely find them!" But it is not the sort of proposition that can enter a theory. For by itself it says only that, if the economic infrastructure changes, there will be some change in the social superstructure, without beginning to suggest what the latter change will be. Most of the sentences of sociology, alleged to be theoretical, resemble this one of Marx's, yet few of our theorists realize it. And while we are always asking that theory guide research, we forget that many statements like Marx's are good guides to research without being good theory.

To constitute a theory, the propositions must take the form of a deductive system. One of them, usually called the lowest-order proposition, is the proposition to be explained, for example, the proposition that the more thoroughly a society is industrialized, the more fully its kinship organization tends towards the nuclear family. The other propositions are either general propositions or statements of particular given conditions. The general propositions are so called because they enter into other, perhaps many other, deductive systems besides the one in question. Indeed, what we often call a theory is a cluster of deductive systems, sharing the same general propositions but having different *explicanda*. The crucial requirement is that each system shall be deductive. That is, the lowest-order proposition follows as a logical conclusion from the general propositions under the specified given conditions. The reason why statements like Marx's may not enter theories is that no definite conclusions may in logic be drawn from them. When the lowest-order proposition does follow logically, it is said to be explained. The explanation of a phenomenon is the theory of the phenomenon. A theory is nothing—it is not a theory—unless it is an explanation.

One may define properties and categories, and one still has no theory. One may state that there *are* relations between the properties, and one still has no theory. One may state that a change in one property will produce a definite change in another property, and one still has no theory. Not until one has properties, and propositions stating the relations between them, and the propositions form a deductive system—not until one has all three does one have a theory. Most of our arguments about theory would fall to the ground, if we first asked whether we had a theory to argue about.

3. FUNCTIONAL THEORIES

As a theoretical effort, functionalism never came near meeting these conditions. Even if the functionalists had seriously tried to meet them, which they did not, I think they would still have failed. The difficulty lay in the characteristic general propositions of functionalism. A proposition is not functional just because it uses the word *function*. To say that a certain institution is functional for individual men in the sense of meeting their needs is not a characteristic proposition of functionalism. Instead it belongs to the class of psychological propositions. Nor is the statement that one institution is a function of another, in the quasi-mathematical sense of function, characteristic. Though many functional theorists make such statements, non-functionalists like myself may also make them without a qualm. The characteristic general propositions of functional theory in sociology take the form: 'If it is to survive, or remain in equilibrium, a social system—any social system—must possess institutions of Type X.' For instance, if it is to survive or remain in equilibrium, a society must possess conflict-resolving institutions. By general propositions of this sort the functionalists sought to meet Durkheim's demand for a truly independent sociological theory.

The problem was, and is, to construct deductive systems headed by such propositions. Take first the terms *equilibrium* and *survival*. If the theorist chose *equilibrium*, he was able to provide no criterion of social equilibrium, especially 'dynamic' or 'moving' equilibrium, definite enough to allow anything specific to be deduced in logic from a proposition employing the term. I shall give an example later. When indeed was a society not in equilibrium? If the theorist chose *survival*, he found this, too, surprisingly hard to define. Did Scotland, for instance, survive as a society? Though it had long been united with England, it still possessed distinctive institutions, legal and religious. If the theorist took *survival* in the strong sense, and said that a society had not survived if all its members had died without issue, he was still in trouble. As far as the records went, the very few societies of this sort had possessed institutions of all the types the functionalists said were necessary for survival. The evidence put in question, to say the least, the empirical truth of the functionalist propositions. Of course the functionalists were at liberty to say: 'If a society is to survive, its members must not all be shot dead', which was true as true could be but allowed little to be deduced about the social characteristics of surviving societies.

Indeed the same was true of the other functional propositions. Even if a statement like: 'If it is to survive, a society must possess conflict-resolving institutions' were accepted as testable and true, it possessed little explanatory power. From the proposition the fact could be deduced that, given a certain society did survive, it did possess conflict-resolving institutions of some kind, and the fact was thus explained. What remained unexplained was why the society had conflict-resolving institutions of a particular kind, why, for instance, the jury was an ancient feature of Anglo-Saxon legal institutions. I take it that what sociology has to explain are the actual features of actual societies and not just the generalized features of a generalized society.

I do not think that members of the functional school could have set up, starting with general propositions of their distinctive type, theories that were also deductive systems. More important, they did not. Recognizing, perhaps, that they were blocked in one direction, some of them elaborated what they called theory in another. They used what they asserted were a limited and exhaustive number of functional problems faced by any society to generate a complex set of categories in terms of which social structure could be analysed. That is, they set up a conceptual scheme. But analysis is not explanation, and a conceptual scheme is not a theory. They did not fail to make statements about the relations between the categories, but most of the statements resembled the one of Marx's I cited earlier: they were not of the type that enter deductive systems. From their lower-order propositions, as from their higher-order ones, no definite conclusions in logic could be drawn. Under these conditions, there was no way of telling whether their choice of functional problems and categories was not wholly arbitrary. What the functionalists actually produced was not a theory but a new language for describing social structure, one among many possible languages; and much of the work they called theoretical consisted in showing how the words in other languages, including that of everyday life, could be translated into theirs. They would say, for instance, that what other people called making a living was called in their language goal-attainment. But what makes a theory is deduction, not translation.

I have said that the question is not whether, in general, functional theories can be real theories, for there are sciences that possess real functional theories. The question is rather whether this particular effort was successful. If a theory is an explanation, the functionalists in sociology were, on the evidence, not successful. Perhaps they could not have been successful; at any rate they were not. The trouble with their theory was not that it was wrong, but that it was not a theory.

4. AN ALTERNATIVE THEORY

Here endeth the destructive part of the lesson. I shall now try to show that a more successful effort to explain social phenomena entails the construction of theories different from functional ones, in the sense that their general propositions are of a different kind, precisely the kind, indeed, that the functionalists tried to get away from. I shall try to show this for the very phenomena the functionalists took for granted and the very relations they discovered empirically. I shall even try to show that, when functionalists took the job of explanation seriously, which they sometimes did, this other kind of theory would appear unacknowledged in their own work.

The functionalists insisted over and over again that the minimum unit of social analysis was the role, which is a cluster of norms. In a recent article, James Coleman has written: ' . . . sociologists have characteristically taken as their starting-point a social system in which norms exist, and individuals are largely governed by these norms. Such a strategy views norms as the governors of social behavior, and thus neatly bypasses the difficult problem that Hobbes posed.'[5] Hobbes's problem is, of course, why there is not a war of all against all.

Why, in short, should there be norms at all? The answer Coleman gives is that, in the kind of case he considers, norms arise through the actions of men rationally calculating to further their own self-interest in a context of other men acting in the same way. He writes: 'The central postulate about behavior is this: each actor will attempt to extend his power over those actions in which he has most interest.' Starting from this postulate, Coleman constructs a deductive system explaining why the actors adopt a particular sort of norm in the given circumstances.

I do not want to argue the vexed question of rationality. I do want to point out what sort of general proposition Coleman starts with. As he recognizes, it is much like the central assumption of economics, though self-interest is not limited to the material interests usually considered by economists. It also resembles a proposition of psychology, though here it might take the form: the more valuable the reward of an activity, the more likely a man is to perform the activity. But it certainly is not a characteristic functional proposition in sociology: it is not a statement about the conditions of equilibrium for a society, but a statement about the behaviour of individual men.

Again, if there are norms, why do men conform to them? Let us lay aside the fact that many men do not conform or conform very indifferently, and assume that they all do so. Why do they do so? So far as the functionalists gave any answer to the question, it was that men have 'internalized' the values embodied in the norm. But 'internalization' is a word and not an explanation. So far as their own theory was concerned, the functionalists took conformity to norms for granted. They made the mistake Malinowski pointed out long ago in a book now too little read by sociologists, the mistake made by early writers on primitive societies, the mistake of assuming that conformity to norms is a matter of '. . . this automatic acquiescence, this instinctive submission of every member of the tribe to its laws . . . ".[6] The alternative answer Malinowski gave was that obedience to norms 'is usually rewarded according to the measure of its perfection, while noncompliance is visited upon the remiss agent'.[7] In short, the answer he gave is much like that of Coleman and the psychologists. Later he added the suggestive remark: 'The true problem is not to study how human life submits to rules—it simply does not; the real problem is how the rules become adapted to life.'[8]

The question remains why members of a particular society find certain of the results of their actions rewarding and not others, especially when some of the results seem far from 'naturally' rewarding. This is the real problem of the 'internalization' of values. The explanation is given not by any distinctively sociological propositions but by the propositions of learning theory in psychology.

The functionalists were much interested in the interrelations of institutions, and it was one of the glories of the school to have pointed out many such interrelations. But the job of a science does not end with pointing out interrelations; it must try to explain why they are what they are. Take the statement that the kinship organization of industrialized societies tends to be that of the nuclear family. I cannot give anything like the full explanation, but I can, and you can too, suggest the beginning of one. Some men organized factories because by so doing they thought they could get greater material rewards than they could get otherwise. Other men entered factories for reasons of the same sort. In so doing they worked away from home and so had to forgo, if only for lack of time, the cultivation of the extended kinship ties that were a source of reward, because a source of help, in many traditional agricultural societies, where work lay closer to home. Accordingly the nuclear family tended to become associated with factory organization; and the explanation for the association is provided by propositions about the behaviour of men as such. Not the needs of society explain the relationship, but the needs of men.

Again, functionalists were interested in the consequences of institutions, especially their consequences for a social system as a whole. For instance, they were endlessly concerned with the functions and dysfunctions of status systems. Seldom did they ask why there should be status systems in the

[6] Bronislaw Malinowski, *Crime and Custom in Savage Society*, Paterson, N.J.: Littlefield, Adams, 1959, p. 11.
[7] Ibid., p. 12.
[8] Ibid., p. 127.

first place. Some theorists have taken the emergence of phenomena like status systems as evidence for Durkheim's contention that sociology was not reducible to psychology. What is important is not the fact of emergence but the question how the emergence is to be explained. One of the accomplishments of small-group research is to explain how a status system, of course on a small scale, emerges in the course of interaction between the members of a group.[9] The explanation is provided by psychological propositions. Certainly no functional propositions are needed. Indeed the theoretical contribution of small-group research has consisted 'in showing how the kinds of microscopic variables usually ignored by sociologists can explain the kinds of social situations usually ignored by psychologists'.[10]

What is the lesson of all this? If the very things functionalists take for granted, like norms, if the very interrelationships they empirically discover can be explained by deductive systems that employ psychological propositions, then it must be that the general explanatory principles even of sociology are not sociological, as the functionalists would have them be, but psychological, propositions about the behaviour of men, not about the behaviour of societies. On the analogy with other sciences, this argument by itself would not undermine the validity of a functional theory. Thermodynamics, for instance, states propositions about aggregates, which are themselves true and general, even though they can be explained in turn, in statistical mechanics, by propositions about members of the aggregates. The question is whether this kind of situation actually obtains in sociology. So far as functional propositions are concerned, which are propositions about social aggregates, the situation does not obtain, for they have not been shown to be true and general.

5. EXPLAINING SOCIAL CHANGE

My next contention is that even confessed functionalists, when they seriously try to explain certain kinds of social phenomena, in fact use non-functional explanations without recognizing that they do so. This is particularly clear in their studies of social change.

Social change provides a searching test for theory, since historical records are a prerequisite for its study. Without history, the social scientist can establish the contemporaneous interrelations of institutions, but may be hard put to it to explain why the interrelations should be what

---

[9] See George C. Homans, *Social Behavior: Its Elementary Forms*, New York: Harcourt, Brace & World, 1961, esp. Ch. 8.

[10] C. N. Alexander, Jr. and R. L. Simpson, 'Balance Theory and Distributive Justice', *Sociological Inquiry*, xxxiv (1964), 182–92.

they are. With historical records he may have the information needed to support an explanation. One of the commonest charges against the functionalist school was that it could not deal with social change, that its analysis was static. In recent years some functionalists have undertaken to show that the charge was unjustified. They have chosen for their demonstration the process of differentiation in society, the process, for instance, of the increasing specialization of occupations. In question as usual is not the fact of differentiation—there is no doubt that the overall trend of social history has been in this direction—but how the process is to be explained.

A particularly good example of this new development in functionalism is Neil Smelser's book, *Social Change in the Industrial Revolution: An Application of Theory to the British Cotton Industry 1770–1840*.[11] The book is not just good for my purposes: it is good, very good, in itself. It provides an enormous amount of well-organized information, and it goes far to explain the changes that occurred. The amusing thing about it is that the explanation Smelser actually uses, good scientist that he is, to account for the changes is not the functional theory he starts out with, which is as usual a non-theory, but a different kind of theory and a better one.

Smelser begins like any true functionalist. For him a social system is one kind of system of action, characterized as follows: 'A social system . . . is composed of a set of interrelated roles, collectivities, etc. . . . It is important to remember that the roles, collectivities, etc., not individuals, are the units in this last case.' Moreover,

all systems of action are governed by the principle of equilibrium. According to the dominant type of equilibrium, the adjustments proceed in a certain direction: if the equilibrium is stable, the units tend to return to their original position; if the equilibrium is partial, only some of the units need to adjust; if the equilibrium is unstable, the tendency is to change, through mutual adjustment, to a new equilibrium or to disintegrate altogether.

Fictionally, 'all social systems are subject to four functional exigencies which must be met more or less satisfactorily if the system is to remain in equilibrium.'[12] Note that by this argument all social systems are in equilibrium, even systems in process of disintegration. Though the latter are in unstable equilibrium, they are still in equilibrium. Accordingly they are meeting more or less satisfactorily the four functional exigencies. You see how useful a deductive system can be in social science? More seriously you will see that definitions of equilibrium are so broad that you may draw any conclusion you like from them.

---

[11] Chicago, Ill.: University of Chicago Press, 1959.
[12] Ibid., pp. 10–11.

But for all the explanatory use Smelser makes of it, this theory and its subsequent elaboration is so much window-dressing. When he really gets down to explaining the innovations in the British cotton textile industry, especially the introduction of spinning and weaving machinery, he forgets his functionalism. The guts of his actual explanation lie in the seven steps through which he says the process proceeds:

Industrial differentiation proceeds, therefore, by the following steps:
(1) Dissatisfaction with the productive achievements of the industry or its relevant sub-sectors and a sense of opportunity in terms of the potential availability of adequate facilities to reach a higher level of productivity.
(2) Appropriate symptoms of disturbance in the form of 'unjustified' negative emotional reactions and 'unrealistic' aspirations on the part of various elements of the population.[13]

I shall not give the other five steps, as I should make the same criticism of them as I now make of the first two. I think they provide by implication a good explanation of the innovations of the Industrial Revolution in cotton manufacturing. But what kind of an explanation is it? Whatever it is, it is not a functional one. Where here do roles appear as the fundamental units of a social system? Where are the four functional exigencies? Not a word do we hear of them. Instead, what do we hear of? We hear of dissatisfaction, a sense of opportunity, emotional reactions, and aspirations. And what feels these things? Is a role dissatisfied or emotional? No; Smelser himself says it is 'various elements of the population' that do so. Under relentless pressure let us finally confess that 'various elements of the population' means men. And what men? For the most part men engaged in making and selling cotton cloth. And what were they dissatisfied with? Not with 'the productive achievements of the industry'. Though some statesmen were certainly concerned about the contribution made by the industry as a whole to the wealth of Great Britain, let us, again under relentless pressure, confess that most of the men in question were concerned with their own profits. Let us get men back in, and let us put some blood in them. Smelser himself makes the crucial statement: 'In Lancashire in the early 1760's there was excited speculation about instantaneous fortunes for the man lucky enough to stumble on the right invention.'[14] In short, the men in question were activated by self-interest. Yet not all self-interests are selfish interests, and certainly not all the innovations of the Industrial Revolution can be attributed to selfishness.

Smelser's actual explanation of technical innovation in cotton manufacturing might be sketched in the following deductive system. I have left out the most obvious steps.

[13] Ibid., p. 29.   [14] Ibid., p. 80.

1. Men are more likely to perform an activity, the more valuable they perceive the reward of that activity to be.
2. Men are more likely to perform an activity, the more successful they perceive the activity to be in getting that reward.
3. The high demand for cotton textiles and the low productivity of labour led men concerned with cotton manufacturing to perceive the development of labour-saving machinery as rewarding in increased profits.
4. The existing state of technology led them to perceive the effort to develop labour-saving machinery as likely to be successful.
5. Therefore, by both (1) and (2) such men were highly likely to try to develop labour-saving machinery.
6. Since their perceptions of the technology were accurate, their efforts were likely to meet with success, and some of them did meet with success.

From these first steps, others such as the organization of factories and an increasing specialization of jobs followed. But no different kind of explanation is needed for these further developments: propositions like (1) and (2), which I call the *value* and the *success* propositions, would occur in them, too. We should need a further proposition to describe the effect of frustration, which certainly attended some of the efforts at innovation, in creating the 'negative emotional reactions' of Smelser's step 2.

I must insist again on the kind of explanation this is. It is an explanation using psychological propositions (1 and 2 above), psychological in that they are commonly stated and tested by psychologists and that they refer to the behaviour of men and not to the conditions of equilibrium of societies or other social groups as such. They are general in that they appear in many, and I think all, of the deductive systems that will even begin to explain social behaviour. There is no assumption that the men in question are all alike in their concrete behaviour. They may well have been conditioned to find different things rewarding, but the way conditioning takes place is itself explained by psychological propositions. There is no assumption that their values are all materialistic, but only that their pursuit of non-material values follows the same laws as their pursuit of material ones. There is no assumption that they are isolated or unsocial, but only that the laws of human behaviour do not change just because another person rather than the physical environment provides the rewards for behaviour. Nor is there any assumption that psychological propositions will explain everything social. We shall certainly not be able to explain everything, but our failures will be attributable to lack of factual information or the intellectual machinery for dealing with complexity—though the computers will help us here—and not to the propositions themselves. Nor is there any assumption here of psychological reductionism, though I used to think there was. For reduction implies that there are general sociological propositions that can then be reduced to psychological ones. I now suspect that there are no general sociological propositions, propositions that hold good of all societies or social groups as such, and that the only general propositions of sociology are in fact psychological.

What I do claim is that, no matter what we say our theories are, when we seriously try to explain social phenomena by constructing even the veriest sketches of deductive systems, we find ourselves in fact, and whether we admit it or not, using what I have called psychological explanations. I need hardly add that our actual explanations are our actual theories.

I am being a little unfair to functionalists like Smelser and Parsons if I imply that they did not realize there were people around. The so-called theory of action made a very good start indeed by taking as its paradigm for social behaviour two persons, the actions of each of whom sanctioned, that is, rewarded or punished, the actions of the other.[15] But as soon as the start was made, its authors disregarded it. As the theory of action was applied to society, it appeared to have no actors and mighty little action. The reason was that it separated the personality system from the social system and proposed to deal with the latter alone. It was the personality system that had 'needs, drives, skills, etc.'[16] It was not part of the social system, but only conducted exchanges with it, by providing it, for instance, with disembodied motivation.[17] This is the kind of box you get into when you think of theory as a set of boxes. For this reason, no one should hold their style of writing against the functionalists. The best of writers must write clumsily when he has set up his intellectual problem in a clumsy way. If the theorist will only envisage his problem from the outset as one of constructing explanatory propositions and not a set of categories, he will come to see that the personal and the social are not to be kept separate. The actions of a man that we take to be evidence of his personality are not different from his actions that, together with the actions of others, make up a social system. They are the same identical actions. The theorist will realize this when he finds the same set of general propositions, including the success and the value proposition mentioned above, are needed for explaining the phenomena of both personality and society.

[15] Talcott Parsons and Edward Shils (eds.), *Toward a General Theory of Action*, Cambridge, Mass.: Harvard University Press, 1951, pp. 14–16.

[16] Smelser, op. cit., p. 10.

[17] Ibid., p. 33.

6. CONCLUSION

If sociology is a science, it must take seriously one of the jobs of any science, which is that of providing explanations for the empirical relations it discovers. An explanation is a theory, and it takes the form of a deductive system. With all its talk about theory, the functionalist school did not take the job of theory seriously enough. It did not ask itself what a theory was, and it never produced a functional theory that was in fact an explanation. I am not sure that it could have done so, starting as it did with propositions about the conditions of social equilibrium, propositions from which no definite conclusions could be drawn in a deductive system. If a serious effort is made to construct theories that will even begin to explain social phenomena, it turns out that their general propositions are not about the equilibrium of societies but about the behaviour of men. This is true even of some good functionalists, though they will not admit it. They keep psychological explanations under the table and bring them out furtively like a bottle of whisky, for use when they really need help. What I ask is that we bring what we say about theory into line with what we actually do, and so put an end to our intellectual hypocrisy. It would unite us with the other social sciences, whose actual theories are much like our actual ones, and so strengthen us all. Let us do so also for the sake of our students. I sometimes think that they begin with more understanding of the real nature of social phenomena than we leave them with, and that our double-talk kills their mother-wit. Finally, I must acknowledge freely that everything I have said seems to me obvious. But why cannot we take the obvious seriously?

IV

FUNCTION AND CAUSE

R. P. DORE

KINGSLEY DAVIS has argued that we should abandon the notion that functionalism is a special form of sociological analysis.[1] It *is* sociological analysis, albeit occasionally clouded by misleading terminology. In at least one reader the effect of his thoughtful and wide-ranging paper was to stimulate reflection on our notions of function and cause and on the relations between them. The starting-point of these reflections was the question: does not Professor Davis's argument rest on a special and hardly universal view of what sociological analysis is or should be?

At one point he commends functionalism as having 'helped to make a place in sociology and anthropology for those wishing to explain social phenomena in terms of social systems, as against those who wished to make no explanation at all, to explain things in terms of some other system or to plead a cause'. Sociological analysis, in other words, is the explanation of social phenomena in terms of social systems. But surely cause-pleading, explanation in terms of other systems, and so on are not the only alternatives. There is another position, equally sociological, equally analytical, which holds that sociologists should search for regularities in the concomitant occurrences of social phenomena, seek to induce causal laws from such regularities, and seek eventually to order such laws into comprehensive theory. According to this view, systematic theory (a logically consistent body of causal laws) is the end product of a long search for causal relations, not a heuristically useful starting-point.

This, perhaps, betrays a preference for 'neat single propositions whose validity is proved but whose significance is not', a preference which Professor Davis condemns as 'scientific ritualism'. It is comforting to reflect that in the natural sciences at least we would not have got far without our ritualists. Newton in developing his systematic theory of mechanics owed a

From *American Sociological Review*, xxvi (Dec. 1961), 843–53. Reprinted by permission of the author and the American Sociological Association.

[1] Kingsley Davis, 'The Myth of Functional Analysis as a Special Method in Sociology and Anthropology', *American Sociological Review*, xxiv (Dec. 1959), 752–72.

good deal to Galileo's neat single proposition about the rate of acceleration of falling bodies.

The difference between these two views which we might characterize as the system approach and the piecemeal approach is not identical with the often imputed distinction between functional and non-functional analysis, but it does seem to be true that only the system approach encourages the use of the concept of function. The piecemeal approach is quite clearly bent on looking for causal relations. The system approach finds the concept of cause and causal law difficult to apply, and often finds functions easier to handle.

Perhaps the best way to justify this assertion would be to analyse closely the relations between the concepts of function and of cause. Let us take as starting-point the question: in what ways can a statement about the function of an institution, a pattern of behaviour, a role, or a norm be translated into a statement about causal relations?

1. FUNCTION—EFFECT

In the first place it is fairly obvious that 'the function of X is to maintain Y' implies that X has some kind of causal influence on Y, and it is presumably this kind of 'translation' Professor Davis had in mind when he denied that functional relations are non-causal. But an analysis of 'causal influence' leads to difficulties. Can we say 'the assertion that, say, the system of stratification has the function of making the division of labour possible implies that among the causes of the division of labour is the system of stratification'? Obviously not if 'the causes of the *origin* of the division of labour' is intended. We have to say something like 'the causes of the persistence of the division of labour'. This suggests that while one can legitimately ask the function of an institution, one cannot ask for the *cause* of an institution; one has to specify cause of origin or cause of persistence. It will be argued later that what this really amounts to is that one can legitimately ask only for the causes of *events*. Let us assume this argument for the moment and formulate this particular relation between function and cause as follows: 'institution X has the function of maintaining institution Y' implies that the recurring events referred to as institution X are among the causes of other events integral to the institution Y (or, can be related by causal laws to other events integral to institution Y).

2. FUNCTION—CAUSE

But this is not the kind of causal relationship implied when it is said that an institution is 'explained' in terms of its function. Here (less often explicitly than implicitly as a result of the ambiguities of the word 'explain') the transition is suggested not from the function of X to the causes of something other than X, but from the function of X to the causes of X itself. When and how may this kind of transition be made?

A small boy's examination of the interior of a watch may lead him to conclude that the function of the balance spring is to control the movement of the balance wheel. He would have little difficulty in using his functional insight to arrive at a causal explanation of the spring's presence—it is there because the man who made the watch realized a need for something to control the movement of the wheel, and the process of ratiocination which ensued led him to put in the spring.

Sociologists are not always precluded from making the same kind of transition from function of X to cause of X. Human institutions are now purposefully designed on a scale rarely attempted before. An analysis of the functions of the Chinese communes leads easily to an explanation of the causes of their existence, for they were created by historically identifiable persons to perform these functions and there may well be minutes of committees which record the process of invention with constant reference to their intended consequences, both those which were to be manifest to the communed Chinese and those which were to be latent to them and manifest only to their leaders.

Perhaps more common is the case where human purpose, based on an awareness of function, is a causal factor not so much in the initiation of an institution as in its growth and development. The Roman circus started well before emperors realized the salutary political functions it shared with bread. It was not until the third century B.C. that, as Radcliffe-Brown has pointed out,[2] the Chinese sociologist, Hsun-Tse, realized the latent psychological and social functions of ancestral rites, but his discovery certainly prompted later Confucian scholars to encourage the deluded masses in a continued belief in the reality of the manifest functions of those rites. Nowadays, with sociologists busily ferreting out latent functions in every nook and cranny of society and their writings gaining general currency, latent functions are not likely to stay latent for long. Here indeed is the complement of the self-fulfilling prophecy—the self-falsifying assertion. The sociologist who contends that X has such and such a latent function in his own society in fact makes that function manifest. The intervention of human purpose to preserve institutions so that they may

[2] A. R. Radcliffe-Brown, *Structure and Function in Primitive Society*, London: Cohen and West, 1952, pp. 157–9.

continue to fulfill their *once* latent functions is likely to occur more frequently as a result.[3]

However, modern sociologists still probably have less direct influence in moulding the institutions of their society than Hsun-Tse had in his, and in any case most sociologists are not imputing such a causal chain when they imply a connection between latent function of X and cause of X. Merton, for instance, clearly is thinking of something else when he speaks, apropos of the Hopi rain dances, of the analysis of their latent function as an *alternative* to describing their persistence 'only as an instance of "inertia", "survival" or "manipulation by powerful subgroups".' [4]

How then, without reference to human awareness of functions, can a statement about the function of an institution be translated into a causal statement about either the origin or the persistence of that institution?

3. SOCIETAL INTEGRATION

One way is to postulate an immanent tendency, universal in human societies, for the parts of the society all to be functionally integrated in the whole. Given such a tendency the function of an institution is its *raison d'être* and hence its cause. The logical grounds for such a postulate seem to be two. First there is the complementarity of roles and institutions; the role of wife implies the role of husband; the specialization of the executive to executive functions implies separate institutions for legislation and litigation, and so on. Such complementarities, however, are of limited range. Let an integrationist try his hand, for instance, at specifying the chains of complementarity which might link the institution of Presidential Elections with that of the burlesque show. The second basis for belief in the integration of societies rests on the supposed integration of the human personality. Since the same individual occupies numerous roles in a variety of institutional contexts and since all individuals are subject to a craving for consistency, it follows that all the institutions of a society must be permeated by the same value-preferences, the same modes of orientations to action, the same patterns of authority, the same world-view, the same sense of time, and so on. But how valid is the assumption of the consistent

---

[3] This raises moral as well as analytical problems when the institutions concerned involve factual beliefs. At the turn of the century John Morley's liberal conscience was somewhat exercised by 'the question of a dual doctrine . . . the question whether it is expedient that the more enlightened classes in a community should . . . not only possess their light in silence, but whether they should openly encourage a doctrine for the less enlightened classes which they do not believe to be true for themselves while they regard it as indispensably useful in the case of less fortunate people' (*On Compromise*, London: Macmillan, 1908, p. 44).

[4] Robert K. Merton, *Social Theory and Social Structure*, rev. edn., Glencoe, Ill.: The Free Press, 1957, p. 65.

personality? Which of us, sophisticates that we are, could confidently claim that he has never been guilty of preferring value *A* to value *B* in one situation and reversing his preference in another? And even if this were not so, this argument would create an *a priori* expectation of social integration only in the case of very simple societies. In such simple societies the number of roles is limited. Every individual in the society may occupy at some stage of his life a high proportion of the total number of roles. In such a society integrated personalities might make for integrated institutions. But this is not the case in large complex societies, segmented into regional and class sub-cultures with specialized personality types and offering a vast multiplication of roles only a tiny fraction of which any one individual will ever find himself performing.

Obviously there are no grounds for expecting such societies to be perfectly integrated. To quote Professor Davis again, 'it would be silly to regard such a proposition as literally true.' And one might add that modification of the proposition from 'always perfectly' to 'usually somewhat' integrated (a) destroys the possibility of its empirical falsification and (b) destroys its value as an automatic means of transition from function to cause.[5]

4. EVOLUTIONARY SELECTION

There remains, however, at least one way in which the sociologist may move on from function to cause—by means of the notions of adaptation and selection developed in the theories of biological evolution. To take the example of stratification and the division of labour, the hypothesis would have to go something like this: for various reasons some societies which began the division of labour also had, or developed, a system of unequal privileges for different groups, others did not. Those which did functioned more efficiently as societies; perhaps they bred more rapidly than, acquired resources at the expense of, and eventually eliminated, the others. Perhaps (and this is an extension of the concept of selection not available to the biologist) their obvious superiority in wealth, power, the arts, standard of

[5] A less ambitious and more precise integrationist thesis such as, for instance, 'the kinship structure and the occupational structure will always be integrated to the degree that the kinship structure does not impose obstacles to such free movement of individuals as the occupational structure requires' still does not allow for automatic transition from function to cause. (Would it be: the family is the way it is because of the occupational structure, or vice versa?) Such a thesis can, however, by specifying areas where causal relations are likely to be found, direct one's thinking towards such empirically testable hypotheses as those implicit in Parsons's discussion of the family. (See e.g. *The Social System*, Glencoe, Ill.: The Free Press, 1951, p. 178.) Such for instance as 'when industrialization proceeds the importance of the conjugal relation in the kinship structure increases.'

living, etc., induced the others to imitate their institutions wholesale, including the principle of stratification; or just conceivably (though here we slip 'human awareness' back into the causal chain) the others bred sociologists who noted the importance of stratification to the superior societies and urged its adoption specifically. At any rate, by one, or a combination, of these processes it now happens that all societies with a division of labour have a system of stratification.

It is an unlikely story, but it seems to be the only kind of story which will make a statement about the latent function of X relevant to a causal explanation of X. And even this, of course, is not a complete causal explanation. The 'various reasons' why some societies had stratification in the first place still need to be explained. For the biologist the place of these 'various reasons' is taken by 'random mutation' and some sociologists, too, are prepared to probe no further.[6]

But often the sociologist can think of specific 'various reasons' which eliminate randomness. Dennis H. Wrong, in his assessment of Davis and Moore on stratification,[7] suggests, for instance, that when the division of labour takes place certain groups acquire greater power in the society by virtue of that division and consequently arrogate to themselves a larger share of material and other rewards. And in this case, if this hypothesis concerning one of the 'various reasons' for the development of stratification in a society is historically validated, or accepted on the basis of what we know in general of human nature, then it could equally explain the development of stratification in any and all societies. The adaptive superiority of stratification due to its function in making the division of labour workable *may* still be relevant, too, but it is only one of a number of possible causal chains, the relative importance of which can only be assessed in the light of the historical evidence.

In any case, if one is looking for the causes of (either the origination or the continuance of) X, it is better to look for causes as such; looking for the functions of X is never a necessary, and not always even a useful, first step.[8]

---

[6] Ruth Benedict, for instance, remarks that 'the course of life and the pressure of the environment, not to speak of the fertility of the human imagination, provide an incredible number of possible leads, all of which, it appears, may serve a society to live by' and, the implication is, it is more or less beyond precise determination why they should utilize one lead rather than another (Ruth Benedict, *Patterns of Culture*, London: Routledge and Kegan Paul, 1949, p. 16).

[7] Dennis H. Wrong, 'The Functional Theory of Stratification', *American Sociological Review*, xxiv (Dec. 1959), 774.

[8] Cf., for instance, George C. Homans and David M. Schneider, *Marriage, Authority and Final Causes*, Glencoe, Ill.: The Free Press, 1955. In suggesting one 'efficient cause' for the development of patrilateral cross-cousin marriage in societies of certain types, namely that such a form of marriage best conforms to the personal interests of the

In point of fact we know from historical evidence that this evolutionary argument relating function to cause is irrelevant to certain social institutions which sociologists describe. The American boss-directed political machine, for instance, is said by Merton to have the functions of providing a centralization of power, of providing necessary services to those who need help rather than justice, of organizing essential, but morally disapproved, sectors of the economy, etc., and as such contributes to the maintenance of the social system as a whole. However, we know that the boss-system developed long after the United States was in direct and aggressive competition with other social groups for resources; we know from historical evidence that there has been no process of selective weeding out of societies involved.

In such cases one can still appeal to a weakened form of the evolutionary argument to relate function to cause by defining causally important conditions not for the original development of the institution but for its later transmission. It would have to go something like this: if the boss-system had not had these effects and so contributed to the smooth working of society, nor had these effects been neutral with respect to the smooth working of society, but had, on the contrary been positively detrimental to society's smooth working, people would have stopped doing it. In other words the fact that this feature was *not dysfunctional* to the workings of the society is a necessary condition of its present existence. It is also a necessary condition that all members of the society were not eliminated by an epidemic of bubonic plague. One could think of many more such negatively defined necessary conditions, all of which play a part, but only a small part, in a full causal explanation.

5. SUMMARY

This seems to exhaust the possible methods by which assertions about the functions of X can be involved in assertions about the causes of the (origin or continuance of) X. The sociologist may not be the least be interested in any of them. Having discovered that, say, social stratification has the function of making the division of labour workable, he may bit content with saying just that—and with perfect justification provided he concedes that he has said nothing about *why* societies are stratified. He may go on to point a corollary of his assertion—that if stratification were

---

members of such societies, they conclude, apropos of Lévy-Strauss's functional, or 'final cause', explanation (that such an institution makes for a 'better', because more organically integrated, society) 'not . . . that [it] is right or that it is wrong, but only that it is now unnecessary' (p. 59). Lévy-Strauss's functional explanation did not lead them to their own causal explanation in any sense except that it prompted them to challenge his assumption that it was all there was to be said on the subject.

abolished the division of labour would become unworkable. This is, indeed, an eminently useful social activity and the kind of analysis which can properly precede attempts at social reform. It is also, incidentally, the kind of activity in which a good many social anthropologists in particular have been professionally engaged in colonial administrations. The practical need to assess the probable effects of changes in institutions wrought by colonial policy has provided an important application of functional analysis which perhaps explains (causally) why so many anthropologists have been content with functional analysis as a legitimate final goal of their activities.

We may sum up the argument so far as follows:

1. In a not very clearly defined way the suggestion that institution X has the function of maintaining Y implies some causal influence of X on Y.

2. Assertions about the functions of an institution X are relevant to assertions about the causes of the origin or the persistence of that same institution X if, and only if: (a) one assumes that the function is manifest to the present actors in, to the present upholders of, or to former upholders or inventors of the institution in question, and as such has played a part in their motives for performing, or inducing others to perform, the institutionalized behaviour involved; (b) one postulated an immanent tendency for the functional integration of a society; (c) one postulates an adaptive superiority conferred by the institution which permitted it, having developed in one society, to spread to others.

These ideas are not particularly new.[9] The reason why they need reiterating is, it seems, largely because of the ill-defined relation between function and cause suggested by the first of our two propositions. It is the main business of this paper to try to improve the definition of that relation and, in the course of doing so, to make a few pertinent remarks about the use of analogies from natural science.

6. SYSTEM AND EVENT

Let us first examine the concept of system. 'How else can data be interpreted', said Professor Davis in his paper, 'except in relation to the larger structures in which they are implicated? How can data on the earth's orbit, for example, be understood except in relation to a system in which they are involved—in this case the solar system or the earth's

---

[9] The clear differentiation of causes and consequences, for instance, and the assertion that one may argue from consequence to cause only via (a) motive or (b) evolutionary theory is to be found in Harry C. Bredemeier, 'The Methodology of Functionalism', *American Sociological Review*, xx (Apr. 1955), 173. He somewhat obscures his first point, however, with the discussion, in the latter part of his paper, of the precise ways in which motives *also* have to be considered even for a discussion of consequences.

climatic system?' Is this, however, a good analogy? There are indeed systems in nature, such as the solar system, the parts of which are in continuous interaction with each other in such a way that causal laws, expressed in the form of differential equations, allow one to predict one state of the system from another prior or later state. In human societies, however, though the money market might be somewhat similar, such systems are rare. Social systems (in the Parsonian manner) are not analogous in that the parts are not *simultaneously* affecting each other in the way in which the sun and the moon simultaneously affect each other by their gravitational attraction. The mutual relation of, say, the system of socialization to the system of political control is mediated by the personality structure, and as such it is a relation which requires a long time interval to work through the whole causal sequence. Parents may well train their children today in ways which are 'significantly congruent' with the ways in which they behave politically today, but, in the other direction, the way in which they now behave politically is affected by the way in which they were trained, not today but a generation ago.

The analysis of systems such as the solar system can dispense with the notion of cause in favour of function—but this, be it noted, is strictly the mathematician's function, not that of the sociologist or of the physiologist.[10] It is not, however, impossible to apply the concept of causal law and causal event to such systems, and to do so might help to elucidate the nature of the distinction we have earlier made between the causes of the origin of, and the causes of the persistence of, institutions. If we are to give a causal explanation of the movement of the moon between 10.00 p.m. and 10.05 p.m. tonight, we would need to refer to the simultaneous events of the movements of the earth and the sun, etc., relating them to it by Newton's law of gravitation. We should also have to mention a previous event—the moon's motion at the point immediately prior to 10.00 p.m.—and relate it to the event in question (its movement between 10.00 and 10.05 p.m.) by means of Newton's first law of motion concerning momentum. Having started on this track we can regress almost indefinitely from

[10] See Bertrand Russell, *Mysticism and Logic*, London: Penguin Books, 1953, p. 184. It would be interesting to know whether Russell's well-known assertion in this paper that the concept of cause was useful 'only in the infancy of a science' and that as a science developed it was replaced by function (mathematical) had any influence in causing sociologists and anthropologists to drop the unfashionable word cause and take up function instead. If so they were the rather naïve victims of the ambiguity of the word function, rather like the lady who heard that bearskins were replacing mink this year and though somewhat puzzled decided that fashion was fashion and went to the party naked. One might add that Russell's assertion that the concept of cause is useful only in the infancy of a science is not incompatible with the claim that 'cause' is still useful for sociology.

event to event back through time (chopping our time continuum arbitrarily into 'events'), the moon's velocity at any particular moment being affected by its velocity the preceding moment, until we get to an earlier traumatic event, namely the moon's supposed wrenching off from the earth. In the whole of this process it is only events which are related to each other by causal laws and only of events that we ask: what are their causes?[11] Similarly—and this is the point of the example—when we talk of 'the cause of the origin of an institution' and 'the cause of the persistence of an institution' we are in both cases asking for the causes of events—in the first case the causes of the particular once-and-for-all events associated with the origin of the institution, and in the second of the recurring events which *are* the institution.

In the light of this view of causal relations, let us now look at the analogy between physiology and sociology often invoked by those who favour sociological explanation in terms of systems. If is often asserted that because the physiologist leaves questions concerning the origin of the heart to the student of evolution and concentrates on tracing its functions as it at present exists, he is not concerned with causes. But this is surely not so. 'The function of the heart in the human being is to pump blood' implies 'the cause of the flow of this blood at this time is the pump of that heart then' and this is as much a causal assertion as 'one of the reasons why animals have hearts is because when random mutation produced the first primitive heart its possessors gained the ability to out-breed the heartless.'

Physiologists and students of evolution have achieved a division of labour which is not formalized among sociologists. Consequently, among sociologists the search for an 'explanation' of an institution is often ambiguous. 'Why is there a system of unequal rewards in this society?' may be answered by some 'because parents tell (this parent and this parent told) their children that some positions in society are more worthy of respect than others, and because employers pay (this employer and this employer paid) more for some kinds of work than others, etc.' This is the

[11] On close analysis it becomes extremely difficult, as Bertrand Russell shows, to define the concept of 'event' (*Mysticism and Logic*, London: Penguin Books, 1953, pp. 176–8; *The Analysis of Mind*, London: Allen and Unwin, 1921, pp. 94–5). The difficulties are, however, not such as to prevent Russell himself from ignoring them in his later work (see e.g. *Human Knowledge*, London: Allen and Unwin, 1948, p. 344), and the common-sense notion of 'event' or 'happening', widened slightly perhaps to include not only 'the eclipse of the moon' but also 'the movement of the moon between 10.00 and 10.01 p.m.' (i.e. not only common-sensically discrete events, but also arbitrarily chopped-up units of continuous processes—a legitimate extension since all 'events', even eclipses, have arbitrarily defined boundaries) is adequate for the purposes of this discussion and, for the moment at least, for the purposes of sociological inquiry.

'physiological' explanation of the recurring events of rewarding particular people with particular acts of deference and so on which is what we mean by stratification. Alternatively the answer might be 'because with the division of labour some groups became more powerful and arrogated privileges to themselves, or because differentiated societies which had systems of stratification proved more successful than those which did not' —the 'evolutionary' explanation of the particular events which led to the institutionalization of certain patterns of behaviour.

7. INSTITUTIONS

It will be noted again that whichever way the question is taken it can be handled as if it were a question about particular events. It is the chief assertion of this paper that ultimately these are the only terms in which causal questions can be framed. But if this is the case, what then is the relation between the particular events observed by the sociologist and his concepts such as stratification, marriage, or socialization—concepts of 'institutions', 'norms', 'behaviour patterns'? Is it not exactly the same as the relation between a particular human heart and *the* human heart for the physiologist? The physiologist's statement that 'the function of the heart is to pump blood' is a summary generalization of statements about the causal relations between the particular events of heart-pump and blood-flow in particular human bodies—events which nowadays recur more than two billion times a second. If the sociologist's statements are to have any empirical reference it is difficult to see how they can be different from this; how, that is to say, the relation between 'John kisses Mary' and 'courtship', or between 'farmer George touched his cap to the lord of the manor' and 'stratification' can be other than the relation between 'the pump of this heart' and 'the pump of the human heart'.

Even sociologists who accept this are often tempted to forget it, partly because while any single heart-pump is very much like another, kisses can vary greatly in intensity, passion, and significance. This is also the reason why it is more important that the sociologist should *not* forget it; it matters very little to the physiologist if he forgets that his abstract human organ is a generalization from particular organs in particular people *because* they are all very much alike.

If it be accepted that the sociologist's 'institutions' are summary generic terms for classes of particular recurring events, then it follows that his statements about the functional interrelations of institutions are generalizations about the causal relations between these recurring events. In other words that 'the system of stratification functions to make the division of labour workable' is a generalized summation of a number of lower-order generalizations to the effect that, for instance, 'men submit to a lengthy medical training because they have the prospect of greater rewards' etc., which are themselves generalizations from statements of particular events ('Jack submitted . . . because he had . . . ').

We might emphasize this assertion that statements about the functional relations between institutions are *only* generalizations about relations between particular events by means of a mathematical analogy (offered only, it might be added, as a didactic illustration and not as a proof). If it is granted that events like 'John (unmarried) passionately kisses Mary (unmarried)' (a) are summarily referred to by such a term as 'romantic courtship' (Σa); and events like 'John (married) hits Mary (married)' (b) are summarily referred to by such a term as 'pattern of marital maladjustment' (Σb), then the statement 'patterns of courtship affect patterns of marital adjustment' is a summary of statements of the nature 'the way John kissed Mary then affects the way he hits her now', and as such is a statement of the nature $\Sigma \, ab$, *not* of the nature $\Sigma \, a \times \Sigma b$.

8. SOCIAL FACTS AND REDUCTIONISM

Some sociologists would part company at this point. They might agree with the above view of the logical nature of constructs like 'institution,' 'behaviour pattern', etc., but still hold that there *is* a $\Sigma a \times \Sigma b$ kind of sense in which institutions can be related over and above the relations of the particular events they describe. It is difficult to see how this can be so. More consistent is the position of those who would hold that concepts like institutions are not, or are not only, generalizations about recurring events. Such arguments might well appeal to the Durkheimian characterization of norms and institutions as 'social facts'. But the position outlined above is in no way incompatible with one interpretation of the Durkheimian view. It is undoubtedly true that the members of a society do have reified concepts of, say, 'marriage', 'romantic love', 'filial conduct' which are both more than and less than generalizations concerning particular relations between particular people. But these reified concepts are part of the *data* of sociology. Having a concept of marriage is (though normally less easily observed) as much an event in society as having a quarrel with one's wife and susceptible of the same kinds of questions and explanations. There is no more reason for the sociologist to adopt for his thinking *about* society the terms used for thinking *in* society (to take, in other words, his analytical tools straight out of his data) than there is for a carpenter to use nothing but wooden saws.

The point might be made clearer if it is stated in the terms of Maurice Mandelbaum's discussion of 'societal facts'.[12] His argument that societal facts are not reducible to statements concerning the actions of individuals rests on an identification of what one might call 'societal (or cultural) concepts' with 'sociologists' concepts'. One can agree with his formulation—that there is a language S, in which concepts like marriage, the banking system, the Presidency, etc., appear; that there is another language P in which we refer to the thoughts and actions of individuals; and that sentences in S cannot be translated wholly into P because some of the thoughts and actions of individuals consist of *using* S. But the contention here is that the sociologist should be speaking in a different language—meta-SP if one likes—which certainly resembles S and was developed from S but is an artificial creation for the purpose of analysing causal relations in society and can only be effective for this purpose if it *is* reducible to P (including all the necessary concepts of S—the words spoken and the thoughts thought by individuals—which P must incorporate). Another way of putting it would be to say that Mandelbaum's arguments that societal facts are not reducible to facts about individuals are really arguments to show that *language* is a necessary part of the sociologist's data for which there can be no substitute. And no one would wish to quarrel with that.[13]

The position outlined above is part of the thesis of 'methodological individualism',[14] the brief debate about which seems to have died down without much interest being shown by professional sociologists. The methodological individualist doctrine which holds that all sociological laws are bound to be such as can ultimately be reduced to laws of individual behaviour is a hard one to refute,[15] but one which few sociologists find

[12] Maurice Mandelbaum, 'Societal Facts', *BritishJ ournal of Sociology*, vi (Dec. 1955), 305–16. Also included in this volume (VI below).

[13] In Parsonian terms the contention here could be put in the form that the analytical categories of the social system are not identical with those of the cultural system. This is indeed what Parsons says (see *The Social System*, Glencoe, Ill.: The Free Press, 1951, p. 15) but in actual practice—in, for instance, his analysis of medical practice in the same book—his method seems to be to take the definition of the role from the cultural system and 'fill it out' with examples of concrete action.

[14] The thesis is outlined in two articles by J. W. N. Watkins, 'Ideal Types and Historical Explanations', *British Journal for the Philosophy of Science*, iii (May 1952), 22–43, and 'The Principle of Methodological Individualism', ibid. iii (Aug. 1952), 186–9.

[15] The two main attacks on Watkins's articles have been those of Leon J. Goldstein ('The Inadequacy of the Principle of Methodological Individualism', *The Journal of Philosophy*, liii (Dec. 1956), 801–13) and E. A. Gellner ('Explanations in History' in *Dreams and Self-Knowledge*, Aristotelian Society Supplementary Volume xxx (1956), 157–76). Goldstein's objection is chiefly that the individualist position 'would leave us with theories the entire content of which were the facts that suggested them in the first place, having no further power of prediction or generalization' and rests on such dubious arguments as that 'to know that in such and such a society descent is reckoned

attractive. The reason is perhaps this: the examples we have given of the particular causal relations actually implied by statements of the functions of institutions were of the type: 'Jack became a doctor because of the prospect of . . . ', 'the way John kissed Mary then affects the way he hits her now.' All imputations of a causal relation imply a causal law. In these cases the relevant laws are laws of individual behaviour—'an individual of such and such training in such and such circumstances will orient present actions to remotely deferred gratifications', 'behavioural dispositions towards individual others built up under the stress of strong biological urges tend to be modified after the satiation of those urges' might be examples. These can be stated in purely behavioural terms. Nevertheless when they are so stated the possibility of further reduction to laws of psychological processes becomes apparent. Psychological reductionism has never appealed to sociologists; it has usually been conceived as a threat to the integrity and importance of sociology. It is difficult to see why. It would be as absurd to argue that because all the laws of social behaviour might ultimately be reducible to psychological terms sociologists should give up sociology and take to psychology, as to hold that chemists should all abandon chemistry since their laws might ultimately be reduced to laws of physics. The antipathy towards the reductionist thesis exists, however, and sociologists have for a long time been intermittently fighting a losing battle to prove (to themselves, it seems, since no one else seems to have been particularly interested) that there *are*

---

in the female line or that residence is avunculocal provides no information about the aspirations and activities of particular persons.' Gellner objects on several grounds; he uses the Durkheimian 'social fact' argument, but eventually admits its irrelevance on approximately the same grounds as are indicated above; he argues also that in practice there may well be a Principle of Indeterminacy that makes it impossible to observe the precise individual causal sequences which account for events which can be generalized about in macroscopic statistical terms (trends in road accidents etc.), but his main point is that a statement in individualist terms *adds* nothing to a statement in holistic terms. There is, he suggests, only neatness and intelligibility to be lost and nothing to be gained in translating 'the committee made this decision' into statements about the processes that went on in the minds of the individual committee members. But the individualist thesis is not one about descriptive statements, but about laws. It holds that if we knew enough such a 'law' as 'committees composed of equal proportions of members of low and high status in societies where a stress is placed on harmonious unanimity will tend to reach unanimous decisions reflecting the wishes of those of higher status' is reducible to a number of 'laws' about individuals, the way in which they are disposed to react when faced with individuals of higher and of similar status, when faced with the demand for an expression of opinion, etc. The *advantage* of these atomistic laws over the holistic one is that they have greater explanatory power; each is applicable to a wider range of situations than just committees, much as the theory of ionization has greater explanatory power than a 'law' dealing with the electrolysis of water, which states that electrodes placed in water give off hydrogen and oxygen and applies only to the specific case of water.

irreducible sociological laws *sui generis*. Is not the resort to 'function' in part a continuation of this warfare by more diplomatic means?

Professor Davis noted that in their studies of social change functionalists behave no differently from other sociologists who claim to be opposed to functionalism. Now, studies of social change are explicitly looking for causes—for the causes of the particular events associated with the origination and changing of institutions. To keep one's nose equally on the scent for causes in the analysis of stable systems, however, involves constant reference to the recurring events which make up the institutional units under study and poses the problem of the kind of reductionism outlined above. The concept of function offers an escape; it blurs the precise causal relations imputed and yet descriptions in terms of functions seem somehow to be causal; it makes it easier for institutions to be treated as ultimate units without constant reference to the empirical content of such concepts;[16] in this way the sociological integrity of sociology is preserved and grand theory concerning social systems becomes possible.

9. VARIOUS SOCIOLOGIES

What, then, of functional*ism*? It is, as Kingsley Davis points out, a name for a variety of methodological and philosophical (following Davis, following Radcliffe-Brown, though 'moral' might be more apposite) positions. It might be useful to elucidate these positions with reference to the two main theses of this paper. These theses are: (1) There is a difference between questions about the functions of an institution and questions about the cause(s) of (the particular one-and-for-all events leading to the origin of, or the recurring events which make up) that institution, and answers to the first kind of question are relevant to answers to the second kind of question only (legitimately) via human motives or evolutionary selection, or (illegitimately) by use of the postulate of necessary integration. (2) Questions about the functions of an institution logically imply questions about the effects of recurring particular events which make up that institution as causes of other recurring particular events.

Functionalists, then, could be any of four types of sociologists. Type (a) sociologists easily accept both of these propositions but find the concept of

---

[16] e.g. Talcott Parsons, op. cit., p. 456. The universalism of the doctor's role is spoken of as having the function of protecting the doctor from involvement in particularistic personal relations with his patients. This sounds like a causal relation but would seem on closer inspection to be a matter of logic: 'a doctor treats his patients all alike' logically implies that he does not treat them as individuals. If the universalism of the doctor's role were something *more* than his treating his patients all alike there would be more than this to Parson's analysis; but it does not seem that this is the case.

function useful because they are chiefly concerned with the way in which changes in one institution in a particular society would affect other institutions, for example, the social reformer or the colonial anthropologist. Type (b) sociologists accept both of these propositions but hold the philosophical view that sociologists should concern themselves only with the kind of causal relationships which have a direct bearing on the equilibrium of the social system (i.e. are [eu]functional or dysfunctional) and not with other causal chains which, being in this special sense 'non-functional', are 'pragmatically unimportant'.[17]

It is this particular philosophical view with its implication that 'stability is all', together with the fact that functionalists of type (a) have usually tended in practice to give reasons for pessimism about the possible scope of social reform, which provide the basis for the charge of functionalist conservatism. Type (c) sociologists are mainly concerned to construct models of social systems and either deny the second of these propositions or occasionally ignore its implications in order to reduce the difficulties of their task. Type (d) sociologists would deny the first of these propositions (usually specifically the charge that the postulate of necessary integration is illegitimate)[18] and, in giving a description of the functions of an institution, would imply that this is also, automatically, a causal explanation of that institution.

A number of alternative positions are possible if these two propositions are accepted. There is the piecemeal approach, outlined at the beginning of this paper, which suggests that sociologists should concern themselves with searching for regularities in the concomitant occurrence of social events with a view to inducing causal laws which might ultimately be ordered in some systematic theory. There is the historical approach which is largely concerned with discovering the causes of the particular once-and-for-all events which explain the origins of institutions. There is the static approach which concentrates on societies which have been stable over long periods of time and seeks for the causal relations between the recurring events which make up their institutions. There is still possible scope for the model-system approach in so far as it seeks to build up a pattern of causal relations such as might pertain to an ideal and entirely stable society, without having recourse to the short cut of functionalists variety (c). There is, finally, the 'issue' approach, the virtues of which have recently been argued with much vehemence by C. Wright Mills. This involves starting from practical

[17] R. K. Merton, op. cit., p. 51.
[18] This is the position from which Hempel has recently attempted to analyse the logic of functional analysis. Carl G. Hempel, 'The Logic of Functional Analysis' in Llewellyn Gross (ed.), *Symposium on Sociological Theory*, Evanston, Ill.: Row, Peterson, 1959, pp. 271–303.

questions which actually worry people, such as 'who is likely to plunge us into a world war', and using for the purpose of elucidation questions about the causes of recurring institutionalized events—so that by knowing why people do things we shall be in a better position to know how to stop them; questions about the once-and-for-all causes—so that by knowing how things got the way they are we shall be in a better position to judge whether that is the way they ought to be; and questions about functions of institutions—so that we would have a better idea of what we would be up against if we tried to change them. All kinds of questions are asked not as ends in themselves but as means to eliciting guides for judgement and action. This is not, perhaps, a scientific pursuit in the way that the other approaches outlined above are scientific, though it is one that has intermittently occupied a great many sociologists of repute.

The differences between these various positions are in part methodological—differences concerning the truth of the two propositions enunciated earlier. In part they are moral differences, about the proper scale of priorities which should guide the sociologist's use of this time. About the methodological issues there is legitimate ground for dispute. But about the 'oughts' implied in these various positions, we can only preach at each other. It would be sad if we stopped preaching, but let us try to keep our sermons and our methodological discussions separate.

V

IDEAL TYPES AND HISTORICAL EXPLANATION

J. W. N. WATKINS

1. INTRODUCTION

IN THIS PAPER I shall consider: first, what sort of creatures ideal types should be if they are to be used in the construction of social theories; and secondly, what we do when we try to explain historical events by applying such theories to them.[1]

From *Readings in the Philosophy of Science*, ed. H. Feigl and M. Brodbeck (New York: Appleton-Century-Crofts Inc., 1953), pp. 723–44. Revised and expanded version of a paper that originally appeared in *The British Journal for the Philosophy of Science* (1952). Reprinted by kind permission of the author and Cambridge University Press.

[1] It has been established by Professor K. R. Popper that the formal structure of a prediction is the same as that of a full-fledged explanation. In both cases we have: (*a*) initial conditions; (*b*) universal statements; and (*c*) deductive consequences of (*a*) plus (*b*). We explain a given event (*c*) by detecting (*a*) and by postulating and applying (*b*); and we predict a future event (*c*) by inferring it from some given (*a*) and postulated (*b*). Nevertheless, I think that in social science explanation and prediction should be considered separately, for two reasons. First, as Professor C. G. Hempel has pointed out in a most illuminating discussion of this problem (see his 'The Function of General Laws in History' in *Readings in Philosophical Analysis*, ed. H. Feigl and W. Sellars (New York, 1949), pp. 462–5) in history we often have to be content (and in fact *are* content) with what he calls an explanation *sketch*, i.e. a somewhat vague and incomplete indication of (*a*) and (*b*) from which (*c*) is not *strictly* deducible. And if we go back to a time when (*a*) but not (*c*) has occurred, this partial sketch of (*a*) and (*b*) will not allow us to predict (*c*). For example, we may be satisfied by the explanation that Smith insulted Jones because Jones had angered him, although we should *not* be prepared to admit that if Jones angers Smith in the future, Smith will necessarily react by insulting Jones.

Secondly, even the social scientist who can provide a *full-fledged* explanation of a past event will run into difficulties if he tries to predict similar events, because they will occur in a system which is not isolated from the influence of factors which he cannot ascertain beforehand. The Astronomer Royal can prepare a Nautical Almanac for 1953 because he is predicting the movements of bodies in a system isolated from extraneous influences, but the Chancellor of the Exchequer cannot prepare an Economic Almanac for 1953 because, even if he possessed sufficient knowledge to explain completely the 1951 levels of prices, production, investment, exports, etc., his predictions of future levels would undoubtedly be upset by unforeseeable, world-wide disturbing factors, the effects of any of which might be cumulative.

Hence, the problem of social prediction raises questions not raised by the problem of historical explanation; and this paper is not concerned with the former.

2. HOLISTIC AND INDIVIDUALISTIC IDEAL TYPES

It is only decent to begin a discussion of ideal types by considering Weber's views; but he held two successive conceptions of what an ideal type should be and do, without, I think, realizing what important differences lay between them.

His earlier version is set out in an article translated under the title ' "Objectivity" in Social Science and Social Policy'.[2] At this time (1904) Weber believed that the social scientist should not try to imitate the natural scientist's procedure of systematically subsuming observation-statements and low-order theories under more comprehensive laws. The social scientist should first decide from what point of view to approach history. Having decided, say, to treat its economic aspect, he should then select from this some unique configuration of activities and institutions, such as 'the rise of capitalism'. Then he should pin down and describe its components. His final task is to draw in the causal lines between these components, imputing 'concrete effects to concrete causes'.[3]

This programme could never be carried out; 'in any actual economic system so many factors are at work simultaneously that the effect of a single factor by itself can never be known, for its traces are soon lost sight of.'[4] And separate facts cannot be linked together as causes and effects with no reference to general laws. However, I will not press these criticisms of a methodological position which Weber tacitly abandoned later.

To assist the social scientist in this task of explaining particular events by relating them to their particular antecedents, Weber proposed his first version of the ideal type. This was to be constructed by abstracting the outstanding features from some (more or less clearly demarcated) historical complex, and by organizing these into a coherent word-picture. The ideality of such a type lies in its simplification and aloofness from detail: it will be free from the detailed complexity of the actuality to be analysed with its aid. As this kind of ideal type emphasizes the 'essential' traits of a situation considered *as a whole*, I call it 'holistic', in contrast with the 'individualistic' ideal type described by Weber in Part I of his posthumous *Wirtschaft und Gesellschaft*.[5]

In this work he held that the social scientist's first task was to build up a generally applicable theoretical system; and for arriving at this he

[2] Max Weber, *The Methodology of the Social Sciences*, trans. and ed. E. A. Shils and H. A. Finch (Illinois, 1949), ch. 2.

[3] Ibid., p. 79.

[4] Walter Eucken, *The Foundations of Economics*, trans. T. W. Hutchison (London. 1950), p. 39.

[5] Translated by A. R. Henderson and Talcott Parsons as *The Theory of Social and Economic Organisation*, introd. by Talcott Parsons (London, 1947).

proposed the use of ideal types similar to the models used in deductive economics. These are constructed, not by withdrawing from the detail of social life, but by formalizing the results of a close analysis of some of its significant details considered in isolation. The holistic ideal type was supposed to give a bird's-eye view of the broad characteristics of a whole social situation, whereas the individualistic ideal type is constructed by inspecting the situations of actual individuals, and by abstracting from these: (*a*) general schemes of personal preferences; (*b*) the different kinds of knowledge of his own situation which the individual may possess; and (*c*) various typical relationships between individuals and between the individual and his resources. An individualistic ideal type places hypothetical actors in some simplified situation. Its premises are: the form (but not the specific content) of the actors' dispositions, the state of their information, and their relationships. And the deductive consequences of these premises demonstrate some principle of social behaviour, e.g. oligopolistic behaviour. The ideality of *this* kind of ideal type lies: (i) in the simplification of the initial situation and in its isolation from disturbing factors; (ii) in the abstract and formal, and yet explicit and precise character of the actors' schemes of preferences and states of information; and (iii) in the actors' rational behaviour in the light of (ii). It is not claimed that a principle of social behaviour demonstrated by an individualistic ideal type will often have an exact empirical counterpart (though the principle of perfect competition has been precisely manifested, for instance in commodity-markets). But economists do claim that there is a limited number of basic economic principles, and that any economic phenomenon is a particular configuration of some of these, occurring at a particular place and time, which can be explained by a synthesis of the relevant ideal types, and by specifying the content of their formal premises.[6]

---

[6] 'This morphological study of economic history reveals a *limited* number of pure forms out of which *all* economic systems past and present are made up.' Eucken, op. cit., p. 10 (my italics). The 'de-idealization' of the pure principles of economic theory which occurs when they are combined into a particular configuration which is applied to an empirical counterpart, is exactly paralleled in the natural sciences. For example, Galileo combined the Law of Inertia (which describes the motion of a body not acted upon by any force—a condition which can never be realized), and the Law of Gravity (which describes the motion of a body in a vacuum which the experimenter cannot obtain), and the principles of air resistance, into a theoretical configuration which allows complete prediction of the trajectories of e.g. cannon-balls, if the initial conditions are known. 'All universal physical concepts and laws ... are arrived at by idealisation. They thereby assume that simple ... form which makes it possible to reconstruct any facts, however complicated, by synthetic combination of these concepts and laws, thus making it possible to understand them' (Ernst Mach, quoted by F. Kaufmann, *Methodology of the Social Sciences* (New York, 1944), p. 87).

Weber was no Platonist; he proposed both kinds of ideal type as heuristic aids which, by themselves, tell you nothing about the real world, but which throw into relief its deviations from themselves. The individualistic ideal type was to assist in the detection of disturbing factors, such as habit and tradition, which deflect actual individuals from a rational course of action—a proposal I shall examine later. Now I shall examine the assumptions underlying Weber's earlier proposal to use holistic ideal types.

One might improve one's appreciation of the shape of a roughly circular object by placing over it an accurate tracing of a circle. This analogy brings out Weber's conception of the purpose, and manner of employing holistic ideal types in three respects. (i) By comparing an impure object with an ideal construction the deviations of the former from the latter are thrown into relief; and Weber did regard this kind of ideal type as a 'purely ideal *limiting* concept with which the real situation . . . is *compared* and surveyed for the explication of certain of its significant components'.[7] (ii) Both the object and the construct are considered *as a whole*. (iii) The analogy involves what is presupposed by the idea of comparison, namely, a simultaneous awareness of the characteristics of both things being compared. And in 1904 Weber did assume that the social scientist can place his knowledge of a real situation alongside his knowledge of an ideal type he has himself constructed, and compare the two.[8] It is the simultaneous knowability of the features of both which enables holistic ideal types to be 'used as conceptual instruments for *comparison* with and *measurement* of reality'.[9]

At this point an awkward question arises: If the characteristics of a historical situation have already been charted *before* the ideal type is brought into play, why bother with ideal types? They are not hypotheses[10] which guide the social scientist in his search for facts, for they are not supposed to be realistic, or empirical. A holistic ideal type is not a guess about reality, but an *a priori* word-picture—in other words, a definition. What Weber's earlier proposal amounts to is that holistic ideal types should be used as explicit definitions of those 'hundreds of words in the historian's vocabulary [which] are ambiguous constructs created to meet the unconsciously felt need for adequate expression and the meaning of which is only concretely felt but not clearly thought out'.[11]

---

[7] *Methodology*, p. 93.
[8] Thus he speaks of 'the relationship between the logical structure of the conceptual system . . . and what is immediately given in empirical reality' (op. cit., p. 96). The term 'immediately given' should not, I think, be taken too seriously. What this phrase does imply is that the social scientist's knowledge of ideal type and corresponding reality are on an equal footing.
[9] Ibid., p. 97.   [10] Ibid., p. 90.   [11] Ibid., pp. 92–3.

Thus the holistic ideal type transpires to be something of a mouse, a mere demand for definitions;[12] and I shudder when I imagine each of those 'hundreds of words' being replaced by lengthy verbal definitions, though such defining *may* be helpful in particular circumstances. For instance, to order and classify a collection of variegated instances it may be necessary to construct a scale with limiting ideal types at either end. The survey of the constitutions of 158 Greek states was probably tidier and more systematic than it would have been if Aristotle's 'Monarchy-Aristocracy-Polity' and 'Tyranny-Oligarchy-Democracy' scales, or some equivalent, had not been used.

But such scales are for classifying facts already analysed, not for analysing raw material; and the real weakness of Weber's earlier proposal lies in the method of historical analysis which was to accompany the use of holistic ideal types. With *individualistic* ideal types, it will be remembered, we *start* with individuals' dispositions, information, and relationships, and work outwards to the unintended consequences of their interaction, (deducing a price-level, for example, from demand and supply schedules). But with *holistic* ideal types the analysis is supposed to proceed in the opposite direction. Here, the historian is supposed to start with the broad (or 'essential') characteristics of an entire historical situation, and then to *descend* to an ever closer definition of its deviations from the ideal type with which it is being compared. In principle, this descent from over-all traits to detailed ingredients might continue until, *at the end of the analysis*, the relevant dispositions, information, and relationships of the people concerned had been established.

The idea that we can apprehend the over-all characteristics of a social situation *before* learning something of the individual situations of the actors in it *appears* to be borne out by a statement such as, 'The British economy in 1850 was competitive.' This statement apparently attributes an over-all characteristic to a demarcated whole, while saying nothing about individuals (just as 'The lake's surface was calm' says nothing about water-particles). Now the unintended merit of the holistic ideal type is that its use forces us to recognize the falsity of this idea. If, in order to assess the competitiveness of the British economy in 1850, we try to establish an ideal type of 'perfect competition' we shall at once find that we can only define it in terms of the preferences, information, and relationships of individuals —an assertion which can be confirmed by turning to any economics text-book. In other words, we shall have established an *individualistic* ideal

---

[12] For a criticism of such demands, see K. R. Popper, *The Open Society and Its Enemies* (London, 1945), Vol. ii, ch. 11, sect. ii.

type.[13] But if knowledge of the general characteristics of a social situation is always derivative knowledge, pieced together from what is known of individuals' situations, then it is not possible for historical analysis to proceed *from* over-all characteristics *towards* individuals' situations. The former is logically derivative from the latter. Weber's earlier conception of an ideal type presupposed that one can detect the essential traits of some historic 'whole' while remaining aloof from the detail of personal behaviour; but this belief is shown to be false when we actually construct such a type. It was probably this experience which later led Weber tacitly to abandon holistic ideal types and the impossible method associated with them, in favour of individualistic ideal types and the method of reconstructing historical phenomena with their aid.[14]

The assertion that knowledge of social phenomena can only be derived from knowledge about individuals requires one qualification. For there are certain overt features[15] which can be established without knowledge of psychological facts, such as the level of prices, or the death-rate (but *not* the suicide-rate). And if we detect more or less regular changes in such overt features we have something eminently suitable for analysis. But some people, over-impressed by the quasi-regularity of, for example, a long-term 'wave' in economic life, have supposed that such a thing possesses a sort of internal dynamic, and obeys its own laws; and that while *it* must therefore be taken as a datum, many other phenomena (such as bursts of

---

[13] Similarly, if we try to construct an ideal type for 'feudalism', say, we shall at once find ourselves speaking of people's obligations and privileges towards their superiors, inferiors, the land, and so on.

[14] What I call a 'holistic ideal type' roughly corresponds to what Eucken called a 'real type', a name he used to denote the 'stages', such as 'city economy', 'early capitalism', 'mature capitalism', through which, according to the Historical School of economists, any economic system develops. He also rejected such types in favour of individualistic ideal types (which he simply called 'ideal types') and he criticized Weber for confusing the two, but from a somewhat different viewpoint to my own. His fascinating book, *The Foundations of Economics*, contains a sustained plea for the fertile marriage of abstract theory and concrete fact, and a powerful criticism of the Historical School for blurring the distinction between the two; whereas I am arguing against methodological holism, and for methodological individualism. Our arguments tend to coincide because 'historicism' is closely related to 'holism': the belief in laws of development presupposes a 'whole' which undergoes the development. (See K. R. Popper, 'The Poverty of Historicism', *Economica*, xi (1944), 91–2.) For Eucken's discussion of real and ideal types, see especially pp. 347–9.

[15] By 'overt feature' I do not mean something which can necessarily be directly perceived—it may be a highly theoretical construct. But whether it be the price of a marked article in a shop-window, or the average level of prices in 1815, an overt feature is something which can be ascertained without referring to people's dispositions, etc. See R. Stone, *The Role of Measurements in Economics* (Cambridge, 1951), p. 9.

inventiveness, emigration movements, outbreaks of war) can be explained as consequences of it.[16]

This is a sort of blasphemy. The Israelites also imputed their fortunes and misfortunes to a superior entity immune from their own activities; but they rightly called this 'God'. But economic cycles do not possess a quasi-divine autonomy. They are mere human creations—not deliberate creations, of course, but the unintended product of the behaviour of interacting people.

For the last few paragraphs a basic methodological principle has been struggling to emerge and the time has come to bring it into the open in order to clarify its meaning and status.

3. THE PRINCIPLE OF METHODOLOGICAL INDIVIDUALISM

This principle states that social processes and events should be explained by being deduced from (a) principles governing the behaviour of participating individuals and (b) descriptions of their situations.[17] The contrary principle of methodological holism states that the behaviour of individuals should be explained by being deduced from (a) macroscopic laws which are *sui generis* and which apply to the social system as a whole, and (b) descriptions of the positions (or functions) of the individuals within the whole.

There is clearly an important difference between these two principles. What are my grounds for accepting the individualistic, and rejecting the holistic, method?

[16] I have written the above with the Russian economist Kondratieff in mind. He asserts that the view that long waves 'are conditioned by causal, extra-economic circumstances and events, such as (1) changes in technique, (2) wars and revolutions, (3) the assimilation of new countries into the world economy, and (4) fluctuations in gold production . . . reverse[s] the causal connections and take[s] the consequence to be the cause' (N. D. Kondratieff, 'The Long Waves in Economic Life', *Readings in Business Cycle Theory*, Blakiston Series (London, 1950), ch. 2, p. 35). In other words, the long wave is *the* fundamental datum, in terms of which even such a strictly individual and psychological matter as human inventiveness is to be explained.

[17] This principle does not apply to the study of purely physical, biological, or behaviouristic properties of human groups. Professor Hayek has drawn a very useful distinction between the 'natural sciences of society', such as vital statistics and the study of contagious diseases, and the 'social sciences' proper (*Individualism and Economic Order* (London, 1949), p. 57). Typical problems of the social sciences are war, unemployment, political instability, the clash of cultures. Professor M. Ginsberg has asserted that principles of historical interpretation 'are not necessarily exclusively psychological or even teleological: there may well be social laws *sui generis* . . .' (*Aristotelian Society, Supplementary Volume* xxi (1947), 'Symposium: The Character of a Historical Explanation', p. 77). The only example he gives of something determined by such laws is phonetic change. But phonetic change is either an unconscious behaviouristic process to be studied by a natural science of society, or a deliberate process, in which case it can be explained individualistically, e.g. in terms of a man's desire to raise his social status by acquiring a superior accent.

(1) Whereas physical things can exist unperceived, social 'things' like laws, prices, prime ministers, and ration-books, are created by personal attitudes. (Remove the attitudes of food officials, shop-keepers, housewives, etc., towards ration-books and they shrivel into bits of cardboard.) But if social objects are formed by individual attitudes, an explanation of their formation must be an individualistic explanation.

(2) The social scientist and the historian have no 'direct access' to the over-all structure and behaviour of a system of interacting individuals (in the sense that a chemist does have 'direct access' to such over-all properties of a gas as its volume and pressure and temperature, which he can measure and relate without any knowledge of gas-molecules). But the social scientist and the historian can often arrive at fairly reliable opinions about the dispositions and situations of individuals. These two facts suggest that a theoretical understanding of an abstract social structure should be derived from more empirical beliefs about concrete individuals.[18]

But neither (1) the truism that social objects are created by personal attitudes, nor (2) the 'invisibility' of social structures, *entail* methodological individualism; they only support it.

(1) The fact that prices, for instance, are charged and paid by people, the fact that they are human creations, does not, by itself, entail that the whole price-system may not be governed by some over-all law which is underivable from propositions about individuals. (2) A holist who denied that 'the English State, for example, is a logical construction out of individual people',[19] and who asserted that it is an organism which develops, and responds to challenges, according to underivable holistic laws, might also admit that only its individual components were visible and that any operational definition of the laws it obeyed would be in terms of individual behaviour.

Moreover, an extremely unlikely circumstance is conceivable in which methodological individualism would have to be demoted from a rule to an aspiration; for it apparently suffers this humiliation in the study of certain non-human societies.

One can see what upsets methodological individualism by considering three different systems of interacting components: (*a*) the solar system as conceived by classical mechanics; (*b*) the economic system as conceived by classical economics; and (*c*) a bee-hive.

---

[18] 'The social sciences ... do not deal with 'given' wholes but their task is to *constitute* these wholes by constructing models from the familiar elements. ...' 'The whole is never directly perceived but always reconstructed by an effort of our imagination.' F. A. Hayek, *The Counter-Revolution of Science: studies on the abuse of reason* (The Free Press, Glencoe, Illinois, 1952), pp. 56 and 214.

[19] A. J. Ayer, *Language, Truth and Logic*, 2nd. ed. (London, 1948), p. 63.

(a) Here, methodological individualism is altogether adequate. The behaviour of the whole system can be explained by applying the inverse square law and the law of inertia to the system's components, if their relative positions, masses, and momenta are known. Indeed, methodological individualism in the social sciences is analogous to the method of resolution and re-composition which characterizes Galilean and Newtonian physics: the method, namely, of analysing a complex whole into its atomic constituents, and into the simplest principles which they obey, and of deductively reconstructing the behaviour of the whole from these.

(b) Adam Smith stated that the individual

generally, indeed, neither intends to promote the public interest, nor knows how much he is promoting it . . . ; by directing [his] industry in such a manner as its produce may be of the greatest value, he intends only his own gain, and he is in this, as in many other cases, led by an invisible hand to promote an end which was no part of his intention (*The Wealth of Nations*, Bk. 4, ch. 2).

But the invisible hand is, strictly, gratuitous and misleading. What Smith actually showed was that individuals in competitive economic situations are led by nothing but their *personal dispositions* to promote unintentionally the public interest. Here again, methodological individualism is altogether adequate.

(c) Mr. E. S. Russell, basing himself on experiments by Rösch, has reported the following strange fact[20] (strange, that is, to the methodological individualist). If young worker-bees (whose normal function is to feed the larvae from their salivary glands) are segregated into one half of a hive sealed off from the other half, in which have been segregated the older worker-bees (whose salivary glands have atrophied and whose normal function is to produce wax from their newly developed wax-glands, and later, to forage), then the following will occur: after two days' dislocation and near-starvation some of the young workers will start foraging and their salivary glands will atrophy prematurely; while the atrophied salivary glands of some of the older workers will revive and continue functioning long after the normal period, enabling them to feed the larvae in their half of the hive. The bees' functions will be increasingly differentiated until the division of labour in both halves approximates that of a whole hive. Here it really is as if individual bees were led by an invisible hand, not merely to promote the interest of the whole half-hive, but to adapt drastically their biological structure in order to do so. It seems extremely difficult to believe that the emergence of these two new systems of specialized functions could be explained individualistically, in terms of the situations and principles

[20] See *The British Journal for the Philosophy of Science*, i (1950), 113–14.

of behaviour of each bee, because all the bees in each half-hive were of a similar type and in approximately the same situation, yet only the requisite number adapted themselves to new functions. Thus each half of the bifurcated bee-hive appears to be an organism in the sense that its components' behaviour is determined by teleological principles which apply to the whole half-hive and which cannot be derived from a knowledge of individual bees—though one hopes that this appearance is misleading and that the re-emergence of specialization will eventually be explained individualistically.

The principle whose status I have been trying to elucidate is a methodological rule which presupposes the factual assertion that human social systems are not organisms in the above sense. There is no evidence to suggest that this presupposition is false; but one cannot assert *a priori* that it is true. What one *can* assert is that *if* any social system were such an organic entity then it would be something utterly different from anything so far imagined. For the only sorts of organism so far imagined are (*a*) physical or biological; (*b*) mental; and (*c*) social; and it will be shown that social systems are none of these.

(*a*) It is at any rate plausible to say that the personalities of a mating couple are sometimes submerged beneath the biological laws of their physical union. But it would be stretching terms to call this a 'social system'; and in the case of such social organizations as the Comintern or the International Red Cross, it is clear that what holds these bodies together is not physical ties but the ideals, loyalties, discipline, and beliefs of their dispersed members.

(*b*) Is the behaviour of a number of individuals ever regulated by some super-individual *mental* entity? It is just possible that this is so in the case of a panicking crowd or of an ecstatic revivalist meeting. But in general, 'group-minds' are very rightly out of fashion; for to impute a big social phenomenon (such as war) to a big mental counterpart (such as a 'nation's' aggressive spirit) is not to explain but to duplicate.[21] Moreover, social phenomena which nobody wants are precisely those whose occurrence most needs explaining; and it would obviously be absurd to impute mass unemployment, for instance, to some mental counterpart such as a 'nation's' laziness.

(*c*) When a sociologist proffers a holistic law the entity whose behaviour it is supposed to determine is usually thought of as a special sort of organism, neither physical nor biological nor mental, but *social*. Alleged

---

[21] This criticism is parallel to Aristotle's chief criticism of Plato's theory of Forms, to the effect that instead of accounting for their perceptible likenesses the Forms merely divert attention to transcendent duplicates. *Met*.992a27.

social entities such as 'The State', 'Capitalism', etc., however, are only hypostatizations of sociological terms. As we have seen, whenever we try to make these terms precise we find ourselves speaking individualistically.

Hence society is not an organism in any existing sense of the term. The ontological basis of methodological individualism is the assumption that society is not some unimagined sort of organism, but really consists only of people who behave fairly intelligibly and who influence each other, directly and mediately, in fairly comprehensible ways.

This section was intended to clarify and justify methodological individualism. We can now revert to the construction and use of ideal types.

4. CONCLUDING REMARKS ON IDEAL TYPES

The argument of section 2 can be summarized thus: An understanding of a complex social situation is always derived from a knowledge of the dispositions, beliefs, and relationships of individuals. Its overt characteristics may be *established* empirically, but they are only *explained* by being shown to be the resultants of individual activities.[22]

All this was recognized by the later Weber. In *The Theory of Social and Economic Organisation* ideal type construction means (not detecting and abstracting the over-all characteristics of a whole situation, and organizing these into a coherent scheme, but) placing hypothetical, rational actors in some simplified situation, and in deducing the consequences of their interaction.

Such intellectual experimenting *may* be fruitful even if some of the premises are very unrealistic. For instance, the concept of a static economy in equilibrium aids the analysis of the changes and disequilibria of actual economies. And gross exaggeration of one factor may show up an influence which would otherwise have been overlooked. This is particularly important in social science where the influence of different factors can seldom be accurately calculated. If E is the *sort* of effect produced by F_1, and if F_1 and E are both present, the social scientist tends to assume that F_1 is *the* cause of E, whereas F_1 may have caused only a *part* of E, and an undetected factor F_2 may have caused the rest of E. For example, the domestic economic policy of country A will be a major influence on its own economy; but this may also be influenced by the domestic economic policy of country B. In order to show up this secondary influence, we might

[22] An explanation may be in terms of the *typical* dispositions of more or less anonymous individuals, or in terms of the peculiar dispositions of specific individuals. (This is the basis of my distinction between 'explanation in principle' and 'explanation in detail.' See p. 733.) Thus, you might try to explain an election result in terms of how 'the Lancashire shop-keeper' and 'the non-party professional man' etc., felt; or, if you had an unlikely amount of knowledge, in terms of the dispositions of each elector.

assume provisionally that A exports *all* its production to, and imports *all* its consumption from, B, and then deduce the effect on A of a change of policy in B.[23]

But that would be a preliminary intellectual experiment. The premisses of a finished ideal type should be sufficiently realistic for it to be applicable to historical situations. I now turn to the problem of application.

5. HISTORICAL EXPLANATION

I shall consider three levels of historical explanation: (I) colligation (where ideal types play no significant role); (II) explanation in principle (which is the field *par excellence* for ideal types); and (III) explanation in detail (where ideal types are mostly constructed *ad hoc*, and rendered increasingly realistic until they become empirical reconstructions).[24]

(I) *Colligation.* The term 'colligation' has been revived by Mr. Walsh[25] to denote a procedure which is important, not because it is methodologically powerful, but because most 'literary' historians do in fact use it when they write, for example, constitutional history. It means 'explaining an event by tracing its intrinsic relations to other events and locating it in its historical context'.[26] Thus we begin to understand why a bill was enacted in May 1640 condemning Strafford to death when we learn of such matters as: his autocratic power in Ireland; Parliament's fear of the Irish army and Pym's ruthlessness as a parliamentary leader; the King's dependence on Parliament to pay indemnities to the Scottish army in the north; and the angry anti-Royalist mob which beset Westminster during the bill's passage. It may also be better understood by being colligated with *subsequent* events. Thus the Long Parliament's later treatment of Laud and Charles suggests that its treatment of Strafford was not eccentric, but part of a campaign against extra-parliamentary power.

However, as Mr. Walsh admits, colligation yields only what he calls a 'significant narrative', which is more than a chronicle, but less than a full explanation, of the events colligated.

(II) *Explanation in Principle.* The principle of the automatic governor can be demonstrated in a simple model which shows that a fall in some

---

[23] I owe this example to Professor J. E. Meade.

[24] Professor F. A. Hayek also draws a distinction between explaining in principle and explaining in detail, but he wishes to distinguish an explanation of why, say, a price will rise under certain conditions, from a quantitative prediction of the amount by which it will rise (*The Counter-Revolution of Science*, pp. 42–3); whereas I wish to distinguish between explanations in terms of *typical* dispositions, etc., and explanations in terms of the characteristics and personal idiosyncrasies of the principal actors concerned.

[25] See W. H. Walsh, *An Introduction to Philosophy of History*, London, 1951, ch. 3, § 3.

[26] Ibid., p. 59.

temperature, voltage, speed, pressure, etc., below a certain level will move a lever which will increase the supply of heat, etc.; and vice versa. Understanding this, you can explain the constant temperature of your car's circulating water *in principle* if you know that an automatic governor controls it, although you do not understand its detailed operation.[27]

Analogous explanations are used in applied economics. Consider the bargaining process. The principle of this is demonstrated in the following ideal type. Two rational agents are postulated. Each possesses one homogeneous, divisible good, and each knows the schedule of those combinations of various portions of his own and the other's good which he would exchange indifferently for the whole of his present good. These premises are highly precise, and also highly formal. Call them α and β. From these it is deduced that only the limits within which a bargain will be struck are determined, and that within those limits the outcome will be arbitrary. Call this consequence ω. Now consider post-war Anglo-Argentinian trade negotiations. Here, we can, I think, detect factors A, B, c, d, ... Z where: A and B are the resources and policies of the trade delegations, and are concrete examples of α and β; c, d, ... are minor factors whose small influences on Z may partly cancel out; and Z is the outcome of the negotiations, the actual instability of Anglo-Argentinian trade relations, which is a rough empirical counterpart of ω. The 'α, β, ω' ideal type explains in principle the 'A, B, c, d, ... Z' situation.[28]

In this example I have assumed that only one main economic principle, demonstrable in a single ideal type, was at work in the historical situation. But the situation will usually be more complex. Consider a wage-bargain. Perhaps there is a closed shop and limited entry into the trade union. The firm, a centrally planned organization, buys its raw materials, which are rationed, through a government agency, and its machinery at the best price it can get from oligopolistic suppliers. By law it must export a proportion of its produce, and the export market is highly competitive. Its home prices are fixed by a cartel agreement.[29] The general situation is inflationary.

[27] It is the principle of an invention rather than its physical detail which is usually described in patents. See M. Polanyi, *The Logic of Liberty* (London, 1951), p. 21.

[28] I owe this example to Professor Lionel Robbins.

[29] The definitions of perfect competition, oligopoly, and monopoly provide, incidentally, good illustrations of the principle of methodological individualism. An entrepreneur faces: (*a*) perfect competition if the price at which he sells is determined for him; (*b*) oligopoly, if he can alter his price, but if this alteration may lead to price changes by his competitors which may force him to make further, undesired alterations to his own price; and (*c*) monopoly, if he can alter his price without causing undesired repercussions. Competition, oligopoly, and monopoly are nothing but the outcome of the behaviour of interacting individuals in certain relationships.

Here, the outcome of the bargaining process will be shaped by a number of economic principles besides that illustrated in the previous example. And in order to understand the whole situation in principle it would be necessary to build up a complex model from the relevant simple ideal types. Here, an '(α, β), (λ, μ), (σ, τ), ... ω' model would be used to explain in principle an 'A, B, c, ... L, M, n, ... S, T, u, ... Z' situation (where c ..., n ..., u ... represent comparatively uninfluential factors).

The social scientist's explanations in principle lack the quantitative precision of explanations in mathematical physics. But he may claim that his explanations are at any rate 'intelligible' and 'satisfying', whereas those of the natural scientist are not. The most universal laws which the latter applies in his explanations and predictions contain terms (e.g. 'elementary quantum of action') whose connotation the layman cannot 'picture' or 'grasp'. Moreover, the status of these most universal laws is probably only temporary: they will probably come to be subsumed under higher-order laws.

But the ultimate premises of social science are human dispositions, i.e. something familiar and understandable (though not introspectable since they are not mental events). They 'are so much the stuff of our everyday experience that they have only to be stated to be recognised as obvious.'[30] And while psychology may try to explain these dispositions, they do provide social science with a natural stopping-place in the search for explanations of overt social phenomena. The social scientist might claim more. The natural scientist cannot, strictly speaking, *verify* valid hypotheses; he can only *refute* false ones.[31] He can say, 'If H, then E. But not-E. Therefore not-H.' But if he says, 'If H, then E. Moreover E. Therefore H' he commits the fallacy of affirming the consequent.[32] But a social scientist might claim that a valid social theory *can* be verified because both its conclusions *and* its premises can be confirmed—'you assent to the former because they correspond with recognized social facts; and you assent to the latter because they correspond with your ideas of how people behave.' An example of the belief that a social theory can be wholly verified by being confirmed at both ends is to be found in Keynes's *General Theory*. There he asserts 'the fundamental psychological law, upon which we are entitled to depend with great confidence ... from our knowledge of human nature ..., that men are disposed, as a rule and on

---

[30] Lionel Robbins, *The Nature and Significance of Economic Science* (London, 1935), p. 79.

[31] See K. R. Popper, *Logik der Forschung* (Vienna, 1935), *passim*.

[32] See F. S. C. Northrop, *The Logic of the Sciences and the Humanities* (New York, 1948), pp. 108–9; and e.g. H. W. B. Joseph, *An Introduction to Logic* (Oxford, 1916), pp. 522–3.

the average, to increase their consumption as their income increases, but not by as much as the increase in their income'; and vice versa.[33] He then shows that the empirical fact that no depression has worsened until 'no one at all was employed' is a deductive consequence of this law.[34] The theory is thus doubly confirmed, and therefore verified: 'it is *certain* that experience would be extremely different from what it is if the law did not hold.'[35] No natural scientist could claim so much for *his* laws. His explanations are 'surprising' in the sense that he explains the familiar in terms of the unconfirmable unfamiliar. But the social scientist explains the familiar in terms of the familiar. The element of surprise in *his* explanations lies in the logical demonstration of connections which had not been seen before between the facts which are prima facie discrete.

But a double caution must be entered against the idea of double confirmation in social science: (i) The same conclusion can, of course, be deduced from different sets of premisses, and we cannot be certain that our set of psychological assumptions is the correct set. (ii) Even if our psychological assumptions *are* correct, and even if we *do* find that their deductive consequences correspond to recognized facts, we may nevertheless be mistaken if we explain these facts as a consequence of those psychological factors. This is because we can seldom calculate the relative influence of different psychological factors.[36] Thus Keynes's belief that people are disposed to save a smaller proportion of their income if their income diminishes may well be correct; his demonstration that this general disposition would not allow depressions to worsen indefinitely is immaculate; and the fact that depressions do not worsen indefinitely is undoubted. It is nevertheless conceivable that *no* depression has been halted because of this disposition. One may have been halted by an outbreak of war, another by an upsurge of confidence, another by a public works policy, and so on. In explaining social phenomena we must not be content with the detection of one factor which, singly, would have produced, after an unstated period, an unstated amount of an effect which may, in any particular situation, have been caused mainly by quite different factors.

If I am right in supposing that social theories derive sociological conclusions from dispositional premisses, we should expect to find that major theoretical advances in social science consist in the perception of

---

[33] *The General Theory of Employment, Interest and Money* (London, 1936), p. 96.
[34] Ibid., p. 252.
[35] Ibid., p. 251 (my italics).
[36] I was myself inclined to accept the idea of double confirmation until Professor Popper pointed out to me the relevance of this consideration.

some typical feature of our mental make-up which had previously been disregarded, and in its formulation in a way which is more deductively fertile and which goes to explain a wider range of facts, than the psychological generalizations relied on hitherto. And this is precisely what we do find. I think that it would be generally conceded that economics is the most mature social science, and that the two most striking advances made in economics during the last century are: (i) the 'revolution' which occurred in the early 1870s when Jevons, Menger, and Walras introduced the concept of marginal utility; and (ii) the Keynesian 'revolution'.

(i) The classical economists saw that the price of a good must be partly determined by the demand for it, and that that demand must reflect the buyers' estimates of the good's utility—and yet diamonds, whose utility is low, fetch a far higher price than water, whose utility is high. So they tried to escape from their dilemma by saying that the price of a good is determined by the cost of its production, though this would obviously be untrue of an unwanted good which had been expensively produced. This difficulty dissolved with the introduction of the idea of the utility, not of a whole good, but of its least important, or 'marginal', unit. For—and this is the recognition of a psychological contour-line which had not been clearly mapped before—it is in terms of that unit that we tend to value a whole good; and the more we have of the same good, the more its marginal utility diminishes. Hence, if diamonds became abundant and water very scarce, their subjectively determined values would be reversed. F. H. Knight has given a vivid description of the elegance and power of the concept of marginal utility:

> To its admirers it comes near to being the fulfilment of the eighteenth-century craving for a principle which would do for human conduct and society what Newton's mechanics had done for the solar system. It introduces simplicity and order, even to the extent of making it possible to state the problems in the form of mathematical functions dealt with by the methods of infinitesimal calculus.[37]

(ii) The reader who is unfamiliar with Keynes's contribution to the theory of employment must take its value on trust, for it is impossible to describe it briefly. But here again we find that what it rests on is the perception and precise formulation of certain human dispositions which Keynes regarded as 'ultimate independent variables',[38] and from which he could deduce such dependent variables (or overt phenomena, as I have called them previously) as the amount of employment and the general level of prices. At the heart of his *General Theory* Keynes placed 'three

---

[37] F. H. Knight, *The Ethics of Competition* (London, 1935), p. 158.
[38] Op. cit., p. 246. Of course, the variables are only 'independent' from the social scientist's point of view. The psychologist would probably consider them 'dependent'.

fundamental psychological factors, namely, the psychological propensity to consume, the psychological attitude to liquidity and the psychological expectation of future yield from capital-assets'.[39]

(III) *Explanation in Detail.* The mark of an explanation in principle is its reliance on typical dispositions and its disregard of personal differences. But it is often impossible to disregard these, for instance, in diplomatic history. Here, the premisses of a historical explanation must be the specific dispositions, beliefs, and relationships of actual people. This is what I call 'explanation in detail'.

So far, I have allowed two questions to lie dormant: (i) What is the status of these dispositions, and wherein lies their explanatory power? (ii) What assumptions concerning people's rationality are we obliged to make when we explain something in terms of their dispositions and beliefs? These questions were not acute so long as explanations in principle were being considered. An explanation requires a general statement as its major premiss; and when we postulate a typical disposition we assert that all men (with trivial exceptions and minor deviations, and, perhaps, within a limited historico-geographical area) are prone to behave in a certain kind of way; and this gives us the generality we require. And we explain in principle by combining types which are, after all, ideal, and which may therefore be expected to contain idealized simplifications of real life, such as the assumption of fully rational behaviour in the light of preferences and beliefs.

But when we turn to explanations in detail these two questions do become acute. For we are here concerned with the variegated dispositions of actual people, and these appear to lack the generality which the major premiss of an explanation needs. And actual people do not behave altogether rationally, which suggests that we cannot go on assuming that they do. I shall discuss the first question under the head of 'Personality', and the second under the head of 'Rationality and Purposefulness'.

(i) *Personality.* A series of occurrences constitutes a person's life, and a complex and evolving system of dispositions constitutes his personality.[40] Dispositions 'are not laws, for they mention particular things or persons.

---

[39] Ibid., pp. 246–7.

[40] I have adopted the terminology of Professor G. Ryle's *Concept of Mind* (London, 1949; see especially ch. 5), but not that book's famous denial that a man has 'privileged access' to his own mind. Sitting beside the driver of a car who turns white and wrenches the steering-wheel over, I may perceive instantaneously *that* he fears an accident, but I do not *feel* his fear. Moreover, the historian is usually in the position of the policeman who tries to reconstruct what happened from skid-marks and reports of witnesses; and for him the dualism between uninterpreted overt behaviour (e.g. Jan Masaryk's fall from a Prague window) and its interpretation in psychological terms is very real.

On the other hand they resemble laws in being partly "variable" as "open".[41] The dispositions which comprise a unique, personality are, so to speak, 'laws' which apply to only one man over a limited period of time It is as if the laws of chemistry concerning, say, mercury, applied only to a period in the life of one solitary bottle of mercury which has come into existence, matured, and will dissolve, and whose twin, we may confidently assume, never has existed, and never will.

All this presupposes that men do have personalities, i.e. that their behaviour is fairly consistent over a period of time if their personalities are not subjected to dissolvent shocks. This assumption of the quasi-permanence of personalities corresponds roughly—very roughly—to the natural scientist's belief in the permanence of the natural order.

The generalizations of psychology fit into this scheme in the following ways: (a) Some attribute a certain disposition to all men. The theory of the association of ideas is an example. (b) Others attribute certain dispositions to a certain type of man, e.g. the 'introvert'. (c) Yet others attempt to describe the dynamics of personality-development, deriving later dispositions from prior determining conditions in the light of psychological theory. (It is this search for the primitive determining conditions which leads back to the 'formative years' of early childhood.) An example is the theory of the 'incest-complex', which asserts that a man who idealized his sister as a child will be prone to hypoaesthesia on marriage.

A disposition attributed to one man is no weaker than the same disposition attributed to all men in explaining and predicting that one man's behaviour. 'X will accept office' can be deduced from the minor premiss 'X believes that if he refuses the office he has been offered he will find himself in the wilderness' in conjunction with either (a) the major premiss, 'All men seek power,' or (b) the major premiss, 'X is a power-seeker'; but whereas (b) may be true, (a) is the sort of statement which is likely to be false because men are not uniform.[42]

Similarly, a detailed description of one man's chess-playing dispositions (his knowledge of the rules, evaluations of the different pieces, and ability to see a certain number of moves ahead) together with his present beliefs about his opponent's intentions and the positions of the pieces,

---

But the following characteristic remarks suggest that Professor Ryle has now modified his original anti-dualism: 'We have . . . a sort of (graduatedly) privileged access to such things as palpitations of the heart, cramps, and creaks in the joints.' 'I have elsewhere argued for the idea that a tickle just *is* a thwarted impulse to scratch. . . . But I do not think now that this will do' ('Feelings', *The Philosophical Quarterly*, i (Apr. 1951), 198–9.

[41] Ryle, *Concept of Mind*, p. 123.

[42] On law-like dispositions of very limited generality, see R. Peters, 'Cure, Cause and Motive', *Analysis*, x, No. 5 Apr. 1950), 106.

imply his next move, which could not be deduced from propositions about chess-players in general in conjunction with a description of the present state of the game.

Thus the idea that the historian's interpretative principles are simply generalizations about human nature, into which he must have special insight, is inadequate.[43] His knowledge of human nature in general has to be supplemented by a knowledge of the peculiar personalities of the principal actors concerned in the situation he is trying to understand, whether his problem be X's behaviour, or the chess-player's next move, or the rise of Christianity, or the Congress of Vienna.

The dispositions which the historian attributes to a personality he is trying to reconstruct resemble scientific laws in two further ways.

(a) They are postulated hypotheses which correspond to nothing observable, although observable behaviour can be inferred from them in conjunction with factual minor premises. Consequently, in judging their validity we want to know, not the mental process by which the historian arrived at them, but their degree of success in accounting for what is known of the man's behaviour. The hypothetical dispositions postulated by the historian who has 'sympathetically identified himself with his hero' may be richer than those of the historian who has not done so, but it is not this which gives them a certificate of reliability. Professor Hempel has put the matter very clearly:

> The method of empathy is, no doubt, frequently applied by laymen and by experts in history. But it does not in itself constitute an explanation; it is rather essentially a heuristic device; its function is to suggest certain psychological hypotheses which might serve as explanatory principles in the case under consideration.[44]

And the historian is no more precluded from reconstructing a strange and unsympathetic personality than is the scientist from reconstructing the behaviour of an atom which does things he would not dream of doing himself.[45]

[43] This idea underlies Mr. Walsh's contribution to the symposium on 'The Character of a Historical Explanation' (*Aristotelian Society, Supplementary Volume* xxi, 1947). From it he infers that, since 'men's notions of human nature change from age to age' we must recognize 'the subjective element which history undoubtedly contains' (p. 66). The point is, do historians' notions of, say, Napoleon's personality change from age to age (not because of the discovery of fresh evidence, etc., but) arbitrarily?

[44] Op. cit., p. 467. Failure to realize this is, I think, the weakness of R. G. Collingwood's *The Idea of History* (ed. T. M. Knox, Oxford, 1946).

[45] Failure to recognize this vitiates, I think, some of the argument in Professor F. A. Hayek's 'Scientism and the Study of Society' (*The Counter-Revolution of Science*, Part One). There, despite all the work done in abnormal psychology, he asserts: 'When we speak of mind what we mean is that certain phenomena can be successfully interpreted on the analogy of our own mind. . . . To recognise mind cannot mean

(b) The dispositions which constitute a personality also resemble scientific laws in that they form a hierarchial system; and this is of considerable methodological importance. It is, of course, essential that the dispositions which a historian attributes to a historical figure should not be mere *ad hoc* translations of known occurrences into dispositional terms. It is no explanation of Brutus's behaviour to say that he was disposed to assassinate Caesar, though it would be a ground for an explanation to say that Brutus was disposed to place his loyalty to the State above his loyalties to his friends, if independent evidence were found to support this hypothesis. Moreover—and it is here that the idea of a hierarchy of dispositions is important—the historian who can explain some aspect of a person's behaviour *up to a certain time* in terms of certain disposition, although his *subsequent* behaviour conflicts with this disposition, must not merely say that at that time the earlier disposition gave way to another. He should find a *higher-order* disposition which helps to explain both earlier and later lower-order dispositions, and hence the whole range of the person's behaviour. For example: suppose that Russian foreign policy is controlled by a consistent integrated personality. Before 1939 Russia was disposed to pursue an anti-fascist foreign policy. But in 1939 came the Russo-German Pact. In order to explain this aberration it is not enough for the historian to say that the anti-fascist disposition was replaced. He must find a higher-order disposition (e.g. 'Russian foreign policy is determined by considerations of national expediency, not by ideological factors') from which, in conjunction with factual premises, the change in policy is derivable. In doing this it is clear that the historian will *not* be translating an occurrence (the signing of the pact) into dispositional terms, but deriving both the occurrence and the change in lower-order dispositions from a more permanent and fundamental disposition.

In conclusion it should be said that the personality of a man in society comprises dispositions both of a more private and temperamental kind, and of a more public and institutional kind. Only certain individuals are disposed to weep during the death-scene in *Othello*, but all policemen are disposed to blow their whistles under certain circumstances and any

---

anything but to recognise something as operating in the same way as our own thinking.' From this false premise he correctly infers the false conclusion that 'history can never carry us beyond the stage where we can understand the working of the minds of the acting people because they are similar to our own' (pp. 77–9). Only a war-like historian can tackle a Genghiz Khan or a Hitler! Moreover, if it were true that people, young and old, do not recognize as mind what they cannot interpret on the analogy of their own mind, they would never learn to speak. For children must unconsciously realize that adult noises differ importantly from their own gibberish in being meaningful before they can begin to understand adult talk.

I hasten to add that I owe much to other parts of Professor Hayek's argument.

Speaker in the House of Commons is disposed to disallow parliamentary criticism of exercises of the Prerogative. And these more public and institutional dispositions, which may vary very little when one man undertakes another's role, can be abstracted from the total, variegated flux of dispositions, and so provide the social scientist with a fairly stable subject-matter.[46]

(ii) *Rationality and Purposefulness.* Before asking what assumptions the historian is obliged to make about the rationality of those whose behaviour he is trying to interpret, we must establish a satisfactory 'definition in use' of the term 'rational behaviour'. Weber defined it, very austerely, as the deliberate and logical choice of means to attain explicit goals, in the light of existing factual knowledge. This is unsatisfactory for two reasons. (*a*) Whitehead said somewhere that 'civilisation advances by extending the number of important operations we can perform without thinking about them.' This morning's tooth-brushing was not irrational because done from habit and not from deliberations on dental hygiene. Our pursuit of goals need not be conscious in order to be rational. (*b*) Behaviour often does not conform to the end-means pattern. I may tell the truth, or go fishing, simply from a desire to do so, with no further end in mind.[47]

We escape these difficulties by saying that a person has behaved rationally if he *would* have behaved in the same way if, with the same *factual* information, he had seen the full *logical* implications of his behaviour, whether he actually saw them or not. And if we define purposeful behaviour as trying (consciously or otherwise) to do or achieve something wanted, it follows that fully rational behaviour is a limiting case of purposeful behaviour.

The historian who tries to interpret overt behaviour must assume that it is purposeful but not necessarily fully rational.[48] Consider a *crime passionel* committed by an enraged husband. A judge who assumed that the husband had behaved purposelessly could reconstruct the event in a number of quite arbitrary ways—perhaps cramp caused his finger to contract round the trigger of a gun which happened to be pointing at his wife's lover. But while the judge must not assume purposelessness he need not assume full rationality. The husband would probably have confined himself to threats and remonstrances if he had paused to consider the less immediate consequences of a violent course of action.

[46] See Hayek, *Counter-Revolution*, p. 34.

[47] 'We invest our capital reluctantly in the hope of getting dividends. . . . But the angler would not accept or understand an offer of the pleasures without the activities of angling. It is angling that he enjoys, not something that angling engenders.' Ryle, *Concept of Mind*, p. 132. See also H. A. Prichard, *Moral Obligation* (Oxford, 1949), pp. 10–11.

[48] See Robbins, op. cit., ch. 4, sect. 5.

The assumption of purposefulness is constantly made by those who attempt the most intensive analysis of human behaviour, i.e. practising psycho-analysts. It has often been pointed out that the psycho-analyst is on the side of rationality in that he tries to cure his patients. More interesting from our point of view is his assumption that the behaviour of an *uncured* patient is thoroughly purposeful. Suppose a patient forgets to wind his watch, and so arrives late at his father's funeral. Unlike the layman, the psycho-analyst will not attribute the stopped watch to accidental forgetfulness, to a purposeless psychic aberration. He will ask his patient *why* he *wanted* his watch to stop—maybe he felt guilty on having a death-wish fulfilled and so created an excuse for avoiding the funeral. This would certainly be purposeful behaviour, and might even be regarded as rational behaviour based on misinformation.[49]

(iii) *Conclusion.* Having considered the status of dispositions and the problem of rationality, we can now return to explanations in detail.

Weber advocated using individualistic ideal types, which depict rational behaviour, to show up the partial irrationality of actual behaviour. But this is unacceptable. Suppose that a historian wishes to interpret a general's behaviour during a battle. He has reconstructed, as best he can, both the dispositions which consitute that aspect of the general's personality with which he is concerned, and the general's information about the military situation. Suppose that, in conjunction, these dictate retreat as the rational course of action, but that the general is known to have given the signal to advance. Now the historian, like the psycho-analyst, will not want to leave puzzling overt behaviour uninterpreted; but according to Weber he should simply call this a deviation from the ideally rational course of action implied by the premises of his theoretical reconstruction of the situation. But since an irrational aberration can be attributed to anything from boredom to panic, this procedure would result in thoroughly arbitrary reconstructions. Rather, this historian must discover the most satisfactory amendment to the premises of his ideal type (constructed more or less *ad hoc* to depict the main features of the general's personality and situation) which will remove the discrepancy between what it implies and what happened. Perhaps there is independent evidence to suggest that the general was more lion-hearted than the historian had supposed; or perhaps he had underestimated the enemy's strength, or, in estimating the immediate consequences of an advance, he had overlooked a more distant undesirable repercussion. When *ad hoc* ideal types are used in detailed historical explanations, they have to be amended and amended until they cease

---

[49] The mixture of rationality and misinformation due to childhood associations which psycho-analysis brings to the surface was pointed out to me by Professor Popper.

being ideal constructs and become empirical reconstructions. The historian who claims to have interpreted a historical situation should be able to show: (*a*) that the behaviour of the actors in it flows from their personalities and situational beliefs; and (*b*) that significant events which no one intended are resultants of the behaviour of interacting individuals.

6. SUMMARY

An individual's personality is a system of unobservable dispositions which, together with his factual beliefs, determine his observable behaviour. Society is a system of unobservable relationships between individuals whose interaction produces certain measurable sociological phenomena. We can apprehend an unobservable social system only by reconstructing it theoretically from what is known of individual dispositions, beliefs, and relationships. Hence holistic ideal types, which would abstract essential traits from a social whole while ignoring individuals, are impossible: they always turn into individualistic ideal types. Individualistic ideal types of explanatory power are constructed by first discerning the form of typical, socially significant, dispositions, and then by demonstrating how, in various typical situations, these lead to certain principles of social behaviour.

If such a principle, or a number of such principles, is at work in a historical situation, the outcome of that situation can be explained anonymously, or in principle, by an application to it of the relevant ideal type, or combination of ideal types. If the idiosyncrasies of the actors concerned significantly influenced the outcome, it must be explained in terms of their peculiar dispositions and beliefs. In either case, the hypothetico-deductive method is used. The hypotheses consist of postulated dispositions, beliefs and relationships of (anonymous or specific) individuals; and their test lies in the correspondence or otherwise between their deductive consequences and what is known of the overt characteristics of the situation being reconstructed. How the historian establishes the overt characteristics of a vanished situation is another story.

VI

SOCIETAL FACTS

MAURICE MANDELBAUM

1. INTRODUCTION

IF ONE adopts Broad's distinction between critical and speculative philosophy, the following paper may be regarded as an attempt to deal with one of the major problems of a critical philosophy of the social sciences. Like all such attempts, this paper faces some difficulties which are not encountered in equally acute form by those who deal with the concepts and methods of the natural sciences. In the first place, the concepts and methods utilized in the natural sciences have been more sharply defined than have been those which social scientists employ. In the second place, there is less disagreement among natural scientists than among social scientists as to the purposes which actually do underlie, or which should underlie, their studies. In the third place, the relations among the various branches of natural science seem to be more easily definable and less subject to dispute than is the case among the social sciences. It is with one aspect of the relations among the various social sciences that this paper will be concerned.

There can scarcely be any doubt that there is at present a considerable measure of disagreement among social scientists concerning the relations which obtain among their various disciplines. For example, there is little agreement as to how the province of 'social psychology' is related to general psychology on the one hand or to sociology on the other. There is perhaps even less agreement as to how sociology and history are related, or whether, in fact, history is itself a social science. Even the province of cultural anthropology which, in its earlier stages, seemed to be capable of clear definition, is now in a position in which its relations to the other fields of social science have become extremely fluid. This type of fluidity in the boundaries of the various social sciences, and the ease with which concepts employed in one discipline spread to other disciplines, has been quite generally regarded as a promising augury for the future of the social sciences. One notes the frequency with which 'integration' is held up as an

From the *British Journal of Sociology*, vi (1955), 305–17. Reprinted by permission of the author and Routledge & Kegan Paul Ltd.

important programmatic goal for social scientists. But such pleas for integration are ambiguous. On the one hand, they may merely signify a recognition of the fact that attempts to understand some concrete problems call for co-operation between persons trained to use the concepts and methods of different social sciences, or that workers in one discipline should be aware of the methods and results of those who work in other fields. On the other hand, what some who plead for 'integration' in social science seem to demand is that the various disciplines should merge into one larger whole. On such a view the goal of integration would be the achievement of a state in which all persons who work in the field of social science would operate with the same set of concepts and would utilize the same methods of inquiry. If I am not mistaken, it is sometimes assumed that the social sciences will have made their greatest advance when the individual social sciences which now exist will have lost their separate identities. In so far as this paper has a practical purpose, its purpose is to indicate that 'integration', taken in this sense, is a mistaken goal for sociologists and psychologists to pursue.[1]

In stating that I wish to argue against what some social scientists believe to be the most promising path which their sciences can follow, it is clear that this paper has what might be termed an injunctive character. I am attempting to rule in advance that certain modes of procedure should or should not be adopted by practising social scientists. To those trained in the critical philosophy of the natural sciences, such a procedure will doubtless seem both foolhardy and perverse. Yet, it is unavoidable. So long as there are fundamental differences among social scientists with respect to the types of concepts and types of method which they actually use, and so long as the criteria by means of which they measure the adequacy of these concepts and methods differ, every attempt to do more than compile a *corpus* of materials for comparison, will involve that the analyst of the social sciences should take his own stand with respect to the matters under debate. Where one can show reasons for the position adopted, the injunctive element in one's analyses cannot be claimed to be wholly arbitrary. It is in proportion to the strength of these reasons that any particular injunctive proposal is to be judged.

However, any proposal as to the relations which ought to obtain between two or more social sciences will presuppose a belief as to what the goal of the social sciences may be. Concerning this topic there is also a considerable amount of debate. However, I believe it possible to formulate a general statement which might be acceptable to all, leaving unprejudiced those specific issues which have divided social scientists into opposed

---

[1] In this paper I shall not be concerned with the other social sciences.

camps. I submit that the following statement would be quite generally acceptable: it is the task of the social sciences to attain a body of knowledge on the basis of which the actions of human beings as members of a society can be understood. This definition of the aim of the social sciences does not rule out the possibility that an understanding of the actions of human beings as members of a society may be instrumental to some further aim, such as that of attaining the means of controlling human behaviour, or of promoting human welfare. (Nor, of course, does it affirm that this is the case.) Furthermore, it is to be noted that in this statement of the aims of the social sciences I have avoided prejudging this issue as to whether the body of knowledge which is sought can be formulated as a system of laws, and whether an understanding of human actions is equivalent to explaining these actions in the sense in which the term 'explanation' is used in the natural sciences. Throughout this paper I wish to avoid raising these questions, and in so far as possible I shall confine my discussion to a neutral terminology which does not prejudge any of these issues. Wherever my language seems to suggest that I am using the model of explanation used in the natural sciences, my point could equally well be phrased in terms which are compatible with the view that the methods and concepts of the social sciences are utterly different from those employed in the natural sciences. And, conversely, where I use the language of 'understanding', my discussion can equally well be rephrased in terms of the language of scientific 'explanation'.

Having now defined what I take to be the task of the social sciences, I can state the aim of this paper. My aim is to show that one cannot understand the actions of human beings as members of a society unless one assumes that there is a group of facts which I shall term 'societal facts' which are as ultimate as are those facts which are 'psychological' in character. In speaking of 'societal facts' I refer to any facts concerning the forms of organization present in a society. In speaking of 'psychological facts' I refer to any facts concerning the thoughts and the actions of specific human beings.

2. AN EXAMPLE OF THE IRREDUCIBILITY OF SOCIETAL CONCEPTS

If it be the case, as I wish to claim, that societal facts are as ultimate as are psychological facts, then those concepts which are used to refer to the forms of organization of a society cannot be reduced without remainder to concepts which only refer to the thoughts and actions of specific individuals.[2] There are many reasons why the type of claim that I am putting

---

[2] The term 'ultimate' may, of course, have other meanings as well. In the present paper, however, I am taking the irreducibility of a set of concepts to be equivalent to the ultimacy of that set of facts to which these concepts refer.

forward has been doubted, and we shall note some of these reasons as we proceed. First, however, it will be well to lend some plausibility to the view by means of an example.

Suppose that I enter a bank, I then take a withdrawal slip and fill it out, I walk to a teller's window, I hand in my slip, he gives me money, I leave the bank and go on my way. Now suppose that you have been observing my actions and that you are accompanied by, let us say, a Trobriand Islander. If you wished to explain my behaviour, how would you proceed? You could explain the filling out of the withdrawal slip as a means which will lead to the teller's behaviour towards me, that is, as a means to his handing me some notes and coins; and you could explain the whole sequence of my action as directed towards this particular end. You could then explain the significance which I attached to the possession of these notes and coins by following me and noting how the possession of them led other persons, such as assistants in shops, to give me goods because I gave them the notes and coins which the bank teller had handed to me. Such would be an explanation of my observed behaviour in terms of the behaviour of other specific individuals towards me. And it might at first glance appear as if an explanation couched in terms of these inter-personal forms of behaviour would be adequate to cover all of the aspects of the case.

However, it would also be necessary for you to inform the stranger who accompanies you that it does not suffice for a person to fill out such a slip and hand it to just anyone he may happen to meet. It would also be only fair to inform him that before one can expect a bank teller to hand one money in exchange for a slip, one must have 'deposited' money. In short, one must explain at least the rudiments of a banking system to him. In doing so one is, of course, using concepts which refer to one aspect of the institutional organization of our society, and this is precisely the point which I wish to make. (And the same point can be made with reference to how Malinowski has explained to *us* the Trobriand Islanders' system of ceremonial exchanges of gifts.) In all cases of this sort, the actual behaviour of specific individuals towards one another is unintelligible unless one views their behaviour in terms of their status and roles, and the concepts of status and role are devoid of meaning unless one interprets them in terms of the organization of the society to which the individuals belong.

To this it may be objected that any statement concerning the status of an individual is itself analysable in terms of how specific individuals behave towards other individuals, and how these in turn behave towards them. Thus it might be claimed that while the explanation of an individual's behaviour often demands the introduction of concepts referring to 'societal status', such concepts are themselves reducible to further statements concerning actual or probable forms of behaviour. Thus, societal concepts might be held to be heuristic devices, summarizing repeated patterns of behaviour, but they would be nothing more: their real meaning would lie in a conjunction of statements concerning the behaviour of a number of individuals.

However, this view is open to serious objection. We have seen in the foregoing illustration that my own behaviour towards the bank teller is determined by his status. If the attempt is now made to interpret his status in terms of the recurrent patterns of behaviour which others exemplify in dealing with him, then *their* behaviour is left unexplained: each of them —no less than I—will only behave in this way because each recognizes the teller of a bank to have a particular status. Similarly, it is impossible to resolve the bank teller's role into statements concerning his behaviour towards other individuals. If one wished to equate his societal role with his reactions towards those who behave in a particular way towards him, it would be unintelligible that he should hand us money when we present him with a withdrawal slip when he stands in his teller's cage, and yet that he would certainly refuse to do so if we were to present him with such a slip when we met him at a party. Bank tellers as well as depositors behave as they do because they assume certain societally defined roles under specific sets of circumstances. This being the case, it is impossible to escape the use of societal concepts in attempting to understand some aspects of individual behaviour: concepts involving the notions of status and role cannot themselves be reduced to a conjunction of statements in which these or other societal concepts do not appear.

[Precisely the same point may be made with respect to attempts to translate societal concepts into terms of the thoughts of individuals rather than into terms of their overt behaviour. If one should wish to say that I acted as I did towards the teller because I foresaw that through my actions he would be led to give me money, one would still have to admit that my anticipation of his response was based upon my recognition of the fact that he was a bank teller, and that the role of a bank teller demands that he should act as the bank's agent, and the function of a bank (so far as each depositor is concerned) is that of being a custodian of legal tender, etc. Thus, in attempting to analyse societal facts by means of appealing to the thoughts which guide an individual's conduct, some of the thoughts will themselves have societal referents, and societal concepts will therefore not have been expunged from our analysis.]

Now I do not wish to claim that an individual's thoughts or his overt actions are wholly explicable in terms of status and roles. Not only does it seem to be the case that some actions may be explained without introducing these concepts, but it is also the case that two individuals, say two bank tellers, may behave differently towards me in spite of the identity in their roles. Thus, one may be friendly and the other hostile or aloof, and the nature of my own behaviour towards them will then differ. Thus it should be apparent that I am not seeking to explain all facets of individual behaviour by means of statements which only refer to societal facts. What I wish to contend is (a) that in understanding or explaining an individual's actions we must often refer to facts concerning the organization of the society in which he lives, and (b) that our statements concerning these societal facts are not reducible to a conjunction of statements concerning the actions of individuals. I take it that almost all social scientists and philosophers would grant the first of these contentions, but that many social scientists and most philosophers would reject the second, insisting that societal facts are reducible to a set of facts concerning individual behaviour.

3. THE CRITERION OF 'IRREDUCIBILITY'

It is now necessary to state the criterion of irreducibility which the foregoing illustration has presupposed.

Let us assume that there is a language, S, in which sociological concepts such as 'institutions', 'mores', 'ideologies', 'status', 'class', etc., appear. These concepts all refer to aspects of what we term 'a society'. That there is a language of this type is clear from the works of sociologists, anthropologists, and historians. It is also clear from the fact that we use such terms as 'the President of the United States', or 'the unmarried children of X'. In order to define the meaning of the latter terms we must make reference to the Constitution of the United States, or to the laws which govern our marriage and kinship systems, and in these references we are employing societal concepts.

There is, of course, also another language, P, in which we refer to the thoughts and actions and capabilities of individual human beings. In making statements in this language (which, for want of a better name, I have called our 'psychological language')[3] we are not using societal

---

[3] It will be noted that what I have termed our psychological language does not include terms such as 'neural paths', 'brain-traces', etc. My argument aims to show that societal facts are not reducible to facts concerning the thoughts and actions of specific individuals; the problem of whether both societal facts and facts concerning an individual's thoughts and actions are explicable in terms of (or, are in some sense 'reducible' to) a set of physical or physiological correlates is not my present concern. It will readily be seen that this is not the point at issue. Those who seek to reduce societal facts to facts concerning individual behaviour are not attempting to speak in physical and physiological terms.

concepts. The differences between these two languages may be illustrated by the fact that the connotation of the term 'the present President of the United States' carries implications which do not follow from the personal name 'Dwight D. Eisenhower', and statements concerning the personality of Dwight D. Eisenhower carry no implications for our understanding of his societal role. This remains true even though we admit that in this case, as in most others, the status of an individual is often causally connected with the nature of his personality, and even though we also admit that an individual's personality is often connected with the fact that he occupies a particular status, or that he functions within this status as he does.

Put in these terms, my thesis that societal facts are irreducible to psychological facts may be reformulated as holding that sociological concepts cannot be translated into psychological concepts *without remainder*. What is signified by the stipulation 'without remainder' must now be made clear.

It would seem to be the case that all statements in the sociological language, *S*, are translatable into statements concerning the behaviour of specific individuals, and thus would be translatable into the language *P*. For example, a statement such as 'the institution of monogamous marriage supplanted the polygynous marriage system of the Mormons' could presumably be translated into statements concerning the actions of certain aggregates of individuals. However, it is by no means certain that such translations could be effected without using other concepts which appear in the sociological language. These concepts too might have their translations into *P*, but the translation of the concepts of *S* into *P* would not be complete if such translations still had to employ other concepts which appear in *S*. It is with respect to incomplete translations of this type that I speak of translations which cannot be effected 'without remainder'.

An analogue of this situation was pointed out by Chisholm in his criticism of C. I. Lewis's theory of knowledge.[4] According to Chisholm, thing-statements cannot be completely reduced to statements concerning sense-data because one must specify the conditions of the appearance of these sense-data, and in doing so one must again use thing-statements. And this is precisely the situation which we found to obtain in our illustration of the behaviour of a person withdrawing money from a bank.

Now, it might be argued (as it has sometimes been argued with respect to Chisholm's contention) that our inability to carry out such translations, without remainder, represents a practical and not a theoretical inability. According to those who take this view, the practical difficulty which is

---

[4] Cf. Chisholm, 'The Problem of Empiricism' in *Journal of Philosophy*, xlv (1948), 512ff. (I am indebted to Roderick Firth for calling my attention to this analogue.)

present arises from the indefinitely long conjunction of statements which we should have to make in carrying out our analyses, and to the fact that some of these statements would involve a foreknowledge of future events. But it is claimed that no theoretically important consequences follow from our inability to complete a detailed analysis of a particular statement; such partical analyses as we can actually make may not have omitted any theoretically significant aspects of the statements which we wish to analyse. Such a rejoinder would be open to two objections, so far as our present discussion is concerned.

First, we are here concerned with the problem of the relations between two empirical disciplines. Therefore, if it be admitted that it is impossible in practice to reduce statements which contain societal terms to a conjunction of statements which only include terms referring to the thoughts and actions of specific individuals, the rejoinder in question might conceivably be significant from the point of view of a general ontology, but it would not affect my argument regarding the autonomy of the societal sciences.

Second, it is to be noted that whatever may be the case regarding Chisholm's argument concerning the relation of sense-data statements to thing-statements, the problem of reducing statements which include societal terms to statements which only concern specific individuals is not merely a question of how we may *analyse* action statements, but how we may *explain* certain facts. It has been my contention that if we are to explain an individual's behaviour when, say, he enters a bank, we must have recourse to societal concepts and cannot merely employ terms which refer to the fact that this individual makes marks on paper, approaches a specific point, hands the marked paper to another individual, etc. He who knew all of this, and who also knew all of the other actions performed by the members of a society, would possess a series of protocol statements, or biographical 'logs'. Even though this set of logs included reference to all of the actions performed by all of the members of the society, no societal concepts would appear in it. However, this information would not make it possible for our omniscient collector of data to explain why the depositor fills out a slip in order to withdraw money, or why the teller will exchange notes and coins for such a slip. Such a transaction only becomes explicable when we employ the concept of 'a bank', and what it means to speak of 'a bank' will involve the use of concepts such as 'legal tender', and 'contract'. Further, what it means to speak of 'a contract' will involve reference to our legal system, and the legal system itself cannot be defined in terms of individual behaviour—even the legal realist must distinguish between the behaviour of judges and policemen and the behaviour of 'just anyone'. Thus, if we are to explain certain forms of individual behaviour we must use societal concepts, and these concepts are not (I have argued) translatable without remainder into terms which only refer to the behaviour of individuals.

Yet it is important to insist that even though societal concepts cannot be translated into psychological concepts without leaving this societal remainder, it is not only possible but is indeed necessary to make the *partial* translation. It is always necessary for us to translate terms such as 'ideologies' or 'banks' or 'a monogamous marriage system' into the language of individual thought and action, for unless we do so we have no means of verifying any statements which we may make concerning these societal facts. Ideologies and banks and marriage systems do not exist unless there are aggregates of individuals who think and act in specific ways, and it is only by means of establishing the forms of their thoughts and their actions that we can apprehend the nature of the societal organization in which they live, or that we can corroborate or disallow statements concerning this organization. Yet, the necessity for this translation of specific sociological concepts into terms of individual behaviour in order that we may verify and refine our sociological statements does not alter the fact that the possibility of making such a translation always involves the necessity for using other societal concepts to define the conditions under which this behaviour takes place. Thus, the translation can never obviate the use of societal concepts and reduce the study of society to a branch of the study of the actions of individuals.

4. OBJECTIONS

In the foregoing discussion I have been at pains to state my position in such a way as to avoid the most usual objections to the general type of view which I hold. However, it will be useful to comment on three objections which have frequently been raised against the view that societal facts are irreducible to psychological facts.[5]

---

[5] When we consider the type of 'irreducibility' which has here been claimed to characterize societal facts, we must be prepared to allow that it may not be the only type of irreducibility to be found among 'existential emergents'. (On the meaning of this term, which has been borrowed from Lovejoy, cf. my 'Note on Emergence', in *Freedom and Reason*, ed. Baron, Nagel, and Pinson, Free Press, Glencoe, Ill., 1951.) I am in fact inclined to believe that there is a stronger form of irreducibility than is here in question. This stronger form may be said to exist between, say, the colour 'red' and brain events or light frequencies. In such cases it might be true that even a *partial* translation cannot be effected. All that I have wished to show is that while it is undeniable that we can and do make partial translations of societal concepts by using psychological concepts, these translations cannot be complete: we must always use further societal concepts to specify the conditions under which the observed forms of societally oriented behaviour take place.

The first of these objections may be termed the ontological objection. It consists in holding that societal facts cannot be said to have any status of their own since no such facts would exist if there were not individuals who thought and acted in specific ways. Now, to hold the view which I hold, one need not deny that the existence of a society presupposes the existence of individuals, and that these individuals must possess certain capacities for thought and for action if what we term a society is to exist. Yet, this admission does not entail the conclusion which is thought to follow from it: one need not hold that a society is an entity independent of all human beings in order to hold that societal facts are not reducible to the facts of individual behaviour. The warrant for the latter position is merely this: all human beings are born into a society, and much of their thought and their action is influenced by the nature of the societies in which they live; therefore, those facts which concern the nature of their societies must be regarded as being independent of them. To be sure, these facts are not independent of the existence of *other* individuals, and it will be from the forms of behaviour of these other individuals that any specific individual will have acquired his own societally oriented patterns of behaviour. But these individuals, too, were born into an already functioning societal organization which was independent of them. Thus, their societally oriented behaviour was also conditioned by an already existing set of societal facts, etc.

To be sure, those who wish to press the ontological objection may insist that at some remote time in the history of the human race there were individuals who were not born into an already existing society, and that these individuals must have formed a societal organization by virtue of certain patterns of repeated interpersonal actions. Thus, they would seek to insist that all societal facts have their origins in individual behaviour, and that it is mistaken to argue, as I have argued, that societal facts are irreducible to the facts of individual behaviour. However, this rejoinder is clearly fallacious. Whatever may have been the origin of the first forms of societal organization (a question which no present knowledge puts us in a position to answer), the issue with which we are here concerned is one which involves the nature of societies as they exist at present. To argue that the nature of present societal facts is reducible to the facts of individual behaviour because the origins of a particular social system grew up out of certain repeated forms of behaviour is a clear example of the genetic fallacy. One might as well argue on the basis of our knowledge of the origins of the Greek drama and of the modern drama that every current Broadway play is really to be understood as a religious festival.

However, the above answer to the ontological type of objection is clearly not sufficient.[6] It is, I hope, adequate to show that one usual form of countering my position is untenable; yet, the essential paradox remains. One can still legitimately ask what sort of ontological status societal facts can conceivably possess if it is affirmed that they depend for their existence on the activities of human beings and yet are claimed not to be identical with these activities. There are, it seems to me, two types of answer which might be given to this question. In the first type of answer one might contend that a whole is not equal to the sum of its parts, and a society is not equal to the sum of those individual activities which go to form it. This familiar holistic answer is not the one which I should be inclined to propose. In the first place, it is by no means certain that the principle of holism (as thus stated) is philosophically defensible. In the second place, such an answer assumes that what may be termed the 'parts' of a society are to be taken to be individual human beings, and this is an assumption which I should be unwilling to make. All of the preceding argument entails the proposition that the 'parts' of a society are specific societal facts, not individuals. If this were not the case, societal concepts could be translated into terms referring to individual behaviour if we had sufficient knowledge of all the interrelations among these individuals. Instead, we have found that an analysis of a statement which concerns a societal fact will involve us in using other societal concepts: for example, that what it means to be a depositor in a bank will involve statements concerning our legal system and our monetary economy. Similarly, what it means to be a college student cannot be defined without recourse to statements concerning our educational system, and such statements cannot be analysed without utilizing concepts which refer to statutory laws as well as to many other aspects of our societal organization. Thus, from the arguments which have been given, it follows that the 'parts' of a society are not individual human beings, but are the specific institutions, and other forms of organization, which characterize that society. Once this is recognized, it remains an open question as to the extent to which any specific society (or all societies) are to be conceived holistically or pluralistically.

The second method of dealing with the ontological objection is the one which I should myself be inclined to adopt. It consists in holding that one set of facts may depend for its existence upon another set of facts and yet not be identical with the latter. An example of such a relationship would be that which a traditional epiphenomenalist would regard as existing between brain events and the concepts of consciousness. Whatever objections one

[6] In what follows I shall only be discussing human societies. The differences between 'animal societies' and human societies are far more striking than are their similarities.

may raise against the epiphenomenalist view of the mind-body relationship, one would scarcely be justified in holding that the position must be false because the content of consciousness could not be different from the nature of brain states and yet be dependent upon the latter. If one has reasons for holding that the content of consciousness *is* different from brain states, and if one also has reason for holding that it *does* depend upon the latter, one's ontology must be accommodated to these facts: the facts cannot be rejected because of a prior ontological commitment. And, without wishing to press my analogy further than is warranted, I can point out that my statement concerning 'the parts' of a society has its analogue in what those who hold to the epiphenomenalist position would say concerning the proper analysis of any statement referring to the content of an individual's field of consciousness. Just as I have claimed that the component parts of a society are the elements of its organization and are not the individuals without whom it would not exist, so the epiphenomenalist would (I assume) say that the parts of the individual's field of consciousness are to be found within the specific data of consciousness and not in the brain events upon which consciousness depends.

These remarks are, I hope, sufficient to dispel the ontological objection to the position which I wish to defend. To be sure, I have not attempted to say what position should be assigned to societal facts when one is constructing a general ontology. To do so, I should have to say much more concerning the nature of societal facts, and I should of course also have to discuss the nature of other types of entity. Here it has only been my concern to suggest that what I have termed the ontological objection to my thesis is by no means as strong as it may at first glance appear to be: the admission that all societal facts depend upon the existence of human beings who possess certain capacities for thought and for action by no means precludes the contention that these facts are irreducible to facts concerning those individuals.

The second of the most usual objections to the thesis that societal facts cannot be reduced to psychological facts is an epistemological objection. This objection may take many forms, depending upon the theory of knowledge which is held by the objector. However, the common core of all such objections is the indubitable fact that societal concepts are not capable of being 'pointed to', in the sense in which we can point to material objects, or to the qualities or activities of these objects. Whenever we wish to point to any fact concerning societal organization we can only point to a sequence of interpersonal actions. Therefore, any theory of knowledge which demands that all empirically meaningful concepts must ultimately be reducible to data which can be directly inspected will lead to the insistence that all societal concepts are reducible to the patterns of individual behaviour.

I shall not, of course, seek to disprove this general theory of knowledge. Yet it is possible to indicate in very brief compass that it is inadequate to deal with societal facts. Since those who would hold this theory of knowledge would presumably wish to show that we can be said to know something of the nature of human societies, and since they would also wish to hold that our means of gaining this knowledge is through the observation of the repeated patterns of activities of individuals, a proof that their theory of knowledge cannot account for our apprehension of the nature of individual action is, in the present context, a sufficient disproof of the epistemological type of objection.

In order to offer such a disproof, let us revert to our illustration of a depositor withdrawing money from a bank. In order to understand his overt actions in entering a bank, filling out a slip, handing it to a teller, receiving notes and coins, and leaving the bank, we must view this sequence of actions as one internally connected series. Yet what connects the elements within the series is the person's intention to withdraw money from his account, and this intention is not itself a directly observable element within the series. Thus, unless it be admitted that we can have knowledge of aspects of human behaviour which are not directly presented to the senses, we cannot understand his behaviour and therefore cannot understand that which we seek to understand, i.e. those societal facts which supposedly are the summations of instances of behaviour of this type. To this, it may of course be objected that we have learned to attribute certain intentions to agents on the basis of our own experienced intentions, and when this introspective experience is combined with our observation of overt behaviour we learn to interpret human actions. Yet if this enlargement of our modes of knowing is allowed, there is no reason to stop with the facts of individual behaviour as the building-blocks of a knowledge of societal facts. Within our own experience we are no less directly aware of our own names, of our belonging to a particular family, of our status as youngsters or elders, etc., than we are of our own intentions. To be sure, our societal status must, originally, have been learned by us in a sense in which our intentions need not presumably have been learned. Yet, once again, we must avoid the genetic fallacy: the origin of our knowledge is not identical with that knowledge itself. Just as the concept of number has a meaning which need not be identical with the experiences through which it was learned, so the concept of a family, or of differentiated status due to age or sex, need not (even for a child) be identical with the experiences through which this concept was first made manifest. And to these remarks it should be added that once we have grasped the idea of status, or of family, or of authority, we can transfer this concept to situations which are initially alien to our own experience (e.g. to new forms of family organization) no less readily than we can apply a knowledge of our own intentions to the understanding of the intentions of those who act in ways which are initially strange to us. The problem of extending our knowledge from our own experience of others is not, I submit, more impossible in principle in the one case than in the other. And if this be so, there is no epistemological reason why we should seek to reduce societal facts to the facts of individual behaviour. Only if it were true that individual behaviour could itself be understood in terms of the supposedly 'hard data' of direct sensory inspection would there be any saving in the reduction of societal facts to facts concerning this behaviour. But, as I have indicated, this is not the case.

The third type of objection to the view which I have been espousing is the objection that such a view interprets individual men as the pawns of society, devoid of initiative, devoid even of a common and socially unconditioned nature, conceiving of them as mere parts of a self-existing social organism.[7] However, such a view I have in fact already rejected. To hold, as I have held, that societal facts are not reducible without remainder to facts concerning the thoughts and actions of specific individuals, is not to deny that the latter class of facts also exists, and that the two classes may interact. Those who have in the past held to the irreducibility of societal facts have, to be sure, often gone to the extreme of denying that there are any facts concerning individual behaviour which are independent of societal facts. Such has not been my thesis. And it is perhaps worth suggesting that if we wish to understand many of the dilemmas by which individuals are faced, we can do no better than to hold to the view that there are societal facts which exercise external constraints over individuals no less than there are facts concerning individual volition which often come into conflict with these constraints.

---

[7] It is to be noted that some societally oriented behaviour is only intelligible when interpreted with respect to *both* a societal concept and an individual's intention (e.g. in our case of a person withdrawing money from a bank). However, other instances of societally oriented behaviour (e.g. customary observances of age and sex differences) do not involve a consideration of the agent's intentions.

VII

METHODOLOGICAL INDIVIDUALISM RECONSIDERED

STEVEN LUKES

IN WHAT follows I discuss and (hopefully) render harmless a doctrine which has a very long ancestry, has constantly reappeared in the history of sociology, and still appears to haunt the scene. It was, we might say, conceived by Hobbes, who held that 'it is necessary that we know the things that are to be compounded before we can know the whole compound' for 'everything is best understood by its constitutive causes', the causes of the social compound residing in 'men as if but even now sprung out of the earth, and suddenly, like mushrooms, come to full maturity without all kinds of engagement to each other.'[1] It was begotten by the thinkers of the Enlightenment, among whom, with a few important exceptions (such as Vico and Montesquieu) an individualist mode of explanation became pre-eminent, though with wide divergences as to what was included in the characterization of the explanatory elements. It was confronted by a wide range of thinkers in the early nineteenth century, who brought to the understanding of social life a new perspective, in which collective phenomena were accorded priority in explanation. As de Bonald wrote, it is 'society that constitutes man, that is, it forms him by social education . . . .'[2] or, in Comte's words, a society was 'no more decomposable into individuals than a geometric surface is into lines, or a line into points'.[3] For others, however, such as Mill and the Utilitarians, 'the Laws of the phenomena of society are, and can be, nothing but the actions and passions of human beings', namely 'the laws of individual human nature'.[4] This debate has recurred in many different guises—in the dispute between

From the *British Journal of Sociology*, xix (1968), 119–29. The author thanks Martin Hollis of the University of East Anglia for his comments on this paper. Reprinted by permission of the author and A. D. Peters & Co.

[1] *The English Works of Thomas Hobbes*, ed. Sir William Molesworth, London, 1839, i. 67; ii. xiv; ii. 109.

[2] L. de Bonald, *Théorie du pouvoir*, Paris, 1854, i. 103.

[3] A. Comte, *Système de politique positive*, Paris, 1851, ii. 181.

[4] J. S. Mill, *A System of Logic*, 9th edn., London, 1875, ii. 469. 'Men are not', Mill continues, 'when brought together, converted into another kind of substance, with different properties.'

the 'historical' school in economics and the 'abstract' theory of classical economics, in endless debates among philosophers of history and between sociologists and psychologists,[5] and, above all, in the celebrated controversy between Durkheim and Gabriel Tarde.[6] Among others, Simmel[7] and Cooley[8] tried to resolve the issue, as did Gurvitch[9] and Ginsberg,[10] but it constantly reappears, for example in reactions to the extravagantly macroscopic theorizing of Parsons and his followers[11] and in the extraordinarily muddled debate provoked by the wide-ranging methodological polemics of Hayek and Popper.[12]

What I shall try to do here is, first, to distinguish what I take to be the central tenet of methodological individualism from a number of

[5] See D. Essertier, *Psychologie et Sociologie*, Paris, 1927.

[6] Cf. E. Durkheim, *Les Règles de la méthode sociologique*, Paris, 1895; 2nd edn., 1901, and G. Tarde, *Les Lois sociales*, Paris, 1898.

[7] See *The Sociology of Georg Simmel*, trans. and ed. with introd. by K. H. Wolff, Glencoe, Ill., 1950, esp. Chs i, ii, and iv (e.g. 'Let us grant for the moment that only individuals "really" exist. Even then, only a false conception of science could infer from this "fact" that any knowledge which somehow aims at synthesizing these individuals deals with merely speculative abstractions and unrealities', pp. 4–5).

[8] See C. H. Cooley, *Human Nature and the Social Order*, New York, 1902. For Cooley, society and the individual are merely 'the collective and distributive aspects of the same thing' (pp. 1–2).

[9] See G. Gurvitch, 'Les Faux Problemes de la sociologie au XIXe siècle', in *La Vocation actuelle de la sociologie*, Paris, 1950, esp. pp. 25–37.

[10] See M. Ginsberg, 'The Individual and Society', in *On the Diversity of Morals*, London, 1956.

[11] See G. C. Homans, 'Bringing Men Back In', *American Sociological Review*, xxix (1964) and D. H. Wrong, 'The Oversocialised Conception of Man in Modern Sociology', *American Sociological Review*, xxvi (1961).

[12] See the following discussions: F. A. Hayek, *The Counter-Revolution of Science*, Glencoe, Ill., 1952, Chs. 4, 6, and 8; K. R. Popper, *The Open Society and its Enemies*, London, 1945, Ch. 14, and *The Poverty of Historicism*, London, 1957, Chs. 7, 23, 24, and 31; J. W. N. Watkins, 'Ideal Types and Historical Explanation', *British Journal for the Philosophy of Science*, iii (1952) (reprinted in H. Feigl and M. Brodbeck, *Readings in the Philosophy of Science*, New York, 1953), 'Methodological Individualism. (note), ibid., 'Historical Explanation in the Social Sciences', ibid. viii (1957); M. Mandelbaum, 'Societal Laws', ibid. (1957). L. J. Goldstein, 'The Two Theses of Methodological Individualism' (note), ibid. ix (1958); Watkins, 'The Two Theses of Methodological Individualism' (note), ibid. x (1959); Goldstein, 'Mr Watkins on the Two Theses' (note), ibid., Watkins 'Third Reply to Mr Goldstein' (note), ibid.; R. J. Scott, 'Methodological and Epistemological Individualism' (note), ibid. xi (1961); Mandelbaum, 'Societal Facts', *British Journal of Sociology*, vi (1955); E. Gellner, Explanations in History', *Proceedings of the Aristotelian Society*, xxx (1956) (these last two articles together with Watkins's 1957 article above are reprinted in P. Gardiner (ed.), *Theories of History*, Glencoe, Ill. and London, 1959, together with a reply to Watkins by Gellner. Gellner's paper is here retitled 'Holism and Individualism in History and Sociology'); M. Brodbeck, 'Philosophy of Social Science', *Philosophy of Science*, xxi (1954); Watkins, 'Methodological Individualism: A Reply' (note), ibid, xxii (1955); Brodbeck, 'Methodological Individualisms: Definition and Reduction" ibid. xxv (1958); Goldstein, 'The Inadequacy of the Principle of Methodological Individualism', *Journal of Philosophy*, liii (1956); Watkins 'The Alleged Inadequacy of

different theses from which it has not normally been distinguished; and second, to show why, even in the most vacuous sense, methodological individualism is implausible.

Let us begin with a set of truisms. Society consists of people. Groups consist of people. Institutions consist of people plus rules and roles. Rules are followed (or alternatively not followed) by people and roles are filled by people. Also there are traditions, customs, ideologies, kinship systems, languages: these are ways people act, think, and talk. At the risk of pomposity, these truisms may be said to constitute a theory (let us call it 'Truistic Social Atomism') made up of banal propositions about the world that are analytically true, i.e. in virtue of the meaning of words.

Some thinkers have held it to be equally truistic (indeed, sometimes, to amount to the same thing) to say that facts about society and social phenomena are to be explained solely in terms of facts about individuals. This is the doctrine of methodological individualism. For example, Hayek writes: 'There is no other way toward an understanding of social phenomena but through our understanding of individual actions directed toward other people and guided by their expected behaviour'.[13] Similarly, according to Popper,

... all social phenomena, and especially the functioning of all social institutions, should always be understood as resulting from the decisions, actions, attitudes, etc. of human individuals, and ... we should never be satisfied by an explanation in terms of so-called 'collectives' ... .[14]

Finally we may quote Watkins's account of 'the principle of methodological individualism':

According to this principle, the ultimate constituents of the social world are individual people who act more or less appropriately in the light of their dispositions and understanding of their situation. Every complex social situation or event is the result of a particular configuration of individuals, their dispositions, situations, beliefs, and physical resources and environment.

Methodological Individualism' (note), ibid. lv (1958); C. Taylor, 'The Poverty of Historicism', *Universities and Left Review* (Summer 1958), followed by replies from I. Jarvie and Watkins, ibid. (Spring 1959); J. Agassi, 'Methodological Individualism,' *British Journal of Sociology*, xi (1960); E. Nagel, *The Structure of Science*, London, 1961, pp. 535–46; A. C. Danto, *Analytical Philosophy of History* Cambridge, 1965, Ch. xii; and W. H. Dray, 'Holism and Individualism in History and Social Science, in P. Edwards (ed.), *The Encyclopedia of Philosophy*, New York 1967.

[13] *Individualism and Economic Order*, London, 1949, p. 6.
[14] *The Open Society*, 4th edn. ii. 98.

It is worth noticing, incidentally, that the first sentence here is simply a (refined) statement of Truistic Social Atomism. Watkins continues:

There may be unfinished or half-way explanations of large-scale social phenomena (say, inflation) in terms of other large-scale phenomena (say, full
employment); but we shall not have arrived at rock-bottom explanations of such
large scale phenomena until we have deduced an account of them from statements
about the dispositions, beliefs, resources and inter-relations of individuals. (The
individuals may remain anonymous and only typical dispositions, etc., may be
attributed to them.) And just as mechanism is contrasted with the organicist idea
of physical fields, so methodological individualism is contrasted with sociological
holism or organicism. On this latter view, social systems constitute 'wholes' at
least in the sense that some of their large-scale behaviour is governed by macro-
laws which are essentially sociological in the sense that they are *sui generis* and
not to be explained as mere regularities or tendencies resulting from the behaviour
of interacting individuals. On the contrary, the behaviour of individuals should
(according to sociological holism) be explained at least partly in terms of such
laws (perhaps in conjunction with an account, first of individuals' roles within
institutions, and secondly of the functions of institutions with the whole social
system). If methodological individualism means that human beings are supposed
to be the only moving agents in history, and if sociological holism means that
some superhuman agents or factors are supposed to be at work in history, then
these two alternatives are exhaustive.[15]

Methodological individualism, therefore, is a prescription for explanation, asserting that no purported explanations of social (or individual)
phenomena are to count as explanations, or (in Watkins's version) as
rock-bottom explanations, unless they are couched wholly in terms of
facts about individuals.

It is now necessary to distinguish this theory from a number of others,
from which it is usually not distinguished. It has been taken to be the same
as any or all of the following:

1. Truistic Social Atomism. We have seen that Watkins, for example,
seems to equate this with methodological individualism proper.

2. A theory of meaning to the effect that every statement about social
phenomena is either a statement about individual human beings or else it is
unintelligible and therefore not a statement at all. This theory entails that
all predicates which range over social phenomena are definable in terms of
predicates which range only over individual phenomena and that all statements about social phenomena are translatable without loss of meaning
into statements that are wholly about individuals. As Jarvie has put it,

[15] Historical Explanation in the Social Sciences' in Gardiner (ed.) *Theories of History*,
p. 505. Cf. '. . , large-scale *social* phenomena must be accounted for by the situations,
dispositions and beliefs of *individuals*. This I call methodological individualism,:
Watkins, 'Methodological Individualism: A Reply', *Philosophy of Science*, xxii (1955),
58 (see n. 12 above).

' "Army" is merely a plural of soldier and *all* statements about the Army can be reduced to statements about the particular soldiers comprising the Army.'[16]

It is worth noticing that this theory is only plausible on a crude verificationist theory of meaning (to the effect that the meaning of p is what confirms the truth of p). Otherwise, although statements about armies are true only in virtue of the fact that other statements about individuals are true, the former are not equivalent in meaning to the latter, nor *a fortiori* are they 'about' the subject of the latter.

3. A theory of ontology to the effect that in the social world only individuals are real. This usually carries the correlative doctrine that social phenomena are constructions of the mind and 'do not exist in reality'. Thus Hayek writes,

The social sciences . . . do not deal with 'given' wholes but their task is to constitute these wholes by constructing models from the familiar elements—models which reproduce the structure of relationships between some of the many phenomena which we always simultaneously observe in real life. This is no less true of the popular concepts of social wholes which are represented by the terms current in ordinary language; they too refer to mental models. . . .[17]

Similarly, Popper holds that 'social entities such as institutions or associations' are 'abstract models constructed to interpret certain selected abstract relations between individuals'.[18]

If this theory means that in the social world only individuals are observable, it is evidently false. Some social phenomena simply can be observed (as both trees and forests can): and indeed, many features of social phenomena are observable (e.g. the procedure of a court) while many features of individuals are not (e.g. intentions). Both individual and social phenomena have observable and non-observable features. If it means that individual phenomena are easy to understand, while social phenomena are not (which is Hayek's view), this is highly implausible: compare the procedure of the court with the motives of the criminal. If the theory means that individuals exist independently of e.g. groups and institutions, this is also false, since, just as facts about social phenomena are contingent upon facts about individuals, the reverse is also true. Thus, as we have seen, we can only speak of soldiers because we can speak of armies: only if certain statements are true of armies are others true of soldiers. If the theory means that all social phenomena are fictional and all individual phenomena are factual, that would entail that all assertions about social

[16] *Universities and Left Review* (Spring 1959), 57.
[17] *The Counter-Revolution of Science*, p. 56.
[18] *The Poverty of Historicism*, p. 140.

phenomena are false or else neither true nor false, which is absurd. Finally, the theory may mean that only facts about individuals are explanatory, which alone would make this theory equivalent to methodological individualism.

4. A negative theory to the effect that sociological laws are impossible, or that lawlike statements about social phenomena are always false. Hayek and Popper sometimes seem to believe this, but Watkins clearly repudiates it, asserting merely that such statements form part of 'half-way' as opposed to 'rock-bottom' explanations.

This theory, like all dogmas of the form 'x is impossible' is open to refutation by a single counter-instance. Since such counter-instances are readily available[19] there is nothing left to say on this score.

5. A doctrine that may be called 'social individualism' which (ambiguously) asserts that society has as its end the good of individuals. When unpacked, this may be taken to mean any or all of the following: (a) social institutions are to be understood as founded and maintained by individuals to fulfil their ends (as in e.g. Social Contract theory); (b) social institutions in fact satisfy individual ends; (c) social institutions ought to satisfy individual ends. (a) is not widely held today, though it is not extinct; (b) is certainly held by Hayek with respect to the market, as though it followed from methodological individualism; and (c) which, interpreting 'social institutions' and 'individual ends' as a non-interventionist state and express preferences, becomes political liberalism, is clearly held by Popper to be uniquely consonant with methodological individualism.

However, neither (b) nor (c) is logically or conceptually related to methodological individualism, while (a) is a version of it.

2

What I hope so far to have shown is what the central tenet of methodological individualism is and what it is not. It remains to assess its plausibility.

It asserts (to repeat) that all attempts to explain social and individual phenomena are to be rejected (or, for Watkins, rejected as rock-bottom explanations) unless they refer exclusively to facts about individuals. There are thus two matters to investigate: (1) what is meant by 'facts about individuals'; and (2) what is meant by 'explanation'?

1. What is a fact about an individual? Or, more clearly, what predicates may be applied to individuals? Consider the following examples:

(i) genetic make-up; brain-states,

[19] Popper himself provides some: see *The Poverty of Historicism*, pp. 62–3.

  (ii) aggression; gratification; stimulus-response,
 (iii) co-operation; power; esteem,
 (iv) cashing cheques; saluting; voting.

What this exceedingly rudimentary list shows is at least this: that there
is a continuum of what I shall henceforth call individual predicates from
what one might call the most non-social to the most social. Propositions
incorporating only predicates of type (i) are about human beings *qua*
material objects and make no reference to and presuppose nothing about
consciousness or any feature of any social group or institution. Propositions incorporating only individual predicates of type (ii) presuppose
consciousness but still make no reference to and presuppose nothing about
any feature of any social group or institution. Propositions incorporating
only predicates of type (ii) do have a minimal social reference; they presuppose a social context in which certain actions, social relations, and/or
mental states are picked out and given a particular significance (which
makes social relations of certain sorts count as 'co-operative', which
makes certain social positions count as positions of 'power' and a certain
set of attitudes count as 'esteem'). They still do not presuppose or entail
any particular propositions about any particular form of group or institution. Finally, propositions incorporating only individual predicates of
type (iv) are maximally social, in that they presuppose and sometimes
directly entail propositions about particular types of group and institution. ('Voting Labour' is at an even further point on the continuum.)

Methodological individualism has frequently been taken to confine its
favoured explanations to any or all of these sorts of individual predicates.
We may distinguish the following four possibilities:

  (i) Attempts to explain in terms of type (i) predicates. A good example is
H. J. Eysenck's *Psychology of Politics*.[20] According to Eysenck, 'Political
actions are actions of human beings; the study of the direct cause of these
actions is the field of the study of psychology. All other social sciences
deal with variables which affect political action indirectly.'[21] (Compare
this with Durkheim's famous statement that 'every time that a social
phenomenon is directly explained by a psychological phenomenon, we
may be sure that the explanation is false.')[22] Eysenck sets out to classify
attitudes along two dimensions—the Radical–Conservative and the
Tough-minded–Tender-minded—on the basis of evidence elicited by
carefully constructed questionnaires. Then, having classified the attitudes,

---

[20] London, 1960.
[21] *Psychology of Politics*, p. 10.
[22] *Les Règles de la méthode sociologique*, p. 103.

his aim is to *explain* them by reference to antecedent conditions and his interest here is centred upon the modifications of the central nervous system.

(ii) Attempts to explain in terms of type (ii) predicates. Examples are Hobbes's appeal to appetites and aversions, Pareto's residues and those Freudian theories in which sexual activity is seen as a type of undifferentiated activity that is (subsequently) channelled on particular social directions.

(iii) Attempts to explain in terms of type (iii) predicates. Examples are those sociologists and social psychologists (from Tarde to Homans)[23] who favour explanations in terms of general. and 'elementary' forms of social behaviour, which do invoke some minimal social reference but are unspecific as to any particular form of group or institution.

(iv) Attempts to explain in terms of type (iv) predicates. Examples of these are extremely widespread, comprising all those who appeal to facts about concrete and specifically located individuals in order to explain. Here the relevant features of the social context are, so to speak, built into the individual. Open almost any empirical (though not theoretical) work of sociology, or history, and explanations of this sort leap to the eye.

Merely to state these four alternative possibilities is to suggest that their differences are more important than their similarities. What do they show about the plausibility of methodological individualism? To answer this it is necessary to turn to the meaning of 'explanation'.

2. To explain something is (at least) to overcome an obstacle—to make what was unintelligible intelligible. There is more than one way of doing this.

It is important to see, and it is often forgotten, that to *identify* a piece of behaviour, a set of beliefs, etc. is sometimes to explain it. This may involve seeing it in a new way, picking out hidden structural features. Consider an anthropologist's interpretation of ritual or a sociological study of (say) bureaucracy. Often explanation resides precisely in a successful and sufficiently wide-ranging identification of behaviour or types of behaviour (often in terms of a set of beliefs). Again, to take an example from Mandelbaum,[24] a Martian visiting earth sees one man mark a piece of paper that another has handed to him through some iron bars: on his being told that the bank teller is certifying the withdrawal slip he has had the action explained, through its being identified. If the methodological individualist is saying that no explanations are possible (or rock-bottom) except those framed exclusively in terms of individual predicates of types (i), (ii), and

---

[23] See *Social Behaviour*, London, 1961.
[24] *British Journal of Sociology* (1955).

(iii), i.e. those not presupposing or entailing propositions about particular institutions and organizations, then he is arbitrarily ruling out (or denying finality to) most ordinarily acceptable explanations, as used in everyday life, but also by most sociologists and anthropologists for most of the time. If he is prepared to include individual predicates of type (iv), he seems to be proposing nothing more than a futile linguistic purism. Why should we be compelled to talk about the tribesman but not the tribe, the bank teller but not the bank? And let no one underestimate the difficulty or the importance of explanation by identification. Indeed, a whole methodological tradition (from Dilthey through Weber to Winch) holds this to be the characteristic mode of explanation in social science.

Another way of explaining is to deduce the specific and particular from the general and universal. If I have a body of coherent, economical, well-confirmed, and unfalsified general laws from which, given the specifications of boundary and initial conditions, I predict (or retrodict) x and x occurs, then, in one very respectable sense, I have certainly explained x.[25] This is the form of explanation which methodological individualists characteristically seem to advocate, though they vary as to whether the individual predicates which are uniquely to constitute the general laws and specifications of particular circumstances are to be of types (i), (ii), (iii), or (iv).

If they are to be of type (i), either of two equally unacceptable consequences follows. Eysenck writes, 'It is fully realised that most of the problems discussed must ultimately be seen in their historical, economic, sociological, and perhaps even anthropological context, but little is to be gained at the present time by complicating the picture too much.'[26] But the picture is already so complicated at the very beginning (and the attitudes Eysenck is studying are only identifiable in social terms); the problem is how to simplify it. This could logically be achieved either by developing a theory which will explain the 'historical, economic, sociological . . . anthropological context' exclusively in terms of (e.g.) the central nervous system or by demonstrating that this 'context' is simply a backdrop against which quasi-mechanical psychological forces are the sole causal influences at work. Since, apart from quaint efforts that are of interest only to the intellectual historian, no one has given the slightest clue as to how either alternative might plausibly be achieved, there seems to be little point in

---

[25] e.g. Hempel calls this 'deductive-nomological explanation'. For a recent defence of this type of explanation in social science, see R. Rudner, *Philosophy of Social Science*, Englewood Cliffs, N.J., 1965. I have not discussed 'probabilistic explanation', in which the general laws are not universal and the *explicans* only makes the *explicandum* highly probable, in the text; such explanations pose no special problems for my argument.

[26] *Psychology of Politics*, p. 5.

taking it seriously, except as a problem in philosophy. Neuro-physiology may be the queen of the social sciences, but her claim remains entirely speculative.

If the individual predicates are to be of type (ii), there is again no positive reason to find the methodological individualist's claim plausible. Parallel arguments to those for type (i) predicates apply: no one has yet provided any plausible reason for supposing that e.g. (logically) pre-social drives uniquely determine the social context or that this context is causally irrelevant to their operation. As Freud himself saw, and many neo-Freudians have insisted, the process of social channelling is a crucial part of the explanation of behaviour, involving reference to features of both small groups and the wider social structure.

If the individual predicates are to be of type (iii), there is still no positive reason to find the methodological individualist's claim plausible. There may indeed be valid and useful explanations of this type, but the claim we are considering asserts that all proper, or rock-bottom, explanations must be. Why rule out as possible candidates for inclusion in an *explicans* (statement of general laws + statement of boundary and initial conditions) statements that are about, or that presuppose or entail other statements that are about, social phenomena? One reason for doing so might be a belief that, in Hume's words, 'mankind are ... much the same in all times in all places.'[27] As Homans puts it, the characteristics of 'elementary social behaviour, far more than those of institutionalised behaviour, are shared by all mankind':

Institutions, whether they are things like the physician's role or things like the bureaucracy, have a long history behind them of development within a particular society; and in institutions, societies differ greatly. But within institutions, in the face-to-face relations between individuals ... characteristics of behaviour appear in which mankind gives away its lost unity.[28]

This may be so, but then there are still the differences between institutions and societies to explain.

Finally, if the claim is that the individual predicates must be of type (iv), then it appears harmless, but also pointless. Explanations, both in the sense we are considering now and in the sense of identifications, may be wholly couched in such predicates but what uniquely special status do they possess? For, as we have already seen, propositions incorporating them presuppose and/or entail other propositions about social phenomena.

[27] D. Hume, *Essays Moral and Political*, ed. T. H. Green and T. H. Grose, London, 1875, ii. 68.
[28] *Social Behaviour*, p. 6.

Thus the latter have not really been eliminated; they have merely been swept under the carpet.

It is worth adding that since Popper and Watkins allow 'situations' and 'interrelations between individuals' to enter into explanations, it is difficult to see why they insist on calling their doctrine 'methodological individualism'. In fact the burden of their concerns and their arguments is to oppose certain sorts of explanations in terms of social phenomena. They are against 'holism' and 'historicism', but opposition to these doctrines does not entail acceptance of methodological individualism. For, in the first place, 'situations' and 'interrelations between individuals' can be described in terms which do not refer to individuals without holist or historicist implications. And secondly, it may be impossible to describe them in terms which do refer to individuals,[29] and yet they may be indispensable to an explanation, either as part of an identifying explanation in the statement of a general law, or of initial and boundary conditions.

[29] e.g. in the cases of rules and terminologies of kinship or of language generally.

VIII

ASSUMPTIONS IN ECONOMIC THEORY

ERNEST NAGEL

SOUND conclusions are sometimes supported by erroneous arguments, and the error is compounded when a sound conclusion is declared to be mistaken on the ground that the argument for it is mistaken. This general observation must serve as my *apologia* for venturing to discuss an important and much debated methodological issue in economics, though not myself an economist. In his well-known essay, 'The Methodology of Positive Economics',[1] Professor Milton Friedman defends the use of abstract (and in particular, neoclassical) theory in economic analysis, in effect by defending the principle that the adequacy of a theory must be judged, not by assessing what he calls the 'realism of its assumptions', but rather by examining the concordance of the theory's logical consequences with the phenomena the theory is designed to explain—a principle which many economists continue to reject, frequently because arguments similar to his seem to them mistaken. I also think that his argument provides no firm support for this principle; and, indeed, my paper is a critique of his defence of it. However, the relevance of my paper is not, I think, limited to Professor Friedman's essay, for I hope to show that despite the inconclusiveness of his argument his conclusion is sound.

1

Since the notions of theory and assumption are central in discussions of the principle at issue, it is convenient to begin by noting some distinctions.

1. The word theory is often used in the social sciences (including economics) rather loosely, to designate almost any general statement, however narrow its intended range of application may be. Thus, the label is commonly given to empirical generalizations (often stated in the form of equations obtained with the help of techniques of curve fitting) that are simply extrapolations from observed statistical regularities, and are

From *American Economic Review Supplementary Volume* (1963), 211–19. Reprinted by permission of the author and the American Economic Association.
[1] It is published in his *Essays in Positive Economics*, Chicago, Ill., 1953. All page references, unless otherwise noted, are to this book.

asserted to hold only for behaviours occurring in a given community during some particular historical period. On the other hand, many economists (including Professor Friedman) employ the word far more selectively, and approximately in the sense associated with it when it occurs in such phrases as 'the Newtonian theory of motion'.

It is this second sense that theory will be used in this paper. Accordingly, an economic theory (e.g. the neoclassical theory of consumer choice) is a set of statements, organized in a characteristic way, and designed to serve as partial premises for explaining as well as predicting an indeterminately large (and usually varied) class of economic phenomena. Moreover, most if not all the statements of a theory have the form of generalized conditionals, which place no spatio-temporal restrictions on the class of phenomena that may be explained with their help. For example, the law of diminishing returns can be expressed in this form: if the quantity of a factor of production is augmented by equal increments, but the quantities of all other factors are kept constant, then the resulting increments in the product will eventually diminish. Space is lacking for discussing adequately the anatomy of theories, but a few additional features distinctive of them must be briefly mentioned.[2]

2. In a given codification of a theory, the statements belonging to it can be divided into three subgroups. The first consists of statements which count as the fundamental ones, and are often called the theory's 'assumptions' (or basic 'hypotheses'); the second subgroup contains the statements that are logically deducible as theorems from statements in the first. However, the term 'assumption' is sometimes also used to refer to the antecedent clause of a conditional theoretical statement in either of these subgroups. This is the way Professor Friedman seems to use the word when, in discussing Galileo's law for freely falling bodies (i.e. 'if a body falls toward the earth in a vacuum, its instantaneous acceleration is constant'), he asks whether this law does in fact 'assume' that bodies actually fall through a vacuum.

The third subgroup of theoretical statements can also be readily characterized, if we recall that many (and perhaps all) statements in the first two subgroups contain expressions which designate nothing actually observable and are not explicitly definable in terms of expressions that do. Familiar examples of such expressions (for easy reference I will call them 'theoretical terms') are 'vacuum' in Galileo's law, 'gene' in biological theory, and 'elasticity of demand at a point' in neoclassical economic theory. Theoretical terms signify either various entities that cannot be specified except by way of some theory which postulates their existence, or certain ideal limits of theoretically endless processes. It is therefore evident that statements containing such terms cannot possibly explain or predict the course of actual events, unless a sufficient number of theoretical terms (but not necessarily all of them) are co-ordinated with observable traits of things. Thus, although the theoretical terms 'instantaneous acceleration' and 'perfectly divisible commodity' describe nothing that can be identified in experience, the expressions do in fact correspond to empirically determinable features in certain actual processes as a consequence of various rules employed (usually tacitly) by physicists and economists. In addition to the two subgroups already mentioned, a theory will in general therefore also contain a third subgroup of statements (though commonly not fully formulated) that indicate among other things such correspondences. It must be emphasized, however, that these statements do not define theoretical terms by way of terms signifying observable traits, so that theoretical terms cannot be eliminated from formulations in which they occur with the help of these statements.[3]

3. One further point deserves mention in this connection. In most disciplines, theoretical formulations (particularly those in the first two subgroups) are normally treated as statements about some subject-matter, so that as in the case of other statements questions about the truth or falsity of such formulations are regarded as significant though difficult to answer. On the other hand, theoretical formulations are sometimes denied the status of 'genuine' statements and are said to be simply rules which are instrumental for drawing inferences from genuine statements but which cannot be properly characterized as true or false. It is impossible in the space available to examine the merits of these opposing views on the status of theories, I have mentioned them to call attention to the fact that a defence of the methodological principle under discussion is intelligible only on the supposition that economic theory is a set of genuine statements, so that considerations of their truth or falsity are not irrelevant to the objectives of economic analysis.

---

[3] This point is of major importance. Professor Friedman also recognizes a category of statements in a theory roughly equivalent to the third subgroup of theoretical statements distinguished above; but he appears to believe that theoretical terms can be eliminated with the help of statements in this category. The point at issue cannot be adequately discussed in short compass, but an example will perhaps make clear why such a belief is dubious. Quantum theory is stated in terms of various theoretical terms, referring to such elementary particles as electrons. However, although physicists are certainly able to apply quantum theory to observable processes with the aid of statements in the third subgroup, such statements of correspondence do not permit the elimination of terms like 'electron' from quantum theory.

2

Professor Friedman rests his argument for the methodological principle on some general reflections concerning the nature of theories *überhaupt*. He notes that a theory cannot explain a class of phenomena, unless it abstracts a small number of 'common and crucial elements' (in terms of which the phenomena may be predicted) from the mass of differing circumstances in which the phenomena are embedded. Accordingly, the assumptions of a satisfactory theory are inescapably 'descriptively false' or 'unrealistic', so that it is pointless to assess the merits of a theory by asking whether or not its assumptions are realistic. The relevant question is whether or not the theory yields predictions which are 'sufficiently good approximations for the purpose at hand'.[4]

However, an assumption may be unrealistic in at least three senses important for the argument, though Professor Friedman does not distinguish them.

1. A statement can be said to be unrealistic because it does not give an 'exhaustive' description of some object, so that it mentions only some traits actually characterizing the object but ignores an endless number of other traits also present. However, no finitely long statement can possibly formulate the totality of traits embodied in any concretely existing thing; and it is difficult to imagine what a statement would be like that is not unrealistic in this sense, or what conceivable use such a statement could have. But in any event, it is with this rather trivial sense of the word in mind that Professor Friedman seems frequently to defend the legitimacy of unrealistic assumptions in economic theory;[5] and although it is not clear whether any economists have maintained a contrary thesis, his defence is fully conclusive.

2. A statement may be said to be unrealistic because it is believed to be either false or highly improbable on the available evidence. Such lack of realism can sometimes be established on the basis of what Professor Friedman calls a 'directly perceived descriptive inaccuracy'; but in general, statements can be shown to be false only 'indirectly', by first deducing from them some of their logical consequences (or implications), and then comparing the latter with 'directly' observed matters of fact. Since it is usually not possible to establish the falsity of theoretical statements directly, Professor Friedman correctly stresses the relevance of this indirect procedure for ascertaining whether a theory is unrealistic. Nevertheless, as he recognizes and even illustrates,[6] the distinction between an assumption and its implications is a sharp one only in a given formulation

---

[4] pp. 14–15.   [5] pp. 18, 25, 32, 35.   [6] pp. 26–7.

of a theory—an implication of some assumption in one formulation may in another formulation be a premiss implying that assumption. Accordingly, his repeated claim that an assumption can be rightly tested for its realism only indirectly obviously needs qualification.

But in any event, if by an assumption of a theory we understand one of the theory's fundamental statements (i.e. those belonging to the first of the three subgroups previously noted), a theory with an unrealistic assumption (in the present sense of the word, according to which the assumption is false) is patently unsatisfactory; for such a theory entails consequences that are incompatible with observed fact, so that on pain of rejecting elementary logical canons the theory must also be rejected. On the other hand, a universal conditional neither asserts nor presupposes that the conditions explicitly stated in its antecedent clause are actually realized; accordingly, a theoretical statement having this logical form is not proved to be false by showing that the specifications in its antecedent are not embodied in some given spatio-temporal region (or for that matter, in any region). Professor Friedman is therefore quite right in maintaining that a theory is not necessarily erroneous merely because its assumptions are unrealistic—provided that he is taken to mean by an 'assumption of a theory', as he sometimes appears to mean, an antecedent clause of some theoretical statement. However, a theory whose assumptions are in this sense unrealistic for a given domain is simply inapplicable in that domain, though it may be applicable in another. But what is to be said of a theory whose assumptions are ostensibly unrealistic for every domain? The aspect of this question that is especially relevant to Professor Friedman's essay is best treated after the third sense of unrealistic has been explained.

3. In many sciences, relations of dependence between phenomena are often stated with reference to so-called 'pure cases' or 'ideal types' of the phenomena being investigated. That is, such theoretical statements (or 'laws') formulate relations specified to hold under highly 'purified' conditions between highly 'idealized' objects or processes, none of which is actually encountered in experience. For example, the law of the lever in physics is stated in terms of the behaviour of absolutely rigid rods turning without friction about dimensionless points; similarly, a familiar law of pricing in economics is formulated in terms of the exchange of perfectly divisible and homogenous commodities under conditions of perfect competition. Statements of this kind contain what have previously been called 'theoretical terms', which connote what are in effect the limits of various non-terminating series and which are not intended to designate anything actual. Such statements may be said to be unrealistic but in a sense different from the two previously noted. For they are not

distinguished by their failure to provide exhaustive descriptions, nor are
they literally false of anything; their distinguishing mark is the fact that
when they are strictly construed, they are applicable to nothing actual.
However, laws of nature formulated with reference to pure cases are
not therefore useless. On the contrary, a law so formulated states how
phenomena are related when they are unaffected by numerous factors
whose influence may never be completely eliminable but whose effects
generally vary in magnitude with differences in the attendant circumstances
under which the phenomena actually recur. Accordingly, discrepancies
between what is asserted for the pure case and what actually happens can
be attributed to the influence of factors not mentioned in the law. Moreover, since these factors and their effects can often be ascertained, the
influence of the factors can be systematically classified into general
types; and in consequence, the law can be viewed as the limiting case of a set
of other laws corresponding to these various types, where each further law
states a modified relation of dependence between the phenomena because
of the influence of factors that are absent in the pure case. In short,
unrealistic theoretical statements (in the third sense of the word) serve as a
powerful means for analysing, representing, and codifying relations of
dependence between actual phenomena.

3

Professor Friedman's discussion of unrealistic assumptions in examples
of theoretical statements drawn from physics and biology sheds important
light on his defence of such assumptions in economic theory. It will
therefore be useful to examine his account of one of these examples.

1. In his discussion of Galileo's law, Professor Friedman notes that the
law is stated for bodies falling in a vacuum, but also declares that the law
'works' in a large number of cases (i.e. it is in sufficiently good agreement
for certain purposes with the actual behaviour of bodies in these cases),
though not in others. He therefore suggests that the law can be restated to
read: under a wide range of circumstances, bodies that fall in the actual
atmosphere behave *as if* they were falling in a vacuum. Indeed, he seems to
think that the law can be rephrased without mentioning a vacuum, as
follows: under a wide range of circumstances, the distance a body falls in
a specified time is given by the formula $s = \frac{1}{2}gt^2$. Accordingly, he main-
tains that the circumstances in which the law works (and is therefore
acceptable) must be specified as 'an essential part' of the law, even though
this specification (and in consequence also the law) may need revision in
the light of further experience.[7]

[7] pp. 18–19

However, as has already been indicated, the term 'vacuum' is a theoretical one, so that Galileo's law in its standard version is formulated for pure cases of falling bodies. Professor Friedman's proposed paraphrase which omits all mention of a vacuum thus rests on the supposition that theoretical terms can in general be replaced by non-theoretical ones, without altering the meaning and function of the statements containing them. But the possibility of such a replacement is dubious on formal grounds alone; and what is more important, the suggestion that unless theoretical terms can thus be eliminated the statements containing them are scientifically otiose, overlooks the rationale for stating laws in terms of pure cases. In point of fact, the proposed paraphrase mistakenly assumes that Galileo's law can be assigned the functions actually performed by statements of correspondence (belonging to the third subgroup of theoretical statements) without impairing the effectiveness of the standard formulation for achieving systematic generality in theoretical physics.

2. The example Professor Friedman uses for the most part in his defence of unrealistic assumptions in economics is the familiar 'rational maximization of returns' hypothesis in the theory of the firm. However, he states it as follows: 'under a wide range of circumstances, individual firms behave *as if* they were seeking rationally to maximize their expected returns and had full knowledge of the data needed to succeed in this attempt.'[8] He freely admits that as a rule businessmen lack such knowledge and do not perform the intricate calculations required for ascertaining the indicated maximum. Indeed, he declares that 'the apparent immediate determinants of business behavior' could be anything at all, e.g. ingrained habit or a chance influence. He nevertheless claims that these admitted facts do not affect the validity of the hypothesis. The relevant evidence, according to him, is the large set of facts in good agreement with various implications of the hypothesis, including the fact that firms whose actions are markedly inconsistent with it do not survive for long.

It is pertinent to ask, however, whether the operative premiss from which these implications really follow is perhaps the supposition, suggested by Professor Friedman's discussion, that is rendered by: 'under a wide range of circumstances, the behavior of individual firms brings them returns approximately equal to a certain magnitude (called the maximum of expected returns by economists)'; or whether the operative premiss is the hypothesis as he formulates it. On the first alternative, most of the matters mentioned in his 'as if' formulation are irrelevant to the substantive content of the hypothesis. In particular, the hypothesis must then not be understood as either asserting or implying that firms conduct their affairs in order

[8] p. 21.

to achieve some objective. To be sure, the statement of the hypothesis contains the expression 'the maximum of expected returns'; nevertheless, this expression simply designates a set of rules used by economists rather than by firms for calculating a certain magnitude. In short, the hypothesis in this case is a somewhat loosely expressed empirical generalization about the returns firms actually receive as the outcome of their overt behaviour, and it specifies no determinants in explanation of that behaviour.[9] Accordingly, although the hypothesis is not an exhaustive description of anything, it is not clear in what sense other than this trivial one the hypothesis is in this case unrealistic if, as Professor Friedman claims, it is in good agreement with experience. On the second alternative, however, it is difficult to avoid reading the hypothesis as saying that firms do seek to maximize their returns in a rational manner, since otherwise it appears to be asserting nothing whatsoever. But the hypothesis must then be understood as dealing with pure cases of economic behaviour, requiring the use of theoretical terms in its formulation which cannot be replaced by non-theoretical expressions. Accordingly, the various facts Professor Friedman freely admits but thinks are irrelevant may in this case be quite pertinent in assessing the merits of the hypothesis.

Professor Friedman's essay does not indicate explicitly which alternative renders the hypothesis as he understands it. In consequence, the essay is marked by an ambiguity that perhaps reflects an unresolved tension in his views on the status of economic theory. Is he defending the legitimacy of unrealistic theoretical assumptions because he thinks theories are at best only useful instruments, valuable for predicting observable events but not to be viewed as genuine statements whose truth or falsity may be significantly investigated? But if this is the way he conceives theories (and much in his argument suggests that it is), the distinction between realistic and unrealistic theoretical assumptions is at best irrelevant, and no defence of theories lacking in realism is needed. Or is he undertaking that defence in order to show that unrealistic theories cannot only be invaluable tools for making predictions but that they may also be reasonably satisfactory explanations of various phenomena in terms of the mechanisms involved in their occurrence? But if this is his aim (and parts of his discussion are compatible with the supposition that it is), a theory cannot be viewed, as he repeatedly suggests that it can, as a 'simple summary' of some vaguely

---

[9] In particular, the hypothesis does not include the assumption, integral to many formulations of neoclassical theory, that firms are purposive agents, whose decisions are based on rationally formed estimates of the relative advantages and risks associated with alternative courses of action open to them. See Frank H. Knight, *Risk, Uncertainty and Profit*, London, 1957, and Paul A. Samuelson, *Foundations of Economic Analysis*, Cambridge, Mass., 1947, Ch. III.

delimited set of empirical generalizations with distinctly specified ranges of application.[10]

Curiously enough, something like the notion that theories can be viewed in this manner underlies one criticism of Professor Friedman's defence of the maximization-of-returns hypothesis. Thus Professor Koopmans argues that if (as Professor Friedman holds) the fact that firms whose behaviour diverges from it are not likely to survive is a basis for accepting the hypothesis, 'we should postulate that basis itself and not the profit maximization which it implies in certain circumstances.'[11] This seems like a recommendation that since a basis for accepting Newtonian gravitational theory is the fact that observed regularities in the motions of the planets are in agreement with various special laws deduced from the theory, we should postulate those regularities rather than the theory—a recommendation that would replace the theory by the empirical evidence for the theory. Such a proposal not only rejects the conception that theories have an explanatory function; it also overlooks the irreplaceable role theories have in scientific inquiry in suggesting how empirical generalizations may need to be corrected, as well as in directing and systematizing further empirical research. Unless I have seriously misunderstood Professor Friedman's essay, he would reject a proposal of this sort. Nevertheless, at various points in his argument he seems to construe theoretical statements in a manner that is almost indistinguishable from what is implied by such a proposal. I have therefore tried in this paper to show where his argument lacks cogency, as well as to indicate why the main thesis he is ostensibly defending is nonetheless sound.

[10] p. 24.
[11] Tjalling C. Koopmans, *Three Essays on the State of Economic Science*, New York, 1957, p. 140.

IX

NEUTRALITY IN POLITICAL SCIENCE

CHARLES TAYLOR

1

I. A FEW years ago one heard it frequently said that political philosophy was dead, that it had been killed by the growth of science, the growth of positivism, the end of ideology, or some combination of these forces, but that, whatever the cause, it was dead.

It is not my intention to rake over the coals of this old issue once more. I am simply using this as a starting-point for a reflection on the relation between political science and political philosophy. For behind the view that political philosophy was dead, behind any view which holds that it *can* die, lies the belief that its fate can be separated from that of political science; for no one would claim that the science of politics is dead, however one might disapprove of this or that manner of carrying it on. It remains a perpetually possible, and indeed important enterprise.

The view was indeed that political science has come of age in freeing itself finally of the incubus of political philosophy. No more would its scope be narrowed and its work prejudiced by some value position which operated as an initial weight holding back the whole enterprise. The belief was that political science had freed itself from philosophy in becoming value-free and in adopting the scientific method. These two moves were felt to be closely connected; indeed, the second contains the first. For scientific method is, if nothing else, a dispassionate study of the facts as they are, without metaphysical presuppositions, and without value biases.

As Vernon van Dyke puts it:

science and *scientific*, then, are words that relate to only one kind of knowledge, i.e., to knowledge of what is observable, and not to any other kinds of knowledge that may exist. They do not relate to alleged knowledge of the normative—knowledge of what ought to be. Science concerns what has been, is, or will be, regardless of the 'oughts' of the situation (*Political Science*). Stanford and London: Stanford University Press, 1960, p. 192).

From *Philosophy, Politics and Society*, 3rd Ser., ed. Laslett and Runciman, (Oxford: Blackwell, 1967), pp. 25–57. Reprinted by permission of the author.

Those who could hold that political philosophy was dead, therefore, were those who held to a conception of the social sciences as *wertfrei*; like natural science, political science must dispassionately study the facts. This position received support from the views of the logical empiricists who had, for philosophers, an extraordinarily wide influence among scientists in general, and among the sciences of man in particular. Emboldened by their teaching, some orthodox political scientists tended to claim that the business of normative theory, making recommendation's and evaluating different courses of action, could be entirely separated from the study of the facts, from the theoretical attempt to account for them.

Many, of course, had doubts; and these doubts seem to be growing today among political scientists. But they do not touch the thesis of the logical separation between fact and value. They centre rather around the possibility of setting one's values to one side when one undertakes the study of politics. The relation between factual study and normative beliefs is therefore thought of in the same traditional positivist way: that the relationship if any is from value to fact, not from fact to value. Thus, scientific findings are held to be neutral: that is, the facts as we discover them do not help to establish or give support to any set of values; we cannot move from fact to value. It is, however, often admitted that our values can influence our findings. This can be thought of as a vicious interference, as when we approach our work with bias which obscures the truth, or as something anodyne and inevitable, as when our values select for us the area of research on which we wish to embark. Or it can be thought of as a factor whose ill effects can be compensated by a clear consciousness of it: thus many theorists today recommend that one set out one's value position in detail at the beginning of a work so as to set the reader (and perhaps also the writer) on guard.

Value beliefs remain therefore as unfounded on scientific fact for the new generation of more cautious theorists as they were for the thinkers of the hey-day of 'value-freedom'. They arise, as it were, from outside factual study; they spring from deep choices which are independent of the facts. Thus David Easton, who goes on to attempt to show that 'whatever effort is exerted, in undertaking research we cannot shed our values in the way we remove our coats' (*The Political System*, New York: Knopf, 1953, p. 225), nevertheless states his acceptance at the outset of the 'working assumption' which is 'generally adopted today in the social sciences', and which 'holds that values can ultimately be reduced to emotional responses conditioned by the individual's total life-experiences' (p. 221). Thus there is no question of founding values on scientific findings.

Emotional responses can be explained by life-experience, but not justified or shown to be appropriate by the facts about society:

The moral aspect of a proposition . . . expresses only the emotional response of an individual to a state of real or presumed facts. . . . Although we can say that the aspect of a proposition referring to a fact can be true or false, it is meaningless to characterize the value aspect of a proposition in this way (ibid.).

The import of these words is clear. For, if value positions could be supported or undermined by the findings of science, then they could not simply be characterized as emotional responses, and we could not say simply that it was *meaningless* (although it might be misleading) to speak of them as true or false.

Political philosophy, therefore, as reasoned argument about fundamental political values, can be entirely separated from political science, even on the mitigated positivist view which is now gaining ground among political scientists. 'Values' steer, as it were, the process of discovery, but they do not gain or lose plausibility by it. Thus although values may be somehow ineradicable from political science, reasoned argument concerning them would seem easily separable (though theorists may differ as to whether this is wise or not: cf. Easton, op. cit.). Indeed, it is hard to see in what such reasoned argument could consist. The findings of science will be relevant to our values, of course, in this sense, that they will tell us how to realize the goals we set ourselves. We can reconstruct political science in the mould of a 'policy science', like engineering and medicine, which shows us how to attain our goals. But the goals and values still come from somewhere else; they are founded on choices whose basis remains obscure.

The aim of this paper is to call into question this notion of the relation of factual findings in politics to value positions, and thus the implied relation between political science and political philosophy. In particular my aim is to call into question the view that the findings of political science leave us, as it were, as free as before, that they do not go some way to establishing particular sets of values and undermining others. If this view is shown to be mistaken, then we will have to recognize a convergence between science and normative theory in the field of politics.

It is usual for philosophers, when discussing this question, to leave the realms of the sciences of man and launch into a study of 'good', or commending, or emotive meaning, and so on. I propose to follow another course here, and to discuss the question first in connection with the disciplines in terms of which I have raised it, namely political philosophy and political science. When we have some understanding of the relations between these two on the ground, as it were, it will be time to see if these are considered possible in the heavens of philosophy.

II. The thesis that political science is value neutral has maximum plausibility when we look at some of its detailed findings. That French workers tend to vote Communist may be judged deplorable or encouraging, but it does not itself determine us to accept either of these judgements. It stands as a fact, neutral between them.

If this were all there is to political science, the debate would end here. But it is no more capable than any other science of proceeding by the random collection of facts. At one time it was believed that science was just concerned with the correlation of observable phenomena—the observables concerned being presumed to lie unproblematically before our gaze. But this position, the offshoot of a more primitive empiricism, is abandoned now by almost everyone, even those in the empiricist tradition.

For the number of features which any given range of phenomena may exhibit, and which can thus figure in correlations, is indefinite; and this because the phenomena themselves can be classified in an indefinite number of ways. Any physical object can be classified according to shape, colour, size, function, aesthetic properties, relation to some process, etc.; when we come to realities as complex as political society, the case is no different. But among these features only a limited range will yield correlations which have some explanatory force.

Nor are these necessarily the most obtrusive. The crucial features, laws or correlations concerning which will explain or help to explain phenomena of the range in question, may at a given stage of the science concerned be only vaguely discerned if not frankly unsuspected. The conceptual resources necessary to pick them out may not yet have been elaborated. It is said, for instance, that the modern physical concept of mass was unknown to the ancients, and only slowly and painfully evolved through the searchings of the later Middle Ages. And yet it is an essential variable in the modern science. A number of more obtrusive features may be irrelevant; that is, they may not be such that they can be linked in functions explanatory of the phenomena. Obvious distinctions may be irrelevant, or have an entirely different relevance from that attributed to them, such as the distinction between Aristotle's 'light' and 'heavy' bodies.

Thus when we wish to go beyond certain immediate low-level correlations whose relevance to the political process is fairly evident, such as the one mentioned above; when we want to explain why French workers vote Communist, or why McCarthyism arises in the United States in the late 1940s, or why the level of abstentionism varies from election to election, or why new African regimes are liable to military take-over, the features by reference to which we can explain these results are not immediately in evidence. Not only is there a wider difference of opinion about them, but we are not even sure that we have as yet the conceptual resources necessary to pick them out. We may easily argue that certain more obtrusive features, those pertaining, say, to the institutional structure, are not relevant, while others less obtrusive, say, the character structure prevalent in certain strata of the society, will yield the real explanation. We may, for instance, refuse to account for McCarthyism in terms of the struggle between Executive and Legislature, and look rather to the development of a certain personality structure among certain sections of the American population. Or else we may reject both these explanations and look to the role of a new status group in American society, newly rich but excluded from the Eastern Establishment. Or we may reject this, and see it as a result of the new position of the United States in the world.

The task of theory in political science, one which cannot be foregone if we are to elaborate any explanations worth the name, is to discover what are the kinds of features to which we should look for explanations of this kind. In which of the above dimensions are we to find an explanation for McCarthyism? Or rather, since all of these dimensions obviously have relevance, how are we to relate them in explaining the political phenomena? The task of theory is to delineate the relevant features in the different dimensions and their relation so that we have some idea of what can be the cause of what, of how character affects political process, or social structure affects character, or economic relations affect social structure, or political process affects economic relations, or vice versa; how ideological divisions affect party systems, or history affects ideological divisions, or culture affects history, or party systems affect culture, or vice versa. Before we have made some at least tentative steps in this direction we don't even have an idea where to look for our explanations; we don't know which facts to gather.

It is not surprising, then, that political science should be the field in which a great and growing number of 'theoretical frameworks' compete to answer these questions. Besides the Marxist approach, and the interest-group theory associated with the name of Bentley, we have seen the recent growth of 'structural-functional' approaches under the influence of systems theory; there have been approaches which have attempted to relate the psychological dimension to political behaviour (e.g. Lasswell), different applications of sociological concepts and methods (e.g. Lipset and Almond), applications of game theory (e.g. Downs and Riker), and so on.

These different approaches are frequently rivals, since they offer different accounts of the features crucial for explanation and the causal relations which hold. We can speak of them, along with their analogues in other sciences, as 'conceptual structures' or 'theoretical frameworks', because they claim to delimit the area in which scientific inquiry will be fruitful. A framework does not give us at once all the variables which will be relevant and the laws which will be true, but it tells us what needs to be explained, and roughly by what kinds of factors. For instance, if we accept the principle of Inertia, certain ways of conceiving bodies and therefore certain questions are beyond the pale. To pursue them is fruitless, as was the search for what kept the cannon-ball moving in pre-Galilean physics. Similarly an orthodox Marxist approach cannot allow that McCarthyism can be explained in terms of early upbringing and the resultant personality structure.

But we can also see a theoretical framework as setting the crucial dimensions through which the phenomena can vary. For it sets out the essential functional relations by which they can be explained, while at the same time ruling out other functional relations belonging to other, rival frameworks. But the given set of functional relations defines certain dimensions in which the phenomena can vary; a given framework therefore affirms some dimensions of variation and denies others. Thus for a Marxist, capitalist societies do not vary as to who wields power, no matter what the constitution or the party in office; supposed variations in these dimensions, which are central to a great many theories, are sham; the crucial dimension is that concerning class structure.

In the more exact sciences theoretical discovery may be couched in the form of laws and be called principles, such as, e.g., of Inertia, or the Rectilinear Propagation of Light. But in the less exact, such as politics, it may consist simply of a general description of the phenomena couched in the crucial concepts. Or it may be implicit in a series of distinctions which a given theory makes (e.g. Aristotle's classification of the types of polity), or in a story of how the phenomena came to be (e.g. the myth of the Social Contract), or in a general statement of causal relations (e.g. Marx's Preface to *A Contribution to the Critique of Political Economy*).

But, however expressed, theoretical discovery can be seen as the delineating of the important dimensions of variation for the range of phenomena concerned.

III. Theoretical discovery of this kind is thus one of the concerns of modern political science, as we have seen. But it also is a traditional concern of what we call political philosophy, that is, normative political theory. It is not hard to see why. Normative theorists of the tradition have also been concerned with delineating crucial dimensions of variation— of course, they were looking for the dimensions which were significant for judging of the value of polities and policies rather than for explaining them. But the two types of research were in fact closely interwoven so that in pursuing the first they were also led to pursue the second.

Aristotle, for instance, is credited with a revision of Plato's threefold classification of political society which enhanced its explanatory value. He substituted for the number criterion a class criterion which gives a more revealing classification of the differences, and allows us to account for more: it made clear what was at stake between democracy and oligarchy; it opened up the whole range of explanations based on class composition, including the one for which Aristotle is known in history, the balancing role of the middle class.

But this revision was not unconnected with differences in the normative theory of the two thinkers. Plato attempted to achieve a society devoid of class struggle, either in the perfect harmony of the *Republic*, or in the single class state of the *Laws*. Aristotle is not above weaving the dream of the ideal state in one section of the *Politics*, but there is little connection between this and the political theory of the rest of the work. This latter is solidly based on the understanding that class differences, and hence divergence of interest and tension, are here to stay. In the light of this theory, Plato's idea in the *Republic* of overcoming class tension by discipline, education, a superior constitution, and so on, is so much pie-in-the-sky (not even very tasty pie in Aristotle's view, as he makes clear in Book II, but that is for other reasons).

Aristotle's insight in political science is incompatible with Plato's normative theory, at least in the *Republic*, and the *Politics* therefore takes a quite different line (for other reasons as well, of course). The difference on this score might perhaps be expressed in this way: both Plato and Aristotle held that social harmony was of crucial importance as a value. But Plato saw this harmony as achieved in the ending of all class conflict; Aristotle saw it as arising from the domestication of this conflict. But crucial to this dispute is the question of the causal relevance of class tension: is it an eradicable blot on social harmony, in the sense that one can say, for instance, that the violent forms of this conflict are? Or is it ineradicable and ever-present, only varying in its forms? In the first case one of the crucial dimensions of variation of our explanatory theory is that concerning the presence or absence of class conflict. In the second case, this dimension is not even recognized as having a basis in fact. If this is so, then the normative theory collapses, or rather is shifted from the realm of political philosophy to that we call Utopia-building. For the idea of a society without class conflict would be one to which we cannot even approach. Moreover, the attempt to approach it would have all the dangerous consequences attendant on large-scale political changes based on illusory hopes.

Thus Plato's theory of the *Republic*, considered as the thesis that a certain dimension of variation is normatively significant, contains claims concerning the dimensions of variation which are relevant for explanation, for it is only compatible with those frameworks which concede the reality of the normatively crucial dimension. It is incompatible with any view of politics as the striving of different classes, or interest groups, or individuals against one another.

It is clear that this is true of any normative theory, that it is linked with certain explanatory theory or theories, and incompatible with others. Aristotle's dimension whereby different constitutions were seen as expressing and moulding different forms of life disappears in the atomistic conception of Hobbes. Rousseau's crucial dimension of the *Social Contract*, marking a sharp discontinuity between popular sovereignty and states of dependence of one form or another, could not survive the validation of the theories of Mosca, or Michels, or Pareto.

Traditional political philosophy was thus forced to engage in the theoretical function that we have seen to be essential to modern political science; and the more elaborate and comprehensive the normative theory, the more complete and defined the conceptual framework which accompanied it. That is why political science can learn something still from the works of Aristotle, Hobbes, Hegel, Marx, and so on. In the tradition one form of inquiry is virtually inseparable from the other.

2

I. This is not a surprising result. Everyone recognized that political philosophers of the tradition were engaged in elaborating on, at least embryonic, political science. But, one might say, that is just the trouble; that is why political science was so long in getting started. Its framework was always set in the interests of some normative theory. In order to progress science must be liberated from all *parti pris* and be value-neutral. Thus if normative theory requires political science and cannot be carried on without it, the reverse is not the case; political science can and should be separated from the older discipline. Let us examine some modern attempts to elaborate a science of politics to see if this is true.

Let us look first at S. M. Lipset's *Political Man* (New York: Doubleday, 1959). In this work Lipset sets out the conditions for modern democracy. He sees societies as existing in two dimensions—conflict and consensus. Both are equally necessary for democracy. They are not mere opposites as a simple-minded view might assume. Conflict here is not seen as a simple divergence of interest, or the existence of objective relations of exploitation, but as the actual working out of these through the struggle for power and over policy.

Surprising as it may sound, a stable democracy requires the manifestation of conflict or cleavage so that there will be struggle over ruling positions, challenges to parties in power, and shifts of parties in office; but without consensus—a political system allowing the peaceful 'play' of power, the adherence of the 'outs' to decisions made by the 'ins', and the recognition by the 'ins' of the rights of the 'outs'—there can be no democracy. The study of the conditions encouraging democracy must therefore focus on the sources of both cleavage and consensus (*Political Man*, p. 21).

And again, 'Cleavage—where it is legitimate—contributes to the integration of societies and organizations' (ibid.). The absence of such conflict, such as where a given group has taken over, or an all-powerful state can produce unanimity, or at least prevent diversity from expressing itself, is a sign that the society is not a free one. De Tocqueville feared (*Political Man*, p. 27) that the power of the state would produce apathy and thus do away even with consensus.

Democracy in a complex society may be defined as a political system which supplies regular constitutional opportunities for changing the governing officials, and a social mechanism which permits the largest possible part of the population to influence major decisions by choosing among contenders for political office (ibid., p. 45).

Such a society requires the organization of group interests to fight for their own goals—provided that this is done in a peaceful way, within the rules of the game, and with the acceptance of the arbiter in the form of elections by universal suffrage. If groups are not organized, they have no real part, their interests are neglected, and they cannot have their share of power; they become alienated from the system.

Now this view can at once be seen to conflict with a Rousseauian view which disapproves of the organization of 'factions', and which sees consensus as arising out of isolated individuals. It also goes against the modern conservative view that to organize people on a class basis gratuitously divides the society. In face of Rousseau, Lipset holds that the absence of close agreement among all concerning the general will is not a sign that something has gone wrong. There are ineradicable basic divergences of interest; they have to be adjusted. If we get to some kind of conflictless state, this can only be because some of the parties have been somehow done down and prevented from competing. For Lipset, absence of conflict is a sure sign that some groups are being excluded from the public thing.

This difference closely parallels the one mentioned above between Plato and Aristotle. Indeed, Lipset points out on several occasions the similarity between his position and that of Aristotle. And it is clear that it is a difference of the same kind, one in which a normative theory is undermined because the reality of its crucial dimension of variation is challenged. A similar point can be made concerning the difference with conservatives who allow for divergence in the state, but resist class parties. Here the belief is that the divergence is gratuitous, that the real differences lie elsewhere, either in narrower or in broader interests, and that these are obfuscated and made more difficult of rational adjustment by class divisions. More, the state can be torn apart if these divisions are played up. Conservatives tend to feel about class in politics as liberals do about race in politics. Once again, Lipset's view would undermine the position, for he holds that class differences are at the centre of politics, and cannot be removed except by reducing the number of players, as it were. They are therefore the very stuff of democratic politics, provided they are moderately and peacefully expressed. The struggle between rich and poor is ineradicable; it can take different forms, that's all.

Attempts to break outside of this range are thus irrational and dysfunctional. Irrational, because based on false premises; and dysfunctional, because the goal of conflictlessness or absence of class tension can only be achieved at the expense of features of the system which most will accept as valuable; by oppressing some segment of the population, or by its apathy and lack of organization. That is, of course, the usual fate of theories with a false factual base in politics; as was remarked above, they are not just erroneous, but positively dangerous.

It can be seen that the value consequences of Lipset's theory are fairly widespread even restricting ourselves to the alternatives which it negates or undermines. An examination of some of the factors which tend to strengthen democracy according to the theory will increase this list of rejected alternatives. Lipset holds that economic development is conducive to the health of democracy, in that, *inter alia*, it narrows gaps in wealth and living standards, tends to create a large middle class, and increases the 'cross-pressures' working to damp down class conflict. For a society cannot function properly as a democracy unless, along with an articulation of class differences, there is some consensus which straddles them. Now Lipset's 'cross-pressures'—typically exercised by religious affiliation, for instance, which cuts across class barriers—are the 'opiates' of a strict Marxist. For they are integrators which prevent the system coming apart at the social seam, and thus prevent the class war from coming to a head. But we are not dealing here simply with two value-judgements about the same facts understood in the same way. The crucial difference is that for Lipset the stage beyond the class struggle does not and cannot exist; the abolition of the conflict in unanimity is impossible; his view is: 'the rich ye have always with you.' But in this case the integrating factors cease to be 'opiates', breeding false consciousness and hiding the great revolutionary potentiality. There is nothing there to hide. Lipset's view therefore negates revolutionary Marxism in a direct way—in the same way as it negates the views above—by denying that the crucial dimensions of variation have reality.

But if we examine this last example a little more closely, we can see even wider normative consequences of Lipset's view. For if we rule out the transformation to the classless society, then we are left with the choice between different kinds of class conflict: a violent kind which so divides society that it can only survive under some form of tyranny, or one which can reach accommodations in peace. This choice, set out in these terms, virtually makes itself for us. We may point out that this does not cover the range of possibility, since there are also cases in which the class conflict is latent, owing to the relative absence of one party. But this is the result of underdevelopment, of a lack of education, or knowledge, or initiative on the part of the underprivileged. Moreover, it unfailingly leads to a worsening of their position relative to the privileged. As Lipset says in the statement of his political position which forms the introduction to the Anchor Edition of *Political Man*, 'I believe with Marx that all privileged classes seek to maintain and *enhance* their advantages against the desire of the under-privileged to reduce them' (Anchor Edition, p. xxii, emphasis in original).

Thus, for Lipset, the important dimension of variation for political societies can be seen as L-shaped, as it were. On the one end lie societies where the divisions are articulated but are so deep that they cannot be contained without violence, suppression of liberty, and despotic rule; on the other end lie societies which are peaceful but oligarchic and which are therefore run to secure the good of a minority ruling group. At the angle are the societies whose differences are articulated but which are capable of accommodating them in a peaceful way, and which therefore are charac-terized by a high degree of individual liberty and political organization.

Faced with this choice, it is hard to opt for anywhere else but the angle. For to do so is either to choose violence and despotism and suppression over peace, rule by consent, and liberty, or to choose a society run more for the benefit of a minority over a society run more for the benefit of all, a society which exploits and/or manipulates over a society which tends to secure the common good as determined by the majority. Only in the angle can we have a society really run for the common good, for at one end is oligarchy based on an unorganized mass, at the other despotism.

Lipset himself makes this option explicit:

A basic premise of this book is that democracy is not only or even primarily a means through which different groups can attain their ends or seek the good society; it is the good society itself in operation. Only the give-and-take of a free society's internal struggles offers some guarantee that the products of the society will not accumulate in the hands of a few power-holders, and that men may develop and bring up their children without fear of persecution (p. 403).

This is a succinct statement of the value position implicit in *Political Man*, but it is wrongly characterized as a 'premise'. The use of this term shows the influence of the theory of value-neutrality, but it is misplaced. It would be less misleading to say 'upshot', for the value position flows out of the analysis of the book. Once we accept Lipset's analysis concerning the fundamental role of class in politics, that it always operates even when division is not overt, and that it can never be surmounted in unanimity, then we have no choice but to accept democracy as he defines it, as a society in which most men are doers, take their fate in their own hands, or have a hand in determining it, and at least reduce the degree to which injustice is done to them, or their interests are unfavourably handled by others, as the good society.

II. But now we have gone far beyond the merely negative consequences noted above for Marxism, conservatism, or Rousseau's general will. We are saying that the crucial dimensions of variation of Lipset's theory not only negate dimensions crucial to other normative theories but support one of their own, which is implicit in the theory itself. But this conclusion, if true, goes against the supposed neutrality of scientific fact. Let us examine it a bit more closely.

We have said above that faced with the choice between a regime based on violence and suppression, and one based on consent, between regimes which serve the interests more or less of all versus regimes which serve the interests only of a minority, the choice is clear. Is this simply a rhetorical flourish, playing on generally accepted values among readers? Or is the connection more solid?

Granted that we wish to apply 'better' and 'worse' to regimes characterized along this dimension, can one conceive of reversing what seemed above to be the only possible judgement? Can one say: yes, a regime based on minority rule with violent suppression of the majority is better than one based on general consensus, where all have a chance to have their interests looked to? Certainly this is not a logically absurd position in itself. But if someone accepted the framework of Lipset and proceeded to make this judgement, surely we would expect him to go on and mention some other considerations which led him to this astounding conclusion. We might expect him to say, that only minorities are creative, that violence is necessary to keep men from stagnating, or something of this kind. But supposing he said nothing of the sort? Supposing he just maintained that violence was better than its opposite, not *qua* stimulus to creativity, or essential element in progress, but just *qua* violence; that it was better that only the minority interest be served, not because the minority would be more creative but just because it was a minority? A position of this kind would be unintelligible. We could understand that the man was dedicating himself to the furtherance of such a society, but the use of the words 'good' or 'better' would be totally inappropriate here, for there would be no visible grounds for applying them. The question would remain open whether the man had understood these terms, whether, e.g., he had not confused 'good' with 'something which gives me a kick', or 'aesthetically pleasing'.

But, it might be argued, this is not a fair example. Supposing our unorthodox thinker did adduce other grounds for preferring violence and majority rule? Surely, then, he would be permitted to differ from us? Yes, but then it is very dubious whether he could still accept Lipset's framework. Suppose, for instance, that one believed (as Hegel did about war) that violence was morally necessary from time to time for the wellbeing of the state. This would not be without effect on one's conception of political science; the range of possible regimes would be different from that which Lipset gives us; for peaceful democratic regimes would suffer a process of stagnation which would render them less viable; they would not in fact be able to maintain themselves, and thus the spectrum of possible regimes would be different from the one Lipset presents us with; the most viable regime would be one which was able to ration violence and maintain it at a non-disruptive level without falling over into stagnation and decay.

But why need this change of values bring along with it a chance in explanatory framework? We seem to be assuming that the evils of internal peace must be such as to have a political effect, to undermine the viability of the political society. Is this assumption justified? Normally, of course, we would expect someone putting forward a theory of this kind to hold that inner violence is good because it contributes to the dynamism, or creativity of people, or progress of the society, or something of the kind which would make peaceful societies less viable. But supposing he chose some other benefits of violence which had nothing to do with the survival or health of political society? Let us say that he held that violence was good for art, that only in societies rent by internal violence could great literature, music, painting be produced? The position, for instance, of Harry Lime in *The Third Man?*

This certainly is a possible case. But let us examine it more closely. Our hypothetical objector has totally forsaken the ground of politics, and is making his judgement on extraneous (here aesthetic) grounds. He cannot deny that, setting these grounds aside, the normal order of preference is valid. He is saying in effect that, although it is better abstracting from aesthetic considerations that society be peaceful, nevertheless this must be overridden in the interests of art.

This distinction is important. We must distinguish between two kinds of objection to a given valuation. It may be that the valuation is accepted, but that its verdict for our actual choices is overridden, as it were, by other more important valuations. Thus we may think that freedom of speech is always a good, while reluctantly conceding that it must be curtailed in an emergency because of the great risks it would entail here. We are in this case self-consciously curtailing a good. The other kind of objection is the one which undermines the valuation itself, seeks to deprive the putative good of its status. This is what Lipset does, for instance, to spiritual followers of Rousseau in showing that their harmony can only be the silence of minority rule.[1] In one case we are conceding that the thing in question does really have the properties which its proponents attribute to it (e.g. that free speech does contribute to justice, progress, human development, or whatever), but we are adding that it also has other properties which force us to proceed against it (e.g. it is potentially disruptive) temporarily or permanently. In the other case, we are denying the condition in question the very properties by which it is judged good (e.g. that the legislation of the society without cleavage emanates from the free conscious will of all its citizens). Let us call these two objections respectively overriding and undermining.

Now what is being claimed here is that an objection which undermines the values which seem to arise out of a given framework must alter the framework; that in this sense the framework is inextricably connected to a certain set of values; and that if we can reverse the valuation without touching the framework, then we are dealing with an overriding.

To go back to the example above. In order to undermine the judgement against violence we would have to show that it does not have the property claimed for it. Now obviously violence has the property of killing and

---

[1] Of course, Rousseau's general will may remain a value in the hypothetical world he casts for it, but that concerns Utopia building, not political philosophy.

maiming which goes some way towards putting it in the list of undesirables, one might think irrevocably; so that it could only be overridden. But here we are not dealing with a judgement about violence *per se*, but rather with one concerning the alternative of peace and violence; and the judgement rests on the ground that violence has properties which peace has not, that the evils obviously attributed to violence are effectively avoided by peace. But if one can show that peace leads to stagnation, and thus to breakdown (and hence eventual chaos or violence) or foreign conquest, then the supposed gap between the two narrows. On the contrary, one is presented with a new alternative, that between more or less concontrolled violence and the destructive uncontrolled kind associated with internal breakdown or foreign conquest. What the undermining job has done is to destroy the alternative on which the original judgement was based, and thus deprive the previously preferred alternative of its differential property for which it was valued.

But any undermining of this kind is bound to alter the explanatory framework of which the original alternative was an essential part. If we cannot maintain a peaceful polity, then the gamut of possibilities is very different, and Lipset is guilty of neglecting a whole host of factors, to do with the gamut tension-stagnation.

To take the other example, let our objector make a case for rule by the minority. Let him claim that only the minority are creative, that if they are not given preference, then they will not produce, and then everyone will suffer. Thus the supposed difference between rule for the minority and that for all, viz. that the ordinary bloke gets something out of the second that he does not out of the first, is set aside; rather the opposite turns out to be the case. The value is undermined. But so is the political framework altered, for now we have an elitist thesis about the importance of minority rule; another variable has entered the picture which was not present in the previous framework and which cuts across it, in so far a the previous framework presented the possibility of good progressive societies run for all.

Let us hold, however, that violence or élite rule is good for painting, and we have an over-ruling; for it remains the case that it would be better to have no violence and everybody getting a square deal, but alas . . . .

Thus the framework does secrete a certain value position, albeit one that can be overridden. In general we can see this arising in the following way: the framework gives us as it were the geography of the range of phenomena in question, it tells us how they can vary, what are the major dimensions of variation. But since we are dealing with matters which are of great importance to human beings, a given map will have, as it were, its own built-in value-slope. That is to say, a given dimension of variation will usually determine for itself how we are to judge of good and bad, because of its relation to obvious human wants and needs.

Now this may seem a somewhat startling result, since it is well known that there are wide differences over what human needs, desires, and purposes are. Not that there is not a wide area of agreement over basic things like life; but this clearly breaks down when one tries to extend the list. There can thus be great disagreement over the putative human need for self-expression or for autonomous development, both of which can and do play important parts in debates and conflicts over political theory.

Does this mean, therefore, that we can reject the previous result and imagine a state of affairs where we could accept the framework of explanation of a given theory, and yet refuse the value-judgements it secretes, because we took a different view of the schedule of human needs?[2] Or, to put it another way, does this mean that the step between accepting a framework of explanation and accepting a certain notion of the political good is mediated by a premiss concerning human needs, which may be widely enough held to go unnoticed, but which nevertheless can be challenged, thus breaking the connection?

The answer is no. For the connection between a given framework of explanation and a certain notion of the schedule of needs, wants, and purposes which seems to mediate the inference to value theory is not fortuitous. If one adopted a quite different view of human need, one would upset the framework. Thus to pursue another example from Lipset, stable democracies are judged better than stable ologarchies, since the latter can only exist where the majority is so uneducated and tradition-bound or narrowed that it has not yet learned to demand its rights. But suppose we tried to upset this judgement by holding that underdevelopment is good for men, that they are happier when they are led by some unquestioned norms, do not have to think for themselves, and so on? One would then be reversing the value-judgement. But at the same time one would be changing the framework. For we are introducing a notion of anomie here, and we cannot suppose this factor to exist without having some important effect on the working of political society. If anomie is the result of the development of education and the breakdown of tradition, then it will affect the stability of the societies which promote this kind of development.

[2] This could involve either an undermining or an overriding of the value-judgement. For we can deny something, a condition or outcome, the property by which it is judged good not only by denying it a property by which it fulfils certain human needs, wants, or purposes, but also by denying that these needs, wants, or purposes exist. And we can override the judgement that it is good by pointing to other needs, wants, or purposes that it frustrates.

They will be subject to constant danger of being undermined as their citizens, suffering from anomie, look for havens of certainty. If men are made unhappy by democracy, then undoubtedly it is not as good as its protagonists make out, but it is not so viable either.

The view above that we could accept the framework of explanation and reject the value conclusion by positing a different schedule of needs cannot be sustained. For a given framework is linked to a given conception of the schedule of human needs, wants, and purposes, such that, if the schedule turns out to have been mistaken in some significant way, the framework itself cannot be maintained. This is for the fairly obvious reason that human needs, wants, and purposes have an important bearing on the way people act, and that therefore one has to have a notion of the schedule which is not too wildly inaccurate if one is to establish the framework for any science of human behaviour, that of politics not excepted. A conception of human needs thus enters into a given political theory, and cannot be considered something extraneous which we later add to the framework to yield a set of value-judgements.

This is not to say that there cannot be needs or purposes which we might add to those implicit in any framework, and which would not alter the framework since their effect on political events might be marginal. But this would at most give us the ground of an overruling, not for an undermining. In order to undermine the valuation we would have to show that the putative need fulfilled was not a need, or that what looked like fulfilling a need, or a want, or a human purpose was really not so, or really did the opposite. Now even an overruling might destroy the framework, if a new need were introduced which was important enough motivationally to dictate quite different behaviour. But certainly an undermining, which implies that one has misidentified the schedule of needs, would do so.

III. It would appear from the above example that the adoption of a framework of explanation carries with it the adoption of the 'value-slope' implicit in it, although the valuations can be overruled by considerations of an extra-political kind. But it might be objected that the study of one example is not a wide enough base for such a far-reaching conclusion. The example might even be thought to be peculiarly inappropriate because of Lipset's closeness to the tradition of political philosophy, and particularly his esteem for Aristotle.

If we wish, however, to extend the range of examples, we can see immediately that Lipset's theory is not exceptional. There is, for instance, a whole range of theories in which the connection between factual base and valuation is built in, as it were, to the conceptual structure. Such is the case of many theories which make use of the notion of function. To fulfil a function is to meet a requirement of some kind, and when the term is used in social theory, the requirement concerned is generally connected with human needs, wants, and purposes. The requirement or end concerned may be the maintenance of the political system which is seen as essential to man, or the securing of some of the benefits which political systems are in a position to attain for men—stability, security, peace, fulfilment of some wants, and so on. Since politics is largely made up of human purposeful activity a characterization of political societies in terms of function is not implausible. But in so far as we characterize societies in terms of their fulfilling in different ways and to different degrees the same set of functions, the crucial dimension of variation for explanatory purposes is also a normatively significant one. Those societies which fulfil the functions more completely are *pro tanto* better.

We can take as an example the 'structural-functional' theory of Gabriel Almond as outlined in his *Politics of the Developing Areas* (Princeton: Princeton University Press, 1963). Among the functions Almond outlines that all polities must fulfil is that of 'interest articulation'. It is an essential part of the process by which the demands, interests, and claims of members of a society can be brought to bear on government and produce some result. Almond sees four main types of structures as involved in interest articulation.[3] Of three of these (institutional, non-associational, and anomic interest groups), he says that a prominent role for them in interest articulation tends to indicate poor 'boundary maintenance', between society and polity. Only the fourth (associational interest groups) can carry the main burden of interest articulation in such a way as to maintain a smooth-running system 'by virtue of the regulatory role of associational interest groups in processing raw claims or interest articulations occurring elsewhere in the society and the political system, and directing them in an orderly way and in aggregable form through the party system, legislature, and bureaucracy'.[4]

The view here is of a flow of raw demands which have to be processed by the system before satisfaction can be meted out. If the processing is inefficient, then the satisfaction will be less, the system will increase frustration, uncertainty, and often as a consequence instability. In this context boundary maintenance between society and polity is important for clarity and efficiency. Speaking of the functions of articulation and aggregation together, Almond says:

[3] *Politics of the Developing Areas*, p. 33.   [4] Ibid., pp. 35–6.

Thus, to attain a maximum flow of inputs of raw claims from the society, a low level of processing into a common language of claims is required which is performed by associated interest groups. To assimilate and transform these interests into a relatively small number of alternatives of policy and personnel, a middle range of processing is necessary. If these two functions are performed in substantial part before the authoritative governmental structures are reached, then the output functions of rule-making and rule application are facilitated, and the political and governmental processes become calculable and responsible. The outputs may be related to and controlled by the inputs, and thus circulation becomes relatively free by virtue of good boundary maintenance or division of labour.[5]

Thus in characterizing different institutions by the way they articulate or aggregate interests, Almond is also evaluating them. For obviously a society with the above characteristics is preferable to one without, where, that is, there is less free circulation, where 'outputs' correspond less to 'inputs' (what people want, claim, or demand), where government is less responsible, and so on. The characterization of the system in terms of function contains the criteria of 'eufunction' and 'dysfunction', as they are sometimes called. The dimension of variation leaves only one answer to the question, which is better?, because of the clear relation in which it stands to men's wants and needs.

Theories of this kind include not only those which make explicit use of 'function', but also other derivatives of systems theory and frameworks which build on the analogy with organisms. This might be thought to include, for instance, David Easton (cf. *A Framework for Political Analysis* Englewood Cliffs, N.J.: Prentice-Hall, 1965, and *A Systems Analysis of Political Life*, New York: Wiley, 1965) and Karl Deutsch (*The Nerves of Government*, Glencoe, Ill: The Free Press, 1963). For the requirements by which we will judge the performance of different political systems are explicit in the theory.

But what about theories which set out explicitly to separate fact from evaluations, to 'state conditions' without in any way 'justifying preferences'? What about a theory of the 'behavioural' type, like that of Harold Lasswell?

IV. Harold Lasswell is clearly a believer in the neutrality of scientific findings. Lasswell is openly committed to certain values, notably those of the democratic society as he defines it, a society 'in which human dignity is realized in theory and fact'.[6] He believes that scientific findings can be

---

[5] Ibid., p. 39.
[6] 'The Democratic Character', in *Political Writings* (Glencoe, Ill.: The Free Press, 1951), p. 473.

brought to bear on the realization of these goals. A science so oriented is
what he calls a 'policy science'. But this does not affect the neutrality of
the findings: a policy science simply determines a certain grouping and
selection of findings which help us to encompass the goal we have set. It
follows that if there are policy sciences of democracy, 'there can also be a
'policy science of tyranny'.[7]

In Lasswell's 'configurative analysis', then, both fact and valuation
enter; but they remain entirely separable. The following passage from the
introduction of *Power and Society* makes the point unambiguously:

The present conception conforms . . . to the philosophical tradition in which
politics and ethics have always been closely associated. But it deviates from the
tradition in giving full recognition to the existence of two distinct components in
political theory—the empirical propositions of political science and the value
judgments of political doctrine. Only statements of the first kind are formulated
in the present work (p. xiii).

Yet the implied separation between factual analysis and evaluation is
belied by the text itself. In the sections dealing with different types of
polity,[8] the authors introduce a number of dimensions of variation of
political society. Polities vary (1) as to the allocation of power (between
autocracy, oligarchy, republic), (2) as to the scope of power (society
either undergoes greater regimentation or liberalization), (3) as to the
concentration or dispersion of power (taking in questions concerning
the separation of powers, or federalism), (4) as to the degree to which a
rule is equalitarian (the degree of equality in power potential), (5) the
degree to which it is libertarian or authoritarian, (6) the degree to which it
is impartial, (7) and the degree to which it is juridical or tyrannical.
Democracy is defined as a rule which is libertarian, juridical, and impartial.

It is not surprising to find one's sympathies growing towards democracy
as one ploughs through this list of definitions. For they leave us little
choice. Dimension (5) clearly determines our preference. Liberty is
defined not just in terms of an absence of coercion, but of genuine re-
sponsibility to self. 'A rule is libertarian where initiative, individuality and
choice are widespread; authoritarian, if obedience, conformity and
coercion are characteristic.'[9] Quoting Spinoza with approval, Lasswell
and Kaplan come down in favour of a notion of liberty as the capacity to
'live by . . . free reason'. 'On this conception, there is liberty in a state
only where each individual has sufficient self-respect to respect others.'[10]

[7] Ibid., p. 471n.
[8] *Power and Society* (New Haven, Conn.: Yale University Press, 1952), Ch. 9,
sections 3 and 4.
[9] Ibid., p. 228.   [10] Ibid., p. 229.

Thus it is clear that liberty is preferable to its opposite. Many thinkers of the orthodox school, while agreeing with this verdict, might attribute it simply to careless wording on the author's part, to a temporary relaxation of that perpetual vigil which must be maintained against creeping value bias. It is important to point out therefore that the value force here is more than a question of wording. It lies in the type of alternative which is presented to us: on the one hand, a man can be manipulated by others, obeying a law and standards set up by others which he cannot judge; on the other hand, he is developed to the point where he can judge for himself, exercise reason, and apply his own standards; he comes to respect himself and is more capable of respecting others. If this is really the alternative before us, how can we fail to judge freedom better (whether or not we believe there are overriding considerations)?

Dimension (6) also determines our choice. 'Impartiality' is said to 'correspond in certain ways to the concepts of "justice" in the classical tradition',[11] and an impartial rule is called a 'commonwealth', 'enhancing the value position of all members of the society impartially, rather than that of some restricted class'.[12] Now if the choice is simply between a regime which works for the common good and a regime which works for the good of some smaller group, there is no doubt which is better in the absence of any overriding considerations.

Similarly dimension (7) is value-determinate. 'Juridical' is opposed to 'tyrannical' and is defined as a state of affairs where 'decisions are made in accord with specified rules . . . rather than arbitrarily'[13] or where a 'decision is challenged by an appraisal of it in terms of . . . conditions, which must be met by rulers as well as ruled'. Since the alternative presented here is *arbitrary* decision, and one which cannot be checked by any due process, there is no question which is preferable. If we had wanted to present a justification of rule outside law (such as Plato did), we would never accept the adjective 'arbitrary' in our description of the alternative to 'juridical'.

As far as the other dimensions are concerned, the authors relate them to these three key ones, so that they too cannot be seen as neutral, although their value relevance is derivative. Thus voluntarization is better for liberty than regimentation, and the dispersion of power can be seen as conducive to juridicalness. In short, we come out with a full-dress justification of democracy, and this in a work which claims neutrality. The work, we are told in the introduction, 'contains no elaborations of political doctrine, of what the state and society *ought* to be'.[14] Even during the very exposition of the section on democracy, there are ritual disclaimers:

11 Ibid., p. 231.   12 Ibid.   13 Ibid., p. 232.   14 Ibid., p. xi.

for instance, when the term 'justice' is mentioned, a parenthesis is inserted: 'the present term, however, is to be understood altogether in a descriptive, non-normative sense'; [15] and at the end of the chapter: 'the formulations throughout are descriptive rather than normatively ambiguous.'[16]

But neutral they are not, as we have seen: we cannot accept these descriptions and fail to agree that democracy is a better form of government than its opposite (a 'tyrannical', 'exploitative', 'authoritarian' rule: you can take your choice). Only the hold of the neutrality myth can hide this truth from the authors.

Of course these sections do not represent adequately Lasswell's total work. Indeed, one of the problems in discussing Lasswell is that he has espoused a bewildering variety of conceptual frameworks of explanation. This is evident from a perusal of *Power and Society* alone, quite apart from his numerous other works. These may all cohere in some unified system, but if this is the case, it is far from obvious. Yet the link between factual analysis and evaluation reappears in each of the different approaches. There is not space to cover them all; one further example will have to suffice here.

In the later psychiatrically oriented works, such as *Power and Personality*, or 'The Democratic Character',[17] the goal explicitly set for policy science is democracy. But the implication that this is a goal chosen independently of what is discovered to be true about politics is belied all along the line. For the alternative to a society where people have a 'self-system' which suits the democratic character is one in which various pathologies, often of a dangerous kind, are rampant. The problem of democracy is to create, among other things, a self-system which is 'multi-valued, rather than single-valued, and . . . disposed to share rather than to hoard or to monopolize.'[18] One might have some quarrel with this: perhaps single-minded people are an asset to society. But after seeing the alternative to multi-valuedness as set out in the 'Democratic Character',[19] one can understand why Lasswell holds this view. Lasswell lays out for us a series of what he describes frankly at one point as 'character deformations'.[20] In talking about the *homo politicus* who concentrates on the pursuit of power, he remarks 'The psychiatrist feels at home in the study of ardent seekers after power in the arena of politics because the physician recognizes the extreme egocentricity and sly ruthlessness of some of the paranoid patients with whom he has come in contact in the clinic' (p. 498).

The point here is not that Lasswell introduces valuation illegitimately by the use of subtly weighted language, or unnecessarily pejorative terms.

[15] Ibid., p. 231.   [16] Ibid., p. 239.
[17] *Political Writings.*   [18] Ibid., pp. 497–8.   [19] Ibid., pp. 497–502.   [20] Ibid., p. 500.

Perhaps politicians do tend to approximate to unbalanced personalities seeking to make up deprivation by any means. The point is that, if this is true, then some important judgements follow about political psychiatry. And these are not, as it were, suspended on some independent value-judgement, but arise from the fact themselves. There *could* be a policy science of tyranny, but then there could also be a medical science aimed at producing disease (as when nations do research into bacteriological warfare). But we could not say that the second was more worthy of pursuit than the first, unless we advanced some very powerful overriding reasons (which is what proponents of bacteriological warfare try—unsuccessfully —to do). The science of health, however, needs no such special justification.

3

I. The thesis we have been defending, however plausible it may appear in the context of a discussion of the different theories of political science, is unacceptable to an important school of philosophy today. Throughout the foregoing analysis, philosophers will have felt uneasy. For this conclusion tells against the well-entrenched doctrine according to which questions of value are independent of questions of fact; the view which holds that before any set of facts we are free to adopt an indefinite number of value positions. According to the view defended here, on the other hand, a given framework of explanation in political science tends to support an associated value position, secretes its own norms for the assessment of polities and policies.

It is of course this philosophical belief which, because of its immense influence among scientists in general and political scientists as well, has contributed to the cult of neutrality in political science, and the belief that genuine science gives no guidance as to right and wrong. It is time, therefore, to come to grips with this philosophical view.

There are two points about the use of 'good' which are overlooked or negated by the standard 'non-naturalist' view: (1) to apply 'good' may or may not be to commend, but it is always to claim that there are reasons for commending whatever it is applied to, (2) to say of something that it fulfils human needs, wants, or purposes always constitutes a prima facie reason for calling it 'good', that is, for applying the term in the absence of overriding considerations.[21]

Now the non-naturalist view, as expressed, for instance, by Hare or Stevenson, denies both these propositions. Its starting-point is the

[21] We might also speak of 'interests' here, but this can be seen as included in 'wants' and 'needs'. Interest may deviate from want, but can only be explicited in terms of such concepts as 'satisfaction', 'happiness', 'unhappiness', etc., the criteria for whose application are ultimately to be found in what we want.

casting of moral argument in deductive form—all the arguments against the so-called 'naturalistic fallacy' have turned on the validity of deductive inference. The ordinary man may think that he is moving from a factual consideration about something to a judgement that it is good or bad, but in fact one cannot deduce a statement concerning the goodness or badness of something from a statement attributing some descriptive property to it. Thus the ordinary man's argument is really an enthymeme: he is assuming some major premiss: when he moves from 'X will make men happy' to 'X is good', he is operating with the suppressed premiss 'What makes men happy is good', for only by adding this can one derive the conclusion by valid inference.

To put the point in another way: the ordinary man sees 'X will make men happy' as the reason for his favourable verdict on it. But on the non-naturalist view, it is a reason only because he accepts the suppressed major premiss. For one could, logically, reject this premiss, and then the conclusion would not follow at all. Hence, that something is a reason for judging X good depends on what values the man who judges holds. Of course, one can find reasons for holding these values. That is, facts from which we could derive the major premiss, but only by adopting a higher major which would allow us to derive our first major as a valid conclusion. Ultimately, we have to decide beyond all reasons, as it were, what our values are. For at each stage where we adduce a reason, we have already to have accepted some value (enshrined in a major premiss) in virtue of which this reason is valid. But then our ultimate major premisses stand without reasons; they are the fruit of a pure choice.

Proposition (1) above, then, is immediately denied by non-naturalism. For in the highest major premisses 'good' is applied to commend without the claim that there are reasons for this commendation. And (2) also is rejected, for nothing can claim always to constitute a reason for calling something good. Whether it does or not depends on the decisions a man has made about his values, and it is not logically impossible that he should decide to consider human needs, wants, and purposes irrelevant to judgements about good and bad. A reason is always a reason-for-somebody, and has this status because of the values he has accepted.

The question at issue, then, is first whether 'good' can be used where there are no reasons, either evident or which can be cited for its application.[22] Consider the following case:[23] There are two segregationists who

[22] In what follows I am indebted to the arguments of Mrs. P. Foot, e.g. to her 'When is a principle a Moral Principle?' in *Aristotelian Society, Supplementary Vol.* xxviii (1954), and her 'Moral Arguments' in *Mind*, A.S.S.V. lxvii (1958), although I do not know whether she would agree with the conclusions I draw from them.

[23] Borrowed with changes from Hare's *Freedom and Reason* (Oxford: Clarendon Press, 1963).

disapprove of miscegenation. The first claims that mixing races will produce general unhappiness, a decline in the intellectual capacity and moral standards of the race, the abolition of a creative tension, and so on. The second, however, refuses to assent to any of these beliefs; the race will not deteriorate, men may even be happier; in any case they will be just as intelligent, moral, etc. But, he insists, miscegenation is bad. When challenged to produce some substitute reason for this judgement, he simply replies: 'I have no reasons; everyone is entitled, indeed has to accept some higher major premiss and stop the search for reasons somewhere. I have chosen to stop here, rather than seeking grounds in such fashionable quarters as human happiness, moral stature, etc.' Or supposing he looked at us in puzzlement and said: 'Reasons? why do you ask for reasons? Miscegenation is just bad.'

Now no one would question that the first segregationist was making the judgement 'miscegenation is bad.' But in the case of the second, a difficulty arises. This can be seen as soon as we ask the question: how can we tell whether the man is really making a judgement about the badness of miscegenation and not just, say, giving vent to a strongly felt repulsion, or a neurotic phobia against sexual relations between people of different races? Now it is essential to the notions 'good' and 'bad' as we use them in judgements that there be a distinction of this kind between these judgements and expressions of horror, delight, liking, disliking, and so on. It is essential that we be able, e.g. to correct a speaker by saying: 'What you want to say would be better put as "miscegenation horrifies me", or "miscegenation makes me go all creepy inside".' Because it is an essential part of the grammar of 'good' and 'bad' that they claim more than is claimed by expressions of delight, horror, etc. For we set aside someone's judgement that X is good when we say: 'All you are saying is that you *like* X.' To which the man can hotly reply: 'I do not like X any more than you do, but I recognize that it is good.'

There must therefore be criteria of distinction between these two cases if 'good' and 'bad' are to have the grammar that they have. But if we allow that our second segregationist is making the judgement 'miscegenation is bad', then no such distinction can be made. A judgement that I like something does not need grounds. That is, the absence of grounds does not undermine the claim 'I like X' (though other things, e.g. in my behaviour, may undermine it). But unless we adduce reasons for it (and moreover reasons of a certain kind as we shall see below) we cannot show that our claim that X is good says more than 'I like X.' Thus a man can only defend himself against the charge that all he is saying is that he likes X by giving his grounds. If there are no grounds, then judgement becomes indistinguishable from expression; which means that there are no more judgements of good and bad, since the distinction is essential to them as we have seen.

Those who believe in the fact-value dichotomy have naturally tried to avoid this conclusion; they have tried to distinguish the two cases by fastening on the use made of judgements of good and bad in commending, prescribing, expressing approval, and so on. Thus, no matter what a man's grounds, if any, we could know that he was making a judgement of good and bad by the fact that he was commending, prescribing, or committing himself to pursue the thing in question, or something of the kind. But this begs the question, for we can raise the query: what constitutes commending, or prescribing, or committing myself, or expressing approval, or whatever? How does one tell whether a man is doing one of these things as against just giving vent to his feelings?

If we can say that we can tell by what the man accepts as following from his stand—whether he accepts that he should strive to realize the thing in question—then the same problem breaks out afresh: how do we distinguish his accepting the proposition that he should seek the end and his just being hell-bent on seeking this end? Presumably, both our segregationists would agree that they should fight miscegenation, but this would still leave us just as puzzled and uncertain about the position of the second. Perhaps we can tell by whether they are willing to universalize their prescription? But here again we have no touchstone, for both segregationists would assent that everyone should seek racial purity, but the question would remain open whether this had a different meaning in the two cases. Perhaps the second one just means that he cannot stand interracial mating, whether done by himself or by anyone else. Similarly, a compulsive may keep his hands scrupulously clean and feel disgust at the uncleanliness of others, even plead with them to follow his example; but we still want to distinguish his case from one who had judged that cleanliness was good.

Can we fall back on behavioural criteria, meaning by 'behaviour' what a man does in contrast to how he thinks about what he does? But there is no reason why a man with a neurotic phobia against X should not do all the things which the man who judges X is bad does, i.e. avoiding X himself, trying to stop others from doing it, and so on.

Thus the non-naturalists would leave us with no criteria except what the man was willing to say. But then we would have no way of knowing whether the words were correctly applied or not, which is to say that they would have no meaning. All that we achieve by trying to mark the distinction by what follows from the judgement is that the same question which we raised about 'X is bad' as against 'X makes me shudder' can be raised about the complex 'X is bad, I/you should not do X' as against the complex 'X makes me shudder, please I/you do not do X.' We simply appeal from what the man is willing to say on the first question to what he is willing to say on the second. The distinction can only be properly drawn if we look to the reasons for the judgement, and this is why a judgement without reasons cannot be allowed, for it can no longer be distinguished from an expression of feeling.[24]

II. This analysis may sound plausible for 'miscegenation is bad', but how about 'anything conducive to human happiness is good'? What can we say here, if asked to give grounds for this affirmation? The answer is that we can say nothing, but also we need say nothing. For that something conduces to human happiness is already an adequate ground for judging it good—adequate, that is, in the absence of countervailing considerations. We come, then to the second point at issue, the claim that to say of something that it fulfils human needs, wants or purposes always constitutes a prima facie reason for calling it 'good'.

For in fact it is not just necessary that there be grounds for the affirmation if we are to take it at its face value as an attribution of good or bad, they must also be grounds of a certain kind. They must be grounds which relate in some intelligible way to what men need, desire, or seek after. This may become clearer if we look at another example. Suppose a man says: 'To make medical care available to more people is good'; suppose, then, that another man wishes to deny this. We could, of course, imagine reasons for this: world population will grow too fast, there are other more urgent claims on scarce resources, the goal can only be obtained by objectionable social policies, such as socialized medicine, and so on. The espousal of any of these would make the opposition to the above judgement intelligible, even it not acceptable, and make it clear

[24] We may use behaviour, of course, to judge which of the two constructions to put on a man's words, but the two are not distinguished by behavioural criteria alone, but also by what a man thinks and feels. It is possible, of course, to challenge a man's even sincere belief that he is judging of good and bad, and to disvalue it on the grounds that one holds it to be based largely on irrational prejudice or unavowed ambitions or fears. Thus our first segregationist may be judged as not too different from our second. For there is some evidence that segregationist ideas can at least partly be assimilated to neurotic phobias in their psychological roots. But this is just why many people look on the judgements of segregationists as self-deception and unconscious sham. 'Really', they are just expressions of horror. But this respects the logic of 'good' as we have outlined it: for it concludes that if the rational base is mere show, then the judgement is mere show. Segregationists, for their part, rarely are of the second type, and pay homage to the logic of 'good' by casting about for all sorts of specious reasons of the correct form.

that it was *this* judgement that was being denied, and not just, say, an emotional reaction which was being countered with another. If, however, our objector said nothing, and claimed to have nothing to say, his position would be unintelligible, as we have seen; or else we would construe his words as expressing some feeling of distaste or horror or sadness at the thought.

But supposing he was willing to give grounds for his position, but none of the above or their like, saying instead, for instance, 'There would be too many doctors', or 'Too many people would be dressed in white'? We would remain in doubt as to how to take his opposition, for we would be led to ask of his opposition to the increase of doctors, say, whether he was making a judgement concerning good and bad or simply expressing a dislike. And we would decide this question by looking at the grounds he adduced for *this* position. And if he claimed to have nothing to say, his position would be unintelligible in exactly the same way as if he had decided to remain silent at the outset and leave his original statement unsupported. 'What is this?' we would say, 'You are against an increase in medical services, because it would increase the number of doctors? But are you just expressing the feelings of dislike that doctors evoke in you or are you really trying to tell us that the increase is bad?' In the absence of any defence on his part, we would take the first interpretation.

It is clear that the problem would remain unsolved, if our opponent grounded his opposition to doctors on the fact that they generally wore dark suits, or washed their hands frequently. We might at this point suspect him of having us on. So that the length or elaboration of the reasoning has nothing to do with the question one way or another.

What would make his position intelligible, and intelligible as a judgement of good and bad, would be his telling some story about the evil influence doctors exercise on society, or the sinister plot they were hatching to take over and exploit the rest of mankind, or something of the kind. For this would relate the increase of doctors in an intelligible way to the interests, needs, or purposes of men. In the absence of such a relation, we remain in the dark, and are tempted to assume the worst.

What is meant by 'intelligibility' here is that we can understand the judgement as a use of 'good' and 'bad'. It is now widely agreed that a word gets its meaning from its place in the skein of discourse; we can give its meaning, for instance, by making clear its relations to other words. But this is not to say that we can give the meaning in a set of logical relations of equivalence, entailment, and so on, that an earlier positivism saw as the content of philosophical endeavour. For the relation to other terms may pass through a certain context. Thus, there is a relation between 'good' and commending, expressing approval, and so on. But this is not to say that we can construe 'X is good', for instance, as *meaning* 'I commend X.'[25] Rather, we can say that 'good' can be used for commending, that to apply the word involves being ready to commend in certain circumstances, for if you are not then you are shown to have been unserious in your application of it, and so on.[26]

The relation between 'good' and commending, expressing approval, persuading, and so on, has been stressed by non-naturalist theorists of ethics (though not always adequately understood, because of the narrow concentration on logical relations), but the term has another set of relations, to the grounds of its predication, as we have tried to show. These two aspects correspond respectively to what has often been called the evaluative, emotive, or prescriptive meaning on one hand (depending on the theory) and the 'descriptive' meaning on the other. For half a century an immense barrage of dialectical artillery has been trained on the so-called 'naturalistic fallacy' in an effort to prize 'good' loose from any set range of descriptive meanings. But this immense effort has been beside the point, for it has concentrated on the non-existence of logical relations between descriptive predicates and evaluative terms. But the fact that one cannot find equivalences, make valid deductive argument, and so on, may show nothing about the relation between a given concept and others.

Just as with the 'evaluative' meaning above, so with the 'descriptive' meaning: 'good' does not *mean* 'conducive to the fulfilment of human wants, needs, or purposes'; but its use is unintelligible outside of any relationship to wants, needs, and purposes, as we saw above. For if we abstract from this relation, then we cannot tell whether a man is using 'good' to make a judgement, or simply express some feeling; and it is an essential part of the meaning of the term that such a distinction can be made. The 'descriptive'[27] aspects of 'good's' meaning can rather be shown

[25] Cf. John Searle's 'Meaning and Speech Acts', *Philosophical Review*, lxxi (1962) 423–32.

[26] Thus, if I say, 'This is a good car', and then my friend comes along and says, 'Help me choose a car', I have to eat my words if I am not willing to commend the car to him, *unless* I can adduce some other countervailing factor such as price, my friend's proclivity to dangerous driving, or whatever. But this complex relationship cannot be expressed in an equivalence, e.g. 'This is a good car' entails 'If you are choosing a car, take this.'

[27] The terms 'descriptive meaning' and 'evaluative meaning' can be seen to be seriously misleading, as is evident from the discussion. For they carry the implication that the meaning is 'contained' in the word, and can be 'unpacked' in statements of logical equivalence. There is rather a descriptive aspect and an evaluative aspect of its role or use, which are, moreover, connected, for we cannot see whether a use of the term carries the evaluation force of 'good' unless we can also see whether it enters into the skein of relations which constitute the descriptive dimension of its meaning.

in this way: 'good' is used in evaluating, commending, persuading, and so on by a race of beings who are such that through their needs, desires, and so on, they are not indifferent to the various outcomes of the world-process. A race of inactive, godless angels, as really disinterested spectators, would have no use for it, could not make use of it, except in the context of cultural anthropology, just as human anthropologists use 'mana'. It is because 'good' has this use, and can only have meaning because there is this role to fill in human life, that it becomes unintelligible when abstracted from this role. Because its having a use arises from the fact that we are not indifferent, its use cannot be understood where we cannot see what there is to be not-indifferent about, as in the strange 'grounds' quoted by our imaginary opponent above. Moreover, its role is such that it is supposed to be predicated on general grounds, and not just according to the likes and dislikes or feelings of individuals. This distinction is essential since (among other things) the race concerned spends a great deal of effort achieving and maintaining consensus within larger or smaller groups, without which it would not survive. But where we cannot see what the grounds could be, we are tempted to go on treating the use of 'good' as an expression of partiality, only of the more trivial, individual kind.

We can thus see why, for instance, 'anything conducive to human happiness is good' does not need any further grounds to be adduced on its behalf. In human happiness, which by definition men desire, we have an adequate ground. This does not mean that all argument is foreclosed. We can try to show that men degenerate in various ways if they seek only happiness, and that certain things which also make men unhappy are necessary for their development. Or we can try to show that there is a higher and a lower happiness, that most men seek under this title only pleasure, and that this turns them away from genuine fulfilment; and so on. But unless we can bring up some countervailing consideration, we cannot deny a thesis of this kind. The fact that we can always bring up such countervailing considerations means that we can never say that 'good' *means* 'conducive to human happiness', as Moore saw. But that something is conducive to human happiness, or in general to the fulfilment of human needs, wants, and purposes, is a prima facie reason for calling it good, which stands unless countered.

Thus the non-neutrality of the theoretical findings of political science need not surprise us. In setting out a given framework, a theorist is also setting out the gamut of possible polities and policies. But a *political* framework cannot fail to contain some, even implicit, conception of human needs, wants, and purposes. The context of this conception will determine the value-slope of the gamut, unless we can introduce counter-vailing considerations. If these countervailing factors are motivationally marginal enough not to have too much relevance to political behaviour, then we can speak of the original valuation as being only overridden. For that part of the gamut of possibilities which we originally valued still has the property we attributed to it and thus remains valuable for us in one aspect, even if we have to give it low marks in another. For instance, we still will believe that having a peaceful polity is good, even if it results in bad art. But if the countervailing factor is significant for political behaviour, then it will lead us to revise our framework and hence our views about the gamut of possible polities and policies; this in turn will lead to new valuations. The basis of the old values will be undermined. Thus, if we believe that an absence of violence will lead to stagnation and foreign conquest or breakdown, then we change the gamut of possibility: the choice no longer lies between peace and violence, but between, say, con-trolled violence and greater uncontrolled violence. Peace ceases to figure on the register: it is not a good we can attain.

Of course, the countervailing factor may not revise our gamut of choices so dramatically. It may simply show that the values of our origi-nally preferred regime cannot be integrally fulfilled or that they will be under threat from a previously unsuspected quarter, or that they will be attended with dangers or disadvantages or disvalues not previously taken into account, so that we have to make a choice as in the peace-versus-good-art case above. Thus not all alterations of the framework will undermine the original values. But we can see that the converse does hold, and all undermining will involve a change in the framework. For if we leave the original framework standing, then the values of its preferred regime will remain as fully realizable goods, even if they are attended with certain evils which force on us a difficult choice, such as that between peace and good art, or progress and psychic harmony, or whatever.

In this sense we can say that a given explanatory framework secretes a notion of good, and a set of valuations, which cannot be done away with—though they can be overridden—unless we do away with the frame-work. Of course because the values can be overridden, we can only say that the framework tends to support them, not that it establishes their validity. But this is enough to show that the neutrality of the findings of political science is not what it was thought to be. For establishing a given framework restricts the range of value positions which can be defensibly adopted. For in the light of the framework certain goods can be accepted as such without further argument, whereas other rival ones cannot be adopted without adducing overriding considerations. The framework can be said to distribute the onus of argument in a certain way. It is thus not neutral.

The only way to avoid this while doing political science would be to stick to the narrow-gauge discoveries which, just because they are, taken alone, compatible with a great number of political frameworks, can bathe in an atmosphere of value neutrality. That Catholics in Detroit tend to vote Democrat can consort with almost anyone's conceptual scheme, and thus with almost anyone's set of political values. But to the extent that political science cannot dispense with theory, with the search for a framework, to that extent it cannot stop developing normative theory.

Nor need this have the vicious results usually attributed to it. There is nothing to stop us making the greatest attempts to avoid bias and achieve objectivity. Of course, it is hard, almost impossible, and precisely because our values are also at stake. But it helps, rather than hinders, the cause to be aware of this.

X

IS A SCIENCE OF COMPARATIVE POLITICS POSSIBLE?

ALASDAIR MACINTYRE

THERE WAS ONCE a man who aspired to be the author of the general theory of holes. When asked 'What kind of hole—holes dug by children in the sand for amusement, holes dug by gardeners to plant lettuce seedlings, tank traps, holes made by roadmakers?' he would reply indignantly that he wished for a *general* theory that would explain all of these. He rejected *ab initio* the—as he saw it—pathetically common-sense view that of the digging of different kinds of holes there are quite different kinds of explanations to be given; why then he would ask do we have the concept of a hole? Lacking the explanations to which he originally aspired, he then fell to discovering statistically significant correlations; he found for example that there is a correlation between the aggregate hole-digging achievement of a society as measured, or at least one day to be measured, by econometric techniques, and its degree of technological development. The United States surpasses both Paraguay and Upper Volta in hole-digging. He also discovered that war accelerates hole-digging; there are more holes in Vietnam than there were. These observations, he would always insist, were neutral and value-free. This man's achievement has passed totally unnoticed except by me. Had he however turned his talents to political science, had he concerned himself not with holes, but with modernization, urbanization, or violence, I find it difficult to believe that he might not have achieved high office in the APSA.

1

The ultimate aim of this paper is constructive; the scepticism which infects so much of my argument is a means and not an end. I do not want to show that there *cannot* be a general science of political action, but only to indicate certain obstacles that stand in the way of the founding of such a science and to suggest that the present practice of so-called political science

From *Against the Self-Images of the Age* (London: Duckworth; New York: Schocken Books, 1971), pp. 260–79. Copyright © 1971 by Alasdair MacIntyre. Reprinted by permission of the author and publishers.

is unlikely to overcome these obstacles. In writing more specifically of *comparative* political science I do not wish to suggest that there could be any other sort of political science; this the APSA recognized when it merged what was its section devoted to comparative politics into the general body. It is with the claim to be using legitimate *comparative* methods which could enable us to advance and to test genuine law-like *cross-cultural* generalizations that I shall initially be concerned. I shall not be concerned to question the possibility of genuine and relevant comparison and even of cross-cultural comparison for other purposes: to exhibit the march of the *Weltgeist* through history, for instance, or to draw moral lessons about the respective benefits of barbarism and civilization. These may or may not be reputable activities; I shall not argue for or against them here. I shall be solely interested in the project of a political *science*, of the formulation of cross-cultural, law-like causal generalizations which may in turn be explained by theories, as the generalizations of Boyle's Law and Dalton's Law are explained by the kinetic theory of gases; all that I say about the problem of comparability must be understood in this particular context. Moreover, my scepticism about any alleged parallel between theorizing about politics and theorizing about gases will not initially be founded on the consideration of the character of human action in general. I shall not argue, for example, that human actions cannot have causes, not just or even mainly because I believe that this proposition is false, but because I believe that, even if its falsity is agreed, we still have substantial grounds for scepticism about comparative political science. My method of proceeding in the first part of my argument will be as follows: I shall examine in turn the claim to have formulated law-like generalizations about political attitudes, about political institutions and practices, and about the discharge of political functions. I shall then in the second part of my argument suggest an alternative strategy to that now customarily employed, although the change in strategy will turn out also to involve change in aim.

2

The study of political culture, of political attitudes, as it has been developed, seems to rest upon the assumption that it is possible to identify political attitudes independently of political institutions and practices. There are at least two reasons for thinking this assumption false. The first derives from Wittgenstein, who pointed out that we identify and define attitudes in terms of the objects toward which they are directed, and not vice versa. Our understanding of the concept of fear depends upon our understanding of the concepts of harm and danger and not vice versa. Our understanding of the concept of an aesthetic attitude depends upon our understanding of the concept of a work of art. It follows that an ability to identify a set of attitudes in one culture as political, and a set of attitudes in some second culture as political, with a view to comparing them must depend upon our having already identified as political in both cultures a set of institutions and practices toward which these attitudes are directed. In other words, the ability to construct comparative generalizations about attitudes depends on our already having solved the problem of how to construct comparative generalizations about institutions and practices. The notion of political culture is secondary to and parasitic upon the notion of political practice.

It follows that a necessary condition of a comparative investigation of political cultures is that the argument about the comparability of political institutions should have a certain outcome; but this is only a necessary and not a sufficient condition. It is also necessary if political attitudes are to be the subject of comparative inquiry that other attitudes shall be susceptible of comparison of a certain kind. I can explain what I mean by this by citing an example from *The Civic Culture* (Princeton: Princeton University Press, 1963) (Chapter IV, pp. 102–5) where Almond and Verba argue that Italians are less committed to and identified with the actions of their government than are Germans or Englishmen, offering as evidence the fact that the Italian respondents, as compared with the English and German respondents to their survey, placed such actions very low on a list of items to which they had been asked to give a rank order in terms of the amount of pride they took in them. At no point do Almond and Verba pause to ask whether the concept of pride is the same in the three different national cultures, that is, to ask whether the different respondents had after all been asked the same question. But in fact the concept of pride (' . . si sente piu' orgoglioso . . ') in Italy is not the same as that of pride in England. The notion of taking pride in Italian culture is still inexorably linked, especially in the south but also in the north, to the notion of honour. What one takes pride in is what touches on one's honour. If asked to list the subjects which touched their honour, many Italians would spontaneously place the chastity of their immediate female relatives high on the list—a connection that it would occur to very few Englishmen to make. These notions of pride and honour partially specify and are partially specified by a notion of the family itself importantly, if imperfectly, embodied in the actualities of Italian family life. Hence we cannot hope to compare an Italian's attitude to his government's acts with an Englishman's in respect of the pride each takes; any comparison would have to begin from the different range of virtues and emotions incorporated in the different social institutions. Once again the project of comparing attitudes independently of institutions and practices encounters difficulties. These particular difficulties suggest that a key question is: what are the units in each culture which are compared to be? To this question I shall of course return; but let me note that the difficulty which I have exemplified in the preceding argument is contingent on Almond and Verba's particular procedures. It does not arise from the project of comparison as such. For the difficulty which arises over any comparison between English and German culture on the one hand, and Italian on the other, from relying on the in fact false assumption that these cultures agree in their concept of pride would not arise in the same way if Italian attitudes were to be compared with Greek, for example. Not that there would not be other and perhaps more subtle pitfalls, but these would not arise merely because concepts of pride and honour are not shared.

We can now pose our problem in the following way: we wish to find identifiable units in different societies and cultures about which we may construct true causal generalizations. Political attitudes, for the two reasons I have given, are implausible candidates; what about political institutions and practices? The first point to be made here is that in turning to the discussion of political institutions and practices we have not left behind the topic of political attitudes. For attitudes to and beliefs about institutions and practices may sometimes be purely external phenomena; that is, the institution or the practice is what it is and does what it does independently of what certain people think and feel about it. But it is an obvious truism that no institution or practice is what it is, or does what it does, independently of what anyone whatsoever thinks or feels about it. For institutions and practices are always partially, even if to differing degrees, constituted by what certain people think and feel about them.

Consider the example of a currency system: a given type of piece of paper or of metal has the value that it has not only because it has been issued by a duly constituted authority, but because it is accepted as having that value by the members of a particular currency-using population. When this condition is not generally satisfied, as in Germany and Austria in 1923, the currency ceases to have value, and thus ceases to be currency. So also with an army: an officer has the authority that he has not only because his commission has been issued by a duly constituted authority, but because he is accepted as having that status by the men serving under him. When this condition is not generally satisfied, as in Russia in 1917, an officer ceases to have authority, and thus ceases to be an officer. Since such beliefs about social institutions are partially constitutive of social institutions, it is impossible to identify the institution except in terms of the beliefs of those who engage in its practices. This fact is ignored in general by those who wish to define political science as the study of political *behaviour*, with a view to thereby providing a public, neutral subject-matter for scientific inquiry. But if we identify behaviour except in terms of the intentions and therefore of the beliefs of the agents we shall risk describing what they are doing as what we would be doing if we went through that series of movements or something like it rather than what they are actually doing. No do we avoid this difficulty merely by finding *some* description of the behaviour in question which both the agents themselves and the political scientist would accept. For clearly both agents and political scientist might apply the description 'voting behaviour' to what they do, but yet have a quite different understanding of what it is to vote. But now what bearing does all this have upon the project of comparing political institutions and practices?

3

I take it that if the generalizations which political scientists construct are to be part of a science, then among the conditions which must be satisfied is this: that we shall be able to distinguish between genuine law-like generalizations and mere *de facto* generalizations which hold only of the instances so far observed. I understand by this distinction, as many others have understood by it, the difference between a generalization the assertion of which commits one to the assertion of a set of corresponding counter-factual conditionals and a generalization which does not so commit one. In the natural sciences the ground for treating a generalization as a law is generally not merely that as a matter of fact no plausible counter-examples have yet been produced. It is also normally required that it be supported by a body of theory. But what then of these generalizations which we wish to assert as genuine law-like generalizations before we have any well-established theory? What about the generalizations of Kepler or of Galileo before Newton formulated his laws? What about Boyle's Law or Dalton's Law before the establishment of the kinetic theory? At this point the problems of confirmation theory become real.

The particular finding of confirmation theory that is relevant is that the degree to which a positive instance does genuinely confirm a generalization is in part a matter of the kind of environment in which it is found. For the greater the extent of the radically different environments in which confirmatory instances of a generalization are found, the less likely it is that the generalization is only confirmed in certain contingent environmental circumstances. Now it is a matter of contingent fact that nature is so structured that this condition is normally realizable. For nature could have been otherwise. If black ravens on being taken into laboratories for pigmentation tests, or if black ravens on being observed in the Arctic—in the course of our seeking confirmation or otherwise of the generalization that all ravens are black—promptly turned into philosophers of science or clouds of dust, generalizations about ravenly nigritude could not be as well founded as they are. But in fact the character of social life is such that in some respects it resembles this imaginary nature rather than nature as it—fortunately for natural scientists—is.

Consider for example the alleged generalization that in two-party electoral systems the two parties will tend to move together in their policies and the alleged explanation for this generalization, that this is because neither party can hope to win those voters attracted by the furthest opposed wing of the other party, but only those nearest to it. Hence where, for example, the parties and their wings can be placed on a Left-Right dimension, each party tends to move its policies towards the centre, having no hope of winning votes from the extreme Right or Left. Now consider two different kinds of attempts to provide counter-examples to this generalization. An example of the first would be Greece before the *coup d'état* of the colonels. This seems to be a straightforward refutation of the generalization, even if we remember that a single counter-example in the natural sciences is never adequate to refute a well-established theory or a generalization with a huge weight of evidence supporting it, such as the generalization that all solids except bismuth, cast-iron, ice, and type metal expand when heated. For here we have nothing like a well-supported theory or generalization, it is rather as if the seventh raven we were to come across was coloured magenta. Now consider a quite different kind of attempt to provide a counter-example.

Suppose that someone were to point to the rival parties in Sierra Leone immediately before the army seized power there, and to offer them as a counter-example. We ought at once to remember what Ruth Schachter wrote of African mass parties: 'They and their cultural affiliates were interested in everything from the cradle to the grave—in birth, initiation, religion, marriage, divorce, dancing, song, plays, feuds, debts, land, migration, death, public order—and not only electoral success.' At once the question cannot but be framed: 'Why do we think of these as parties, rather than as, say, churches?' The answer, that they have some of the marks of American political parties, and that they call themselves parties, does nothing to show that in fact the meaning of 'party' is not radically changed when the cultural context is radically changed, or that even if it is not changed the description has not become inapplicable. The intentions, the beliefs, the concepts which inform the practices of African mass parties provide so different a context that there can be no question of transporting the phenomena of party to this context in order to provide a suitably different environment for testing our generalization. Where the environment and where the culture is radically different the phenomenon is viewed so differently by those who participate in it that it is an entirely different phenomenon. In just this respect does society differ from nature. That is to say, the provision of an environment sufficiently different to make the search for counter-examples interesting will normally be the provision of an environment where we cannot hope or expect to find examples of the original phenomenon and therefore cannot hope to find counter-examples.

Note that my thesis is not that to transplant a phenomenon such as party is to subject it to causal influences which transform it. That is doubtless true. But the difficulty of studying political parties in alien social environments to test a generalization constructed about political parties in familiar social environments is not like the difficulty of studying viruses: that their own causal properties and/or those of the environment cause them to mutate too rapidly and too often. If this were the type of difficulty that we encountered in formulating cross-cultural generalizations about politics, then we might well ask if we could not insulate the object of study in its new environment from the disturbing causal influences at work. To ask this would be to mistake my point which is not about causal interference with the phenomenon of party, but with the absence of the same concept of party, or perhaps of any concept of party, as we understand it, in the alien culture.

Let me now consider a possible objection to this thesis which would base itself upon my choice of examples. A quite different choice of examples might provide us with more plausible candidates for cross-cultural generalization. Consider the alleged (and quite possibly false) generalization that in the government of cities, if a single non-transferable vote for single members is the method of election, then there will be over a certain time-span a tendency for a two-party system to flourish. This seems to hold in the United States. But it might hold in other alien environments, even environments of an exotic kind, where we could identify the system as two-party, even if unclear in what sense the parties were parties. But this is surely therefore an example of at least a possible cross-cultural comparison which provides us with a law-like generalization and is therefore lethal to my entire thesis. Let me at once concede that I take this generalization to be law-like in that it does indeed entail counter-factual conditionals, and let me further concede that the counter-factuals in question might be true. But I do not concede that it injures my thesis. Why not?

The reason for not conceding that this example, if true, would injure my thesis is intimately connected with the fact that I should not be extremely surprised if the generalization in question did turn out to be true of cities outside North America as well as in North America. For what could make the generalization true, if true, is that voters prefer in general not to waste their votes in voting on matters that concern the administration of their daily lives; and it requires only a minimal and a very untheoretical understanding of the electoral system produced by such a voting procedure to understand that in the majority of cases votes for a third party will be wasted. The considerations from which we can deduce *this* particular generalization are thus concerned with human rationality in general; they do not have any specific connection with politics and they do not belong to political science, but to our general understanding of rationality. This will be true of all generalizations which concern the formal structures of human argument, even if they appear in political clothing, furnishing us with explanations of particular political choices and actions. So it must be, for example, with all applications of the theory of games to politics.

My thesis about the legitimacy or otherwise of the project of accumulating a stock of cross-cultural generalizations about political behaviour to furnish the empirical foundation for a political science, as I have developed it so far, can now be stated distinctively: *either* such generalizations about institutions will necessarily lack the kind of confirmation they require *or* they will be consequences of true generalizations about human rationality and not part of a specifically political science.

To complete this part of my argument I must now make three further observations. The first is that my statement of the difficulties in constructing true and warranted cross-cultural generalizations about political institutions is obviously akin to the arguments which some anthropologists —notably Edmund Leach and Walter Goldschmidt—have developed about cross-cultural generalizations in their discipline. But Goldschmidt has then argued that it is not institutions, but functions, or rather institutions only as serving certain functions, which we ought to aspire to compare; and this contention has already been advanced by some political scientists. We are, that is to say, to begin by identifying the same function in different societies and then to inquire how quite different institutions have this same effect; for I take it that to say that X performs, serves, or discharges a given function always entails that X is the cause of a particular effect, even if this does not exhaust the meaning of the statement in which function was ascribed. It is certainly not a final objection to this project that most political scientists who have tried to specify the functions in question have produced nothing but statements about institutions and their effects in which the word 'function' may appear, but could be replaced not only without loss, but with gain, 'Wherever the political party has emerged, it appears to perform some common functions in a wide variety of political systems . . . the organization called the party is expected to organize public opinion and to communicate demands to the centre of governmental power and decision . . . the party must articulate to its followers the concept and meaning of the broader community . . . the party is likely to be involved in political recruitment . . . These similarities of function . . . suggest that the political party emerges when the activities of a political system reach a certain degree of complexity, or whenever the notion of political power comes to include the idea that the mass public must participate or be controlled.'[1] In a passage like this, the notion of function can be replaced entirely by either the notion of effect or the notion of purpose. When we so replace it, we notice also that the transition from premise to tentative conclusion requires no reliance on any factual generalizations anyway; it is merely a matter of drawing out the consequences of definition. But even if in the writing of political scientists as sophisticated as LaPalombara and Weiner the function of the use of 'function' is unclear, it does not follow that this has to be so. But the condition of its not being so is that we should have some criteria for identifying the functions served by political institutions which is other than, and independent of, the aims and purposes of political agents and the effects of political institutions. The provision of such a criterion would require the identification of a system, using the word 'system' precisely, so that concepts of feedback and equilibrium are applicable on the basis of quantitative data which will provide values for variables in differential equations. I scarcely need stress the remoteness of this goal from the present state of all political science; if we match the requirements that have to be satisfied to identify such a system—which would involve, for example, being able to distinguish between change that is part of the movement of items through the system, change that is itself part of the structuring of the system, and change that is the system decaying by providing ways of measuring rates of change for all three—then a work like David Easton's *A Systems Analysis of Political Life* looks like a mad, millenarian dream. I therefore take it that any attempt to answer my argument by suggesting that cross-cultural generalizations about institutions may be provided by means of a prior account in terms of functions is bound to fail.

[1] J. LaPalombara and M. Weiner, eds., *Political Parties and Political Development* (Princeton, N.J.: Princeton University Press, 1966).

My second observation is that my argument does not imply any under-valuation of the importance of the work done by political scientists in establishing both the facts about particular institutions and the very limited generalizations they do establish. That the conditions under which these generalizations hold necessarily remain unclear to us for the kind of reason that I have given does not mean that we do not need the best that we can get in this case, which is what they give us; only this kind of accumulation of data in no way leads toward the construction of a science. I shall later suggest an alternative context in which these empirical labours could perhaps be viewed more constructively. For the moment I note that it is Machiavelli who ought to be regarded as the patron saint of political studies and not Hobbes, and for this reason: Hobbes believed—as presumably Almond and LaPalombara and Easton (although Easton, in ways that I do not entirely understand, tried to distinguish his enterprise from that of Hobbes) believe—that the fortuitous, the surprising, the unpredicted, arise in politics only because our knowledge of political motions is less adequate than our knowledge of planetary motions. Given time, labour, and foundation grants—the contemporary version of royal patronage—an unpredicted revolution—but for the sheer complexity of human affairs—ought to be as disgraceful to political scientists as an unpredicted eclipse to astronomers. But Machiavelli realized that in political life *fortuna*, the bitch goddess of unpredictability, has never been dethroned. To any stock of maxims derived from empirically founded generalizations the student of politics must always add one more: 'And do not be surprised if in the event things turn out otherwise.' The need to include this maxim follows from my argument, just as it follows from Machiavelli's.

My third observation is that in the history of political theory we have more than once been here before, and notably in the dispute between James Mill and Macaulay. James Mill argued, although in the interests of a quite different conclusion, even more that we cannot find reliable empirical generalizations about political behaviour: 'Absolute monarchy under Neros and Caligulas . . . is the scourge of human nature. On the other side, the public of Denmark . . . under their absolute monarch are as well governed as any people in Europe . . . the surface of history affords, there-fore, no certain principles of decision.' Mill then proceeded to argue from this that we ought to turn instead to the type of psychology favoured by the utilitarians for our explanations, that there is no specifically political science. Against him Macaulay argued that the empirical facts about government *do* yield genuine law-like generalizations, not least generalizations of a kind which enable us to predict future actions with great confidence. And it is clear that this practical use of law-like generalizations provides Macaulay with a crucial motive. The claim to technical expertise on the part of the political scientist is closely bound up with the defence of the possibility of formulating law-like generalizations. If the latter fails, the former is gravely impaired. When in our time on the basis of *his* generalizations Lipset predicts totalitarian horrors as the outcome of widespread political participation, he turns out to be the true heir of Macaulay who, on the basis of *his* generalizations, predicted cultural ruin if 'the great number' were allowed to participate in government; 'they will commit waste of every sort in the estate of mankind, and transmit it to posterity impoverished and desolate', so that 'in two or three hundred years, a few lean and half naked fishermen may divide with owls and foxes the ruins of the greatest of European cities . . . ' In both Macaulay and Lipset the claims of political science are closely linked to a claim about the political status of the political scientist, to a claim about the possession of political expertise, which entitles the political scientist to advise government. This claim too demands inquiry; but a prerequisite for such inquiry is a further development of my central argument.

4

My doubts about identifying institutions in different cultures as 'the same' and therefore as interestingly different are of course compatible with a recognition of the massive fact that the same actions are regularly performed in quite different cultures. One class of such actions are those that derive from implicit imitation. It is of course not necessarily or always the case that if one person imitates another he does what the other does. Indeed it is sometimes the condition of successful imitation that he who imitates shall not do what the other does precisely in order to seem to do what the other does. But when the intention to perform the same action as another *is* present, we always have an intelligible question as to why, if the corresponding action or its consequences or both are not the same as those produced by the agent imitated, they are not so. Of course it may be that even a particular intention to perform certain actions cannot be intelligibly embodied in some cultures; *Don Quixote* is the classical example. But we do have clear cases where the same intention is embodied in two different cultures, such intentions as to apply Roman Law or the Code Napoléon, or to bring about some particular course of economic development. What we shall achieve if we study the projects springing from such intentions are two or more histories of these projects, and it is only after writing these histories that we shall be able to compare the different outcomes of the same intention. We shall not, that is to say, begin by collecting data in the hope of formulating causal generalizations; we shall begin by looking at cases where a will to achieve the same end was realized with greater or lesser success in different cultural contexts.

There is of course a notable formula which seems to prescribe this approach: 'Men make their own history, but they do not make it just as they please. They do not make it under circumstances chosen by themselves, but under circumstances directly encountered, given and transmitted from the past.' But when Marx wrote these words he did not discriminate what was implied by this approach from a search for causal generalizations, and he does not do so at least in part because he treats what he calls the circumstances of action only as a causally effective and limiting enivronment and not in addition, or rather primarily, as a context of meaning-conferring symbols and rules. So Marx speaks of 'the burden of history' in the very next sentence and Engels speaks of history as a 'series of parallelograms of forces', and it is this model of Engels which creates for Plekhanov the problem of the role of the individual in history (since an individual can be no more than a point at which some force operates). But the question with which Marx began in the *Eighteenth Brumaire* does not require an answer in terms of causal generalizations and parallelograms of forces. For what Marx asks then is why, when someone aspires to perform the same actions as a predecessor in some earlier cultural period—as the English Puritans aspired to be Old Testament Israelites or the French Revolutinary Roman republicans or Louis Napoléon to do the deeds of Napoleon I—the actions should be so different. A full answer to Marx's question would provide a genuine starting-point for historical comparison, but such an answer could only be provided by first writing a history of each of these episodes.

I therefore take it that if we wish to have a science of comparative politics, one first step is the writing of a series of comparative histories; that comparative history is a more fundamental discipline than comparative politics. But then the crucial question arises: what can we legitimately expect the study of comparative history to yield? And one of the best ways of answering this question is to ask what the study of comparative history has in fact yielded. Consider for example Isaac Deutscher's thesis about revolutions. Deutscher asserted that in the English, French, and Russian revolutions the same 'broad scheme of revolutionary development' could be discerned. This scheme involves three stages: a first stage in which 'popular energy, impatience, anger and hope' burst out, and 'the party that gives the fullest expression to the popular mood outdoes its rivals, gains the confidence of the masses and rises to power'; a second stage in which during the war on behalf of the revolution the leaders of the revolutionary party and the people are so well in accord that the leaders 'are willing and even eager to submit their policies to open debate and to accept the popular verdict'; and a third stage in which weariness and ruthlessness divide party and people, so that the revolutionary party cannot listen to, but must indeed suppress the voice of the people, thus in consequence splitting itself between the holders of revolutionary power and the caretakers of the purity of revolutionary doctrine. This pattern holds of 'any party of the revolution, whether it be called Independent, Jacobin or Bolshevik'.

That there are such patterns revealed by the rare studies of comparative history that we already possess and that there will be more is clear. But how are we to understand them? When we assert the recurrence of such a pattern, what are we asserting? Deutscher himself, following Engels and Plekhanov, understood this pattern of revolutionary behaviour deterministically. Hence followed his very different assessment of Trotsky's relation to Stalin from Trotsky's own non-deterministic assessment of that relationship. Deutscher treats each stage, as he specified it, as satisfying both a necessary and a sufficient condition for the occurrence of the next stage, as he specified it; hence he takes it that Trotsky, the caretaker of revolutionary purity, could not but have failed to hold power, since maintaining the revolutionary doctrine and holding power are causally incompatible.

The evaluation of Deutscher's specific contentions about revolution is not relevant to my present argument; but the contention Deutscher almost takes for granted, namely that the discernment of recurring patterns in history has as its end-product the formulation of law-like generalizations, is precisely what I want to question. For when I suggested that the study of comparative politics would certainly benefit from, and perhaps require, a prior writing of comparative history, I did not intend to imply that what comparative history will provide us with is merely a stock of more adequate materials for the construction of these cross-cultural, law-like generalizations which the present methods of orthodox political science aspire to but in fact fail to provide; that the comparative history is not so much an alternative, as merely a necessary prelude to proceeding as before. What I want to suggest is that it is characteristic of the causal knowledge which history does provide us with that the antecedent conditions in terms of which we explain historical outcomes are sometimes necessary conditions for the occurrence of some specific outcome, but are never sufficient. If this is so, then the patterns which we discern in comparative history will always be *de facto* guides yielding Machiavellian maxims, rather than Hobbesian laws. But is it so? Is comparative political science, even when based on comparative history, precluded from formulating law-like generalizations?

To cast light on this, compare the situation of the political scientist with that of the political agent. The political agent confronts a situation in which he wishes to produce certain outcomes. He wishes, for example, to maintain two-party democracy in a new state, or he wishes to overthrow that state by revolutionary action. The situation he confronts consists of other political agents: party politicians, soldiers, trade union leaders, trade union rank and file, and so on. Some of each of these groups are keen readers of such works as *Political Man, Voting, Permanent Revolution*, and so on. Each of these derives certain inductively grounded maxims from these works; in an earlier age the maxims had different sources—Livy, Plutarch, what Napoleon did, or political folk wisdom—but the situation was essentially the same. The difficulty in applying the maxims is that the factors in the situation confronting the agent include the beliefs of every other agent about what each agent other than himself will do in applying the maxims, including the beliefs of every agent about what every other agent believes about his beliefs. 'I know you know I know you know I know' is a crucial piece of poetic wisdom for political as well as for sexual behaviour. The perception of any pattern or regularity in the behaviour of the other actors, or in the behaviour characteristic of this particular type of situation, is what particularly invites deviation from the pattern. 'They all knew what Napoleon would have done', said Grant of the Union generals. 'The trouble was that the rebel generals didn't know about Napoleon.'

The key part that beliefs play in defining political situations, and the fact that beliefs are always liable to be altered by reflection upon the situation, including reflection about the beliefs of other agents, has a crucial consequence: that we cannot ever identify a determinate set of factors which constitute the initial conditions for the production of some outcome in conformity with a law-like regularity. To claim that we could identify such regularities and such sets of factors would be to claim that we can understand what occurs in politics independently of a knowledge of the beliefs of the agents, for it would be to claim that the beliefs do not play a causal role in political outcomes.

It makes no difference at this point if the alleged law-like regularity is framed in probabilistic terms: when the alleged probability of an outcome is 0.7, the prediction is as vulnerable to reflection by agents as when the alleged probability of an outcome is 1. The conclusion that political agents are bound to be prone to error in their predictions of what other agents will do, and hence of political outcomes, has one important merit other than that of following validly from my premises: it would appear to be true. Nor is its truth incompatible with the fact that some political agents produce more correct predictions than others. It would perhaps be cynical to explain this latter fact by pointing out that given an entirely random relationship between prediction and outcome in a sufficiently large population of predictors, predictions, and outcomes, certain predictors would consistently predict correctly, just as certain predictors would consistently predict incorrectly. But without resorting to either cynicism or the theorems of statistics one can point out that success at prediction in practical affairs, including political affairs, can never be embodied into a method which can be taught, precisely because the maxims relied upon are open-textured and open-ended, and the sense of when which maxim is relevant cannot itself be unpacked into a set of maxims.

It may be asked: when I conclude that political agents cannot find law-like generalizations to aid them in their actions (other of course than those crucial and rock-like law-like generalizations of the physical senses which are available to us all, such that a bullet accelerates in the way that all moving bodies do, and that when a man's skull is crushed by an ice pick he dies), what is the force of 'cannot'? Do I mean only that we have at the moment no technique for identifying determinate sets of antecedent conditions of the relevent kind, but that such a technique might well be discovered? Or do I mean that there is some confusion in the nature of such a technique? Am I saying what the limits of inquiry are *as of now*, or what the limits *as such* are?

I am strongly inclined to say that at the moment we have no grounds for answering this question as it stands in either way. We lack even the most minimal theoretical background against which to raise such questions. To say this is not to ignore the empirical work done by both psychologists and sociologists on such topics as prejudice, cognitive dissonance, and the relation of roles to beliefs; it is to say that the results of empirical studies in this field (which are not always obviously consistent with each other) are exceptionally difficult to interpret and to assess, in part just for the type of reason that I have given.

What I have been arguing in this latter part of my essay is that the political agent cannot rely on law-governed regularities in his activities. But just those premises, which entail that conclusion, entail that the political scientist is in no better position in this respect than the political agent. The political scientist may claim to know more (quantitatively, as it were) than many political agents; but his knowledge is not of a different kind, and there seems no reason to believe that the chances that he will be able to apply the inductively grounded maxims which he derives from his studies in the course of political action successfully are any higher than they are for any other political agent.

If this is so, then the case for Machiavelli against Hobbes rests not merely on the impossibility of testing these law-like generalizations to which a true science of comparative politics would have to aspire; it derives also from the nature of the subject-matter of political science. For the most that any study of comparative politics based upon comparative history can hope to supply us with in the foreseeable future is *de facto* generalizations about what has been an obstacle to or has facilitated certain types of course of action. There is available for the formulation of this type of generalization no vocabulary for political scientists which is essentially more sophisticated than the vocabulary of political agents themselves. And the advice given by political scientists turns out to be simply the advice given by a certain genre of political agent, agents as partial, as socially conditioned, as creative, and as wayward as any others.

To this the defender of orthodox political science might well feel bound to reply as follows. *Qua* scientist, he may claim, he has a vocabulary that is not available to political agents; and he has this neutrality precisely because he restricts himself to the facts and to theorizing about them in an uncommitted way. Your redefinition of the tasks of political studies would, he might complain, destroy this neutrality. For the model of explanation implicit in your view of the relation of comparative history to comparative politics is as follows: men in two different cultures seek to implement the same intention in action. Either their actions or the consequences of their actions may differ. If they do, by examining what was present in the one case and absent in the other, you make inferences as to what the obstacles or diversions were in either or both cases. You then explain in terms of the presence or absence of these obstacles or diversions the success or failure of the respective projects. But this is in fact a model of explanation familiar in our everyday understanding of action; and when we apply it in everyday life we cite as explanations for the success or failure of men's projects, not merely the external obstacles which they faced or the lack of such obstacles, but such factors as their reasonableness or unreasonableness, their courage or their weakness, their willingness or reluctance to commit injustice, and so on. That is to say, your model of explanation is that used by ordinary men in their political and other actions to assess themselves and each other and it is of the essence of this mode of explanation that we may cite in explanation evaluations both of intelligence and of moral character. The strength of orthodox comparative political science, this objector will go on, is that it has broken decisively with the evaluative commitments of the world of action. Just because it aspires to study these scientifically, it cannot share them. It must instead be objective in a sense that requires that it be neutral and value-free.

I accept from this objection the characterization of my own standpoint. It would certainly be an open empirical question whether it ever was in fact true that this or that project failed because of the unreasonableness or the injustice of the agents; but *a priori* nothing could rule out the possibility of these being true and relevant explanations. Political science would become in a true sense a moral science. But I do not take this to be in any way an objection. For what is the alternative, as it is exemplified in comparative political science as it is now usually practised?

The type of comparative political science of which I have been highly critical is indeed generally and deeply committed to the view that its inquiries and explanations are indeed value-free. This results in an attempt to allow evaluative expressions into political life only in intentional contexts, in oratio obliqua, or in quotation marks. Hence, as John Schaar has pointed out,[1] such notions as those of legitimacy are in fact defined in terms of belief. Lipset says that 'Legitimacy involves the capacity of the system to engender and maintain the belief that the existing political institutions are the most appropriate ones for the society' (*Political Man*, p. 77) and Robert Bierstedt writes that 'In the tradition of Weber, legitimacy has been defined as the degree to which institutions are valued for themselves and considered right and proper.'[2] These definitions are clearly mistaken in any case; not only would there by no contradiction in holding that a government was entirely legitimate, but that its institutions were morally ill suited to a particular society, but in a society where this latter was widely believed, it would not follow either that the government was, or that it was considered, illegitimate. But it is not mere definitional ineptitude that I am concerned with here. Suppose that we define, as Lipset and the Weberian tradition according to Bierstedt do, evaluation in terms so that where 'X' is an evaluative expression it is always defined so that 'A is X' is equivalent in meaning to an expression of the form 'A' is believed by some class of persons to be Y' where 'Y' is another evaluative expression. Suppose further that, as both Lipset and some Weberians do, we try to explain legitimacy in terms of stability or vice versa. What is clear is that the original definitional move has pre-empted on a crucial causal and explanatory question: is it only beliefs about what is legitimate, what is appropriate, what is right which can be causally effective, or can the legitimacy of an institution, the appropriateness of an institution or an

<hr/>

[2] 'Legitimacy in the Modern State', in Green and Levison (eds.), *Power and Community*, (New York: Random House, 1970).

[3] 'Legitimacy', in *Dictionary of Social Sciences* (London: Tavistock, 1964), p. 386.

action, or the rightness or the justice of an action, themselves be causally effective? The definitional move of Lipset and Bierstedt removes *a priori* the possibility of a certain class of characteristics of intention and agency being relevant in giving causal explanations.

Lipset and Bierstedt are thereby taking sides in an ancient philosophical argument: is it important for the ruler to be just, or is it only important for him to be thought to be just? What Lipset and Bierstedt do in defining legitimacy is not unlike what Thrasymachus did in defining justice and what Glaucon and Adeimantus did in developing Thrasymachus' case. We may now recall that Thrasymachus too claimed to be merely reporting how the world went, to be a neutral and value-free observer. My thesis on this last point can indeed be summarized as follows: to insist that political science be value-free is to insist that we never use in our explanations such clauses as 'because it was unjust' or 'because it was illegitimate' when we explain the collapse of a policy or a regime; and to insist on this is to agree with Thrasymachus—even if for different reasons—that justice plays no part and can play no part in political life. The insistence on being value-free thus involves the most extreme of value commitments. Hence I take it to be no objection to the methodology which I propose that it is clearly not able to purge its explanations of evaluative elements.

Note that I have offered no arguments at this point for believing that Thrasymachus is, as a matter of fact, mistaken; what I have done is to suggest that those who maintain the stance of orthodox comparative political science are committed by their starting-point and not by the empirical findings to the view that he was right. And this raises one more kind of doubt about their view. For the response to my parable about the man who aspired to be the author of the general theory of holes might well have been that such a man is intellectually misguided, but practically harmless. When, however, one has to recognize that this kind of intellectual mistake is allied to a Thrasymachean attitude to morality, it becomes clear that if this type of enterprise is to be ranked as a joke, it must be classed with the more dangerous kinds of practical jokes.

XI

WHAT IS STRUCTURALISM?[1]

W. G. RUNCIMAN

So MUCH has been written about 'structuralism' that to add to it may seem to call for some excuse. But it is precisely the volume and diversity of the literature[2] which prompts this paper. My purpose is not to attempt to review this literature or to criticize any one portion of it in detail, but simply to inquire at a general level how far structuralism can be said to constitute a distinctive doctrine or method in the analysis either of societies as such or of their myths and ideas.

1

Very broadly, the term 'structure' serves to mark off questions about the constituents of the object under study from questions about its workings. In sociology (or anthropology or history), therefore, questions about 'structure' can be answered in as many ways as there are held to be kinds of constituents of societies. The old-fashioned answer would be to say that societies are made up of institutions; the fashionable answer would be to say that they are made up of messages. But they can equally well be held to be made up of groups, or relationships, or classes, or roles, or exchanges, or norms and sanctions, or even shared concepts and symbols. There is always the risk of lapsing unwittingly into metaphor, as in the discredited analogy of society as an organism. But beyond this, the test of one answer as against another can only lie in its explanatory value in the

From *Sociology in its Place and other Essays* (Cambridge: Cambridge University Press, 1970), pp. 45–58. Originally published in the *British Journal of Sociology*, xx (1969), 253–65. Reprinted by permission of the author and Routledge & Kegan Paul Ltd.

[1] This paper was read in an earlier draft at a staff seminar in the Department of Sociology at the University of Leicester in January 1967, and I should like to express my thanks to the members of the seminar for their comments. Since it was written, the second and third volumes of Claude Lévi-Strauss's *Mythologiques* have been published, but I have not tried to revise it in order to take account of them: for a useful and up-to-date (if rather summary) discussion by a qualified critic, see Edmund Leach, *Claude Lévi-Strauss*, London, 1970.

[2] Much of the more recent literature is in French. I have given references to English versions wherever available, but I have once or twice made slight modifications to the translation.

context where it is employed. The only common assumption underlying all the answers is that if a society (like anything else) is to be satisfactorily explained, then the question 'what is it made of?' will have to be answered as well as, if not actually prior to, the question 'why does it do what it does?'

This, however, is to say very little—so little, in fact, as to lend support to the well-known remark of Kroeber that to invoke the word 'structure' in the discussion of societies or cultures (or organisms, or crystals, or machines) adds nothing 'except to provoke a degree of pleasant puzzlement'.[3] But two other assumptions can be said to be built into the notion of structure apart from the assumption that the object in question is, as Kroeber puts it, 'not wholly amorphous'. The first is the assumption of a more specific interconnectedness: thus the term 'social structure' is said by Fortes, for example, to draw attention to the 'interconnection and interdependence, within a single system, of all the different classes of social relations found within a given society'.[4] The second is the assumption that form can usefully be divorced from content: Fortes, in the same passage, credits Lowie with first bringing out 'the very obvious but fundamental fact that closely similar, if not identical, forms of social relationship occur in widely separate societies and are expressed in varied custom'.[5] It is not simply, therefore, that the notion of 'structure' presupposes distinguishable elements, but that these elements constitute a system which displays a minimum persistence over time and is in principle comparable with other similarly identifiable systems. Hence social structure can be defined in such phrases as 'the assemblage of the main recurrent institutional patterns in the society, seen as complexes of roles'.[6]

But once the notion of structure is seen to overlap, or even to collapse into, the notion of system, what follows? A system is best defined simply as a set of connected variables. The term may carry the additional implication that the definitive set is the set yielding single-valued transformations; but the important emphasis is on variables as opposed to 'things'.[7] The 'structure' of a social collectivity, therefore, is a vector whose components are whatever variables the investigator has reason to regard as best able

---

[3] A. L. Kroeber, *Anthropology*, New York, 1948, p. 325 (Contrast with this, for example, the remark of R. S. Peters, *The Concept of Motivation*, London, 1958, p. 7, that 'in explaining human actions we, like anthropologists, must all in the first place be structuralists').

[4] Meyer Fortes, 'The Structure of Unilineal Descent Groups', *American Anthropologist*, lv (1953), 22.

[5] Ibid.

[6] Dorothy Emmet, *Rules, Roles and Relations*, London, 1966, p. 145.

[7] Cf. e.g. Leach, *Rethinking Anthropology*, London, 1961, p. 7: 'Considered mathematically, society is not an assemblage of things but an assemblage of variables.'

to explain how it works. Of course there underlies the notions both of structure and system the assumption that there is some ascertainable pattern which the investigator will, given sufficient patience and sagacity, lay bare. But this means simply that the interrelations between the variables isolated are not random; and this is the assumption without which scientific inquiry in any field whatever would be hopeless. In this sense there will be nothing distinctive about a 'structural' theory; in fact, any and all sociological explanations will be 'structuralist'.

Perhaps, however, it can be argued that 'structural' theories are distinguished from 'non-structural' in terms of their conception of societies as coherent and integrated wholes between whose components the internal interrelations are particularly strong. On this view, the rival doctrine which structuralism sets out to deny is the doctrine that institutions can be explained individually and as such in non-comparative and largely historical terms. Now it is certainly true that some anthropologists who have adopted what they would be prepared to call a 'structural' approach have meant something like this by it. But it is still implausible to claim that 'structuralism' constitutes a distinctive doctrine. In the first place, its contrary is a straw man which no sociologist, anthropologist, or historian would nowadays wish to defend; and in the second, 'structuralism' taken in this sense becomes in the end more or less indistinguishable from another of its presumable rivals—the functionalism of Malinowski. All theories of society presuppose some interrelation between societies' components; indeed, this is so by definition. But the strength of particular interrelations, or the priority to be accorded to particular variables, are matters for empirical study. There is little point in laying down *a priori* that the components of society are *strongly* interrelated and labelling the assumption 'structuralism'.

It is true that there is a clear distinction between structure on one side and both history and function on the other. But this does not by itself justify the escalation of a difference of emphasis into a clash of doctrines. Every historical explanation has implicit reference to structure; every structural explanation has implicit reference to origin and function. The rivalry between them is not between one theory and another but between one aspect and another of the particular theory employed.[8] It might be argued against this that the revolution in linguistics which has had so marked an influence on 'structural' anthropology was a revolution in

---

[8] Cf. G. Lautéri-Laura, 'Histoire et structure dans la connaissance de l'homme' *Annales*, xxii (1967), 796: 'Nous ne pouvons guère isoler, non plus, des champions supposés de l'une et de l'autre tendance, car, à vrai dire, la dichotomie est à l'intérieur de chacun d'eux.'

doctrine, and that Saussure himself was insistent on the incompatibility of synchronic with historical explanation. But even in linguistics, this looks in retrospect less like a doctrine than a methodological battle-cry,[9] and as such it has been progressively modified through Troubetzkoy and Jakobsen down to Chomsky. There is no such thing as a purely synchronic sociological explanation any more than an explanation in terms of a unique and self-insulated historical sequence; and the attempt to construct one would have as little explanatory value in the one case as in the other.[10] Even Lévi-Strauss, who has made the strongest claims for structural linguistics as the paradigm of sociological explanation, is quite explicit about the simultaneous importance of diachronic analysis.[11] *Pace* Saussure, there is no justification for turning the distinction between them into an incompatibility.

The only sense in which it might be plausible to regard structuralism as a distinctive sociological doctrine is the sense in which it is assumed not merely that separate structures can be broken down into their components, but also that there is a general isomorphism *between* structures. But the use of the term is still misleading. To say that ostensibly dissimilar structures are isomorphic and that this isomorphism is not coincidental is to say no more than that the same theory explains both. It says nothing about the content of the theory. All successful theories are isomorphic to the phenomena they set out to explain. To say that structuralism is the doctrine of isomorphism between structures must, presumably, mean the belief in a *universal* isomorphism—what Merleau-Ponty describes as 'the programme of a universal code of structures, which would allow us to deduce them from one another by means of transformation-rules'.[12] But then this is no less and no more than the belief in a general theory of the social sciences. How far this belief may be well founded, nobody is at present in a position to say. But if there is a general theory, its validity will

[9] Cf. Paul Ricoeur, 'La Structure, le mot, l'événement', *Esprit* (May 1967), p. 807.

[10] Cf. e.g. F. G. Bailey, *Tribe, Caste and Nation*, Manchester, 1960, p. 9: 'I cannot think of any examples of a purely static analysis of a society'; or Fernand Braudel, 'La Longue Durée', *Annales*, xiii (1968), 739: 'un arret instantané, suspendant toutes les Durées, est presque absurde toujours'; or Braudel's reference in *La Méditerranée et le monde mediterranéen à l'époque de Philippe II*, 2nd edn., Paris, 1966, i. 325, to '... des structures sociales, donc à des mécanismes lents à s'user'.

[11] Claude Lévi-Strauss, 'Les Limites de la notion de structure en ethnologie', in R. Bastide (ed.), *Sens et usages du terme structure dans les sciences humaines et sociales*, The Hague, 1962, p. 42: 'Mais toute structure n'est-elle pas bi-dimensionelle?'; or *The Scope of Anthropology*, London, 1967, p. 23; or 'Social Structure', in *Structural Anthropology*, New York, 1963, p. 312 (with particular reference to Fortes, 'Time and Social Structure: an Ashanti Case Study', in Fortes (ed.), *Social Structure: Studies Presented to A. R. Radcliffe-Brown*, Oxford, 1949, pp. 54–84).

[12] Maurice Merleau-Ponty, 'From Mauss to Claude Lévi-Strauss', in *Signs*, North-western University, 1964, p. 118.

depend on its substantive content, not on any particularly intimate connection with the notion of 'structure'. A general theory will be 'structuralist' in the sense that all socio-psychological theories are structuralist; it will be neither more nor less so if it turns out to be, let us say, a cybernetic theory rather than an economic one. If a commitment to 'structuralism' means only the optimistic belief that a general theory of human behaviour will one day be validated, it is hard to see why this particular term (or any other) is needed for it.

On the other hand, the fact that the term *does* often carry this implication helps to account for some of the enthusiasm and controversy which it continues to generate. In this respect, 'structure' is very like 'system'. The amount of controversy is not simply the result of an excessive concern with matters of terminology. It arises because of the strong difference of view which there has always been between those who do and those who do not believe in the possibility of a general theory of society. Much of the literature which has accumulated around the term 'system' is centred on the claim that it makes possible the formulation of hypotheses of a higher generality than could have been reached without it. But even if this claim is valid—which it may well be—the injunction 'look at it as a system' is uncomfortably like the injunction 'talk prose'. All interrelated variables constitute a system by definition, and that system has a structure by definition. For the sociologist, the two notions carry with them a substantive doctrine only if the injunction is not merely to look at society as a system, but to look at it as a system *of* something. To say merely that society is a system, and has a structure, will explain nothing at all.

It might, however, still be suggested that 'structuralism' constitutes not so much a distinctive doctrine as a distinctive method. Whatever may be said about the doctrines propounded by Saussure, it can hardly be denied that he did inaugurate a new method for the study of language which has proved outstandingly rewarding. But it remains true that the success of this method in linguistics lies in the specific demonstration that language can be broken down into components for whose analysis the method of Saussure and his successors is appropriate; and if this is 'structuralism', then what it means is, in effect, the replacement of less clear and rigorous analyses by more clear and rigorous ones. In the case of 'social' structure, it is true that to look, with Radcliffe-Brown, at actual social relations is very different from looking, with Lévi-Strauss, at formal relations between formal relations.[13] But it in no way follows that the more abstract model,

---

[13] Radcliffe-Brown does, as Lévi-Strauss allows (*Structural Anthropology*, p. 303), distinguish between 'actual relations' and 'the form of the structure' (*Structure and Function in Primitive Society*, London, 1952, p. 192); but he is still insistent that 'the components of social structure are *persons*' (Introduction, p. 4).

even if it proves the more useful, is therefore entitled to lay exclusive claim to 'structuralist' method.

In the version of Lévi-Strauss, the essence of 'structuralist' method seems to lie in the construction of deliberately abstract models by the artificial breaking-down of the object under study and its subsequent reconstitution in terms of essentially relational properties. But isn't this true of science in general? To borrow again from Merlau-Ponty, 'the objects which science constructs . . . are always bundles of relations.'[14] Nor is there anything distinctively 'structuralist' about the recognition that an explanatory model *is* a construction—that, in the phrase of Roland Barthes, it is 'l'intellect ajouté a l'objet'.[15] The only force in the injunction of structuralism as a method would seem to lie, as with it as a doctrine, in the emphasis placed on the search for isomorphism. But the success of the method, if it can be so called, will rest not on the search for isomorphism by itself but on the extent to which it leads to a valid reduction —that is, to a demonstration that one class of phenomena can be strictly identified with another. It is, of course, true that such reductions can constitute major scientific discoveries and that they are worth looking for no less in the social than the physical sciences. But the discoveries are not arrived at by means of any methodological axiom derived from the notion of 'structure'. They are arrived at by finding that the laws governing two discrete classes of phenomena are isomorphic, that the constants are identical and that the two sets of terms are empirically interchangeable.[16] It may well be that there is both an isomorphism of laws and an inter-changeability of concepts between apparently discrete areas of social phenomena. But the explanatory value of the discovery will depend on the empirical identification. The value of the methodological injunction 'look for isomorphism' (or, equally, 'look for "total" phenomena') is that its implications are reductionist, not that it argues a methodological parallel between the study of language and the study of society.

In effect, the point is the same whether structuralism is put forward as a doctrine or as a method. 'Look at society as a system (or structure)' is trivial where 'look at society as a system (or structure) of information exchanges' is not. But if the suggestion that society should be looked at in cybernetic terms turns out to be useful, there will be nothing peculiarly 'structuralist' about it. On this basis it could just as well be claimed that Durkheim's dictum 'Tell me the code of domestic morality and I will tell you the social organisation' is a dictum of 'structuralism'. But this means

---

[14] Maurice Merleau-Ponty, *The Structure of Behaviour*, London, 1965, p. 142.
[15] Roland Barthes, 'L'Activité structuraliste' in *Essais critiques*, Paris, 1964, p. 215.
[16] See May Brodbeck, 'Models, Meaning and Theories', in Llewellyn Gross (ed.), *Symposium on Sociological Theory*, Evanston, Ill., 1959, pp. 392ff.

merely (as Durkheim himself makes clear) that societies develop that morality they need.[17] If this is true, it is not because of the fact that social organization and morality are in some sense isomorphic but because there is a demonstrable causal relation between them. As a doctrine, 'societies are structures' means little more than 'societies are societies'; as a method, 'look for the structure' means little more than 'look for the right explanation', or, perhaps, 'the explanation lies deeper than you think.'

2

It may be, however, that to question the distinctive content of a 'structural' approach to societies as a whole is to misconceive its scope. Perhaps its virtue—whether methodological or doctrinal—lies not in the traditional area of 'social structure' so much as in the particular field of ritual and ideas. On this view, the merit of Lévi-Strauss is that he 'succeeds in doing for myth what Radcliffe-Brown did for social structure'—that is, he succeeds in showing that myths can only be explained in terms of their position within 'the total myth structure of the culture concerned'.[18] But once again, what exactly is distinctive about this? It is fair to say that certain forms of historical explanation of myth are more palpable rivals to Lévi-Strauss's approach than is 'non-structural' to 'structural' sociology; Lévi-Strauss is, for example, explicitly concerned to reject the explanation of myth in terms of Jungian archetypes. But the explanations which he offers in his turn must still be explanations by origin if they are to be explanations at all. There is no need to dispute the verdict of Firth that Lévi-Strauss 'has amply shown in these fields [of myth and totemism] what Freud showed elsewhere, that thought is not random but structured'.[19] No doubt, too, this demonstration depends to a significant degree on synchronic comparisons. But if it is demonstrably the case that the Oedipus myth is an attempt to reconcile the incompatible beliefs that man is autochthonous and that he is not autochthonous, or that the story of Asdiwal gives expression to the strain inherent in a system of cross-cousin marriage which is patrilocal at the same time as matrilateral, or that a myth purporting to explain the origin of clan names is in general likely to be 'demarcative rather than aetiological',[20] this does not follow simply from the particular rearrangement of the elements of the myth which have been selected. It can only follow from the further evidence cited to

[17] Emile Durkheim, *Moral Education*, New York, 1961, p. 87.
[18] Nur Yalman, 'The Raw: the Cooked: Nature: Culture', in Leach (ed.), *The Structural Study of Myth and Totemism*, London, 1967, p. 73.
[19] Raymond Firth, 'Twins, Birds and Vegetables', *Man*, N.S. i (1966), 2.
[20] Lévi-Strauss, *The Savage Mind*, London, 1966, p. 230.

show that this rearrangement, and not any other, furnishes the clue to the original composition and subsequent preservation (with such accretions as may be) of the myth in question.

Against this, it might be said that 'structural' explanations of myth, even if they must in some sense be explanations by origin, are explanations by origin of a peculiar kind, since what is required is not the tracing of a pedigree but the deciphering of a code. Thus Leach, for example, draws an explicit parallel between the mythography of Lévi-Strauss and the decipherment of Linear B[21]. But the parallel is a dangerous one. The notion of a code presupposes the notion of an original of which the coded version is a translation. There was no doubt in anyone's mind that Linear B was a script; the question was a question of meaning, which was solved when Ventris and Chadwick effectively showed that Linear B was Greek. But it is a very different matter to speak of 'decoding' *Hamlet* or *Moby Dick*. To claim to have 'decoded' a work of art is legitimate only in such special cases as an allegorical painting or a novel *à clef*. It is still possible to argue that works of art can be explained in terms of *unconscious* symbolism (and it is, perhaps, worth remarking that Lévi-Strauss in his autobiography pays tribute to the triple influence on his intellectual development of Marxism, geology, and psycho-analysis). But this too will be defensible only in terms of solving the problem of origin. It is not enough to produce a 'structural' parallel between the components of the work of art and the presumptive content of the artist's repressed impulses and fantasies. It has also to be shown that the artist *was* under the influence of these repressed impulses and that he *therefore* produced the work of art whose symbolism can be 'decoded' along these lines.

At this point, the partisans of 'structuralism' will be likely to reply that they are still not required to proffer a conventional explanation by origin, but only to show that an ostensibly haphazard complex can be accounted for by a logical reduction which is both more economical and more coherent. Thus Leach says of the kinship terminology of the Jinghpaw that it 'impressed me as highly complex, yet it must be, I argued, *from the users' point of view*, the simplest possible logical system consistent with the rules of the society'.[22] An excellent simple example is furnished by the Hanunoo system of personal pronouns, which is palpably illogical if set out in terms of the traditional categories of first, second, and third persons singular and plural but which makes perfect sense in terms of the three dimensions of minimal/non-minimal membership, inclusion/exclusion of the speaker, and inclusion/exclusion of the listener.[23] Here, the

---

[21] *The Structural Study of Myth and Totemism*, p. xviii.
[22] 'Jinghpaw Kinship Terminology', in *Rethinking Anthropology*, p. 50.

solution is immediately satisfying (and serves at the same time to support the view that the thought of primitive peoples is much less illogical than used to be supposed). But we are still, even in these cases, dealing with explanation by origin, for the presumption underlying the argument is that the Jinghpaw or Hanunoo or anybody else will not in fact have developed and preserved an inexplicable terminology. In other words, the question of motive is taken for granted. But where it comes to the explanation of myth, it is precisely the reason for which the myth has been composed, added to, and preserved that we wish to know.

Lévi-Strauss himself is well aware of the need to rebut the charge that 'structural' explanation of myth is arbitrary. In *Le Cru et le cuit* his rebuttal rests partly on the criteria of coherence and economy and partly on the self-denying ordinance whereby the investigator is forbidden to switch at will from logical to historical explanations of variations in the *mythe de rèfèrence*.[24] But this still leaves open the question of content. Here Lèvi-Strauss's argument appears to rest on the analogy between myth and music. But although it is evident that the musicologist can demonstrate a formal structure common to different individual compositions of which neither the listeners, the performers, nor even the composer need necessarily be aware, it is less clear how far this constitutes the explanation for which the sociologist will be seeking. It is entirely legitimate to break down a myth or work of art paradigmatically (to borrow a term from the linguists) instead of syntagmatically. Indeed, this is a commonplace of literary and artistic criticism of many different schools. But the fact that a piece of music is a fugue explains neither why Bach wrote it nor why twentieth-century Europeans still like to listen to it. Lévi-Strauss appears to reject the question of content on the grounds that structure, unlike form, does not *have* a content, but *is* content;[25] but this is merely (if I understand him) another way of making the point that the 'structural' view of anything is as a set of variables. If the conclusion of Lévi-Strauss's mythography is that 'Myths serve to provide an apparent resolution, or "mediation", of problems which by their very nature are incapable of

[23] H. C. Conklin, 'Lexicographical Treatment of Folk Taxonomies', in F. W. Householder and S. Saporta (eds.), *Problems in Lexicography*, Bloomington, Ind., 1962, pp. 119–41, cited by Nicholas Ruwet, 'La Linguistique générale aujourd'hui', *Archives Européennes de Sociologie*, v (1964), 306–7.

[24] *Le Cru et le cuit*, Paris, 1964, pp. 155–6.

[25] In 'L'Analyse morphologique des contes russes', *Int. J. Slavic Linguistics and Poetics* (1960), quoted by J. Pauillon, 'Présentation', in *Les Temps Modernes* (Nov. 1966), p. 782: 'la forme se définit par opposition à un contenu qui lui est extérieur; mais la structure n'a pas de contenu: elle est le contenu même, appréhendé dans une organisation logique conçue comme propriété du réel.'

any final resolution',[26] this is an explanation by origin no less than is a Freudian or Jungian explanation, or a more conventionally 'structuralist' anthropological explanation relating ritual to social organization, or a 'genetic-epistemological' explanation in the manner of Piaget.[27] Whatever is meant by the 'structure' of myth, the components must in the end be related to the meaning and thus the structure to the content.

Thus in practice, 'structural' mythography does not deny (how could it?) that 'To study form it may be sufficient to describe it. To explain form one needs to discover and describe the processes that generate the form.'[28] For Lévi-Strauss, the matrix to be deduced from the juxta-position and 'structural' reduction of all known myths will disclose the fundamental (and irresolvable) preoccupations of man in his relations to nature; and these will in turn be traceable to a fundamental biochemical account of the constituents of the human mind. It is a further assumption that human thought is essentially binary, and that this fact can in turn be related to the binary neuro-physiological mechanisms operating in the brain; but an isomorphism of this kind is neither a necessary nor, for that matter, a very significant assumption. All psychological explanations must be compatible with at least one possible neurological model;[29] but the function of binary thinking could be performed by any number of different mechanisms, and, conversely, binary neurological mechanisms could yield any number of 'fundamental' modes of thought which need not be binary themselves. In any case, this aspect of the question is outside the scope of the present paper. I am not here concerned with what particular explanation by origin is the correct one; nor am I qualified to pass comment on any specific interpretation of a particular myth. The concern of this paper is with the question how far 'structuralism' constitutes a distinctive kind of analysis; and the answer seems to be that although the explanations of myth offered by Lévi-Strauss are substantively different from those put forward by others, and although he has been consciously influenced by post-Saussurean linguistics to a degree that others have not, there is still no clear sense in which rival explanations of myth are 'non-structuralist',

[26] Leach, 'The Legitimacy of Solomon', *Archives Européennes de Sociologie*, vii (1966), 80.

[27] Piaget himself is claimed as a 'structuralist' by Jean Viet, *Les Méthodes structuralistes dans les sciences sociales*, The Hague, 1965, pp. 53–8; but such a wide range of authors in different fields is similarly included by Viet as in effect to support the argument that no useful theory in the social sciences will ever be *non*-structuralist.

[28] Fredrik Barth, *Models of Social Organization*, Royal Anthropological Institute, 1966, p. v.

[29] See Jerry A. Fodor, 'Explanations in Psychology', in Max Black (ed.), *Philosophy in America* (London, 1965), p. 176.

or 'structuralist' explanations are not explanations by origin and content in the orthodox sense.

3

But is there yet another possible interpretation? When Firth, in 1955 announced that 'the air of enchantment which for the last two decades has surrounded the "structuralist" point of view has now begun to be dispelled',[30] he evidently did not foresee the vogue which a renovated 'structuralism' was to enjoy under the influence of Lévi-Strauss. But it might be argued that the transition from Radcliffe-Brown to Lévi-Strauss represents not so much the transition from one sociology to another as from sociology to philosophy. It is noticeable that Lévi-Strauss's 'structuralism' has attracted the attention of philosophers and literary critics to a degree that the 'structuralism' of English-speaking social anthropology has never done. Might it then be that this newer variant should be seen less as a doctrine of what societies are and how their workings are to be explained than as a fresh attempt to resolve for social science as a whole the perennial conflict between idealism and empiricism?

The brief discussion of Lévi-Strauss's mythography in the preceding section suggested already that a 'structuralist' interpretation of ideas must sooner or later confront the problems of meaning as well as origin. At this point, both the ethnographer and the psychologist must give way to the epistemologist. Lévi-Strauss clearly accepts this. A philosopher by training and perhaps to some degree by temperament, he is well aware of what he is doing in proffering an explanation of culture by reference to the ultimate constituents of the human mind. Indeed, he has not only been labelled a Kantian but has accepted the label—he is only concerned to make clear that it is not a 'transcendental' Kantianism but a Kantianism transposed into the 'domaine ethnologique'.[31] Now this could be read simply as a determination to preserve, even in the search for 'Kantian' universals, a dogmatic empiricism modelled on the physical sciences. But compare the following passage, which, apart from its lack of a specific reference to ethnography, could almost have been written by Lévi-Strauss himself:

> Philosophy is related by regular laws to the sciences, to art and society. From this relationship its tasks arise. Ours is clearly marked out for us: to follow Kant's critical path to the end, and establish an empirical science of the human mind in collaboration with workers in other fields; our task is to get to know the laws which govern social, intellectual and moral phenomena.

[30] Raymond Firth, 'Some Principles of Social Organization', in *Essays on Social Organization and Values*, London, 1964, p. 59.

[31] Réponse à quelques questions', *Esprit* (Nov. 1963), p. 631. Cf. *Le Cru et le cuit*, p. 19.

The author here, far from being an orthodox empiricist, is Dilthey, in his inaugural lecture at Basle;[32] and although it is in general a mistake to spend too much time tracing ideological parallels (even the method of 'binary selection' can be traced back to Plato's *Sophist*), the parallel between Lévi-Strauss and Dilthey is not, perhaps, as far-fetched as it seems.

One obvious objection to it is the physicalist basis of Lévi-Strauss's psychology. But where Piaget, for example, finds the source of the isomorphism between thought and the world, for which the central nervous system furnishes the mechanism, in the 'sociogenesis' of the human intellect, Lévi-Strauss finds it in the structural continuities of myth. Indeed, it is his explicit claim that his epistemology is ethnological instead of psychological. But by forfeiting Piaget's kind of grounds for the rejection of 'transcendentalism', he lays himself open to the same charge as the 'empirical science of the human mind' of Dilthey. For if Lévi-Strauss's 'mythography' is not, any more than Dilthey's 'hermeneutics', grounded in empirically testable psychological theory, then the perennial question of ultimate origin will be no less open (and damaging) in the one case as the other. It is not enough to base a theory of the human mind on structural ethnography plus the assumption of biochemical isomorphism, because this will leave the investigator's own conclusions open to the charge of a regress. Piaget, at least, can claim immunity from the regress by invoking the standards of public testability for his explanation of the origins of logical thought, and thereby his own psychological theory. I am not qualified to judge how far Piaget's attempt will he held to be successful. But it is impossible to see how the theory of Lévi-Strauss could be validated in any analogous way within the framework of its own assumptions. It always remains to be asked why the mythography of Lévi-Strauss is not itself a myth; and he himself, in *Le Cru et le cuit*, disarmingly admits of his 'third-order code' that 'on n'aura pas tort de la tenir pour un mythe; en quelque sorte, le mythe de la mythologie.'[33] We are unavoidably forced back, at the end of the structuralist exercise, to the traditional questions of origin and meaning; and there is nothing in Lévi-Strauss to show that the philosophical appeal of 'ethnological' Kantianism rests in the end on an epistemological foundation any less 'Kantian' than that of Kant himself.

The isomorphism of thought and the world is a familiar preoccupation of philosophy: to the Wittgenstein of the *Tractatus* just as much as to Lévi-Strauss, the fundamental categories of human thought mirror the structure of the world although not directly asserting anything about it. The role of logic in the epistemology of the early Wittgenstein is not

[32] H. A. Hodges, *Wilhelm Dilthey: an Introduction*, London, 1944, p. 115.
[33] Op. cit., p. 20.

unlike the role of myth in the epistemology of Lévi-Strauss; and in a sense, this is only to be expected, since it is part of Lévi-Strauss's purpose to show that 'the kind of logic in mythical thought is as rigorous as that of modern science.'[34] But having said that the fundamental categories of human thought, whether revealed by ethnography or by introspection, are somehow isomorphic to the world, how are we ever to demonstrate either the nature or the cause of this connection without lapsing into a regress? The same dilemma faces the Kantianism not only of Dilthey but likewise of Lévi-Strauss. Lévi-Strauss is entitled to argue that his theory is based on 'experience' in a way that Wittgenstein's or Kant's are not and do not claim to be. But to the degree that his theory is, like theirs, an epistemological theory, the search for ethnographic generalizations merely defers the problem which it is alleged to solve. The status of Lévi-Strauss's ultimate constituents is not modified by the fact that he bases them on a 'structural' reduction of universal myths rather than the 'thought-experiments' of the traditional logician.

It should be clear that to say this is not to deny the importance of the notion of isomorphic patterning (or 'structure') to epistemology as well as to communication theory—an importance of which Wittgenstein was no less aware than Lévi-Strauss or Leach.[35] But it would be unwarranted to claim for the new 'structuralism' that it resolves the philosophical difficulties which were not resolved by Dilthey or Wittgenstein or Kant himself. It is perfectly possible that philosophical discussion on these topics will be permanently influenced by the findings of 'structuralist' ethnography. Epistemology is not debated in a vacuum. The findings of psychology, for example, can drastically modify philosophers' doctrines of 'sense-data', and there is nothing inherently misconceived in the claim of Lévi Strauss to have demonstrated the mistakes both of Peirce in defining proper names as 'indices' and of Russell in putting forward demonstrative pronouns as the logical model of proper names.[36] But it is one thing to claim that the findings of ethnography can influence philosophers' doctrines; it is another to claim that they can solve either psychologists' or philosophers' problems. Not only are the epistemological difficulties of the 'ultimate constituents of the human mind' not resolved by Lévi-Strauss's mythography; they are not bypassed by it either. 'Structuralism' does not

---

[34] 'The Structural Study of Myth', in *Structural Anthropology*, p. 230.

[35] Cf. e.g. Leach, 'Men and Machines' ,*Listener* (23 Nov. 1967), p. 663, on the transmission of isomorphism from speaker's head, voice, microphone, and transmitter to listener's receiver, loudspeaker, ears, and brain with Wittgenstein, *Tractatus* 4.0141 on the isomorphism between musical idea, score, sound-waves, and the groove on the gramophone record.

[36] *The Savage Mind*, p. 215.

succeed in showing how the epistemological status of the 'mythe de la mythologie' can be vindicated by that mythology itself, and if the debate between empiricists and idealists will ever be settled, it will not be by appeal to it.

<h1 style="text-align:center">4</h1>

This rapid and rather cavalier survey of a complex topic cannot suggest more than a very tentative general conclusion. But if my argument is at all well founded, it suggests that 'structuralism', whether in its Anglo-Saxon or its Gallic version, should not be claimed to constitute a novel, coherent, and comprehensive paradigm for sociological and anthropological theory. Whether viewed as a doctrine or a method (and the two should in any case not be too sharply distinguished) 'structuralism' as such does not, on examination, stand for a more distinctive standpoint than a belief in the applicability of rigorous models to social behaviour; and this is equally true whether it is taken to apply to societies as a whole or only to their rituals and beliefs, or even, at a more explicitly philosophical level, to the theoretical presuppositions of social-scientific investigation itself.

At the same time, it would be altogether wrong to draw from this argument the implication that the exponents of 'structuralism' have not both made important contributions to specialist topics and also suggested ideas of wider relevance for social theory in general. Indeed, it may well be that Lévi-Strauss and his followers will extend his empirical studies beyond what is still a relatively circumspect range of societies and institutions, and that this will have valuable implications over wide areas of the social sciences. But it has not been the purpose of this paper to try to forecast the future of anthropological theory. I have merely been concerned to suggest that 'structuralist' theory may not be distinctive to quite the degree that is apt to be claimed for it.

XII

PROBLEMS OF INTERPRETIVE SOCIOLOGY

ALFRED SCHUTZ

1. CAUSAL ADEQUACY AND MEANING ADEQUACY

WEBER makes the distinction between the two concepts quite clear at an early point in his *Wirtschaft und Gesellschaft*:

We apply the term *adequacy on the level of meaning* to the subjective interpretation of a coherent course of conduct, when, and in so far as according to our habitual modes of thought and feeling, its component parts, taken in their mutal relation, are recognized to constitute a typical complex of meaning. It is more common to say 'correct'. The interpretation of a sequence of events will, on the other hand, be *causally adequate* in so far as, according to established generalizations from *experience*, there is a probability that it will always actually occur in the same way. An example of *adequacy on the level of meaning* in this sense is what is, according to our current *norms* of calculation or thinking, the correct solution to an arithmetical problem. On the other hand, a causally adequate interpretation of the same phenomenon would concern the statistical probability that, according to verified generalizations from experience, there would be a 'correct' or 'erroneous' solution of the same problem. This also refers to currently accepted norms, but includes taking account of typical errors or of typical confusions. Thus causal explanation depends on being able to determine that there is a probability, which, in the rare ideal case, can be numerically stated, but is always in some sense calculable, that a given observable event (overt or subjective) will be followed or accompanied by another event.

A *correct* causal interpretation of a concrete course of action is arrived at when the overt action and the motives have both been correctly apprehended, and at the same time their relation has become *meaningfully* comprehensible. A correct causal interpretation of typical action means that the process which is claimed to be typical is shown to be both adequately grasped on the level of meaning and at the same time the interpretation is to some degree causally adequate. If adequacy in respect to meaning is lacking, then no matter how high

From *The Phenomenology of the Social World*, (London: Heinemann Educational; Evanston, Ill.: Northwestern University Press, 1967), pp. 230–6, 239–49. Reprinted by permission of the author and publishers.

The translators have supplied references to Weber's work in English translation wherever possible. All translators' notes are enclosed in square brackets.

the degree of uniformity and how precisely its probability can be numerically determined, it is still an *incomprehensible statistical* probability, whether dealing with overt or subjective processes. On the other hand, even the most perfect adequacy on the level of meaning has causal significance from the sociological point of view only insofar as there is some kind of proof for the existence of a *probability* that the action *in fact* normally *takes* the course which has been held to be meaning-adequate. For this there must be some degree of determinable frequency of approximation to an average or a pure type.

Statistical uniformities constitute understandable types of action in the sense of this discussion, and thus constitute 'sociological generalizations', only when they can be regarded as manifestations of the understandable subjective meaning of a course of social action. Conversely, formulations of a rational course of subjectively understandable action constitute sociological types of empirical processes only when they can be empirically observed with a significant degree of approximation. It is unfortunately by no means the case that the actual likelihood of the occurrence of a given course of overt action is *always* directly proportional to the clarity of subjective interpretation.[1]

We shall now seek to bring these remarks of Weber into accord with the requirements of our own theory. Let us begin with the concept of causal adequacy. A sequence of events is causally adequate to the degree that experience teaches us it will probably happen again. The concept of causal adequacy relates, therefore, to that objective context of meaning which is social science itself. That certain acts are followed by certain other acts is a generalization founded (1) in everyday life in my interpretation of my own experiences and (2) in social science, in a scientific complex of knowledge. In both cases the generalization is achieved through a synthesis of recognition. But this should in nowise be identified with knowledge of the conscious experience of the other person or with knowledge of the 'intended meaning' of his action. A sequence of events is, therefore, causally adequate if it is in accord with past experience. Here it is immaterial whether the events in question add up to a human action or whether they are nothing more than a series of happenings in the world of nature. As a matter of fact, the concept of causal adequacy was first advanced by the physiologist Johannes von Kries[2] in connection with certain problems involved in the calculating of probabilities. His aim was to make a contribution to the theory of legal accountability in criminal law, but he introduced the idea as a general concept independent of any specific application. There are weighty objections against the use of the word 'causal' in sociological discourse. For when we formulate judgements of causal

---

[1] Weber, *Wirtschaft und Gesellschaft* (Tübingen: Mohr, 1922) pp. 5–6 [E.T., pp. 99–100].

[2] 'Über den Begriff der objektiven Müglichkeit und einige Anwendungen delsseben', *Vierteljahrsschrift für wissenschaftliche Philosophie* (1888), pp. 180ff.; on the concept of causal adequacy see esp. pp. 201f. With respect to Max Weber's concept, cf. the essay devoted to this theme in *Gesammelte Aufsätze zur Wissenschaftslehre* (Tübingen: Mohr, 1922), pp. 78ff.

adequacy in the social sciences, what we are really talking about is not causal necessity in the strict sense but the so-called 'causality of freedom', which pertains to the end-means relation. Therefore, one cannot really speak of a causal relation in the general sense postulated by Kries[3] so long as one confines oneself to the external event, the objective context of meaning, and so forth. However, if one interprets the concept in Weber's sense, then the postulate of causal adequacy is identical with what we have previously called 'the postulate of the coherence of experience'. A type construct is causally adequate, then, if it is probable that, according to the rules of experience, an act will be performed (it does not matter by whom or in what context of meaning) in a manner corresponding to the construct.

But this formulation is still lacking in precision. If I start out from a real action as my datum, then every ideal-typical construct that I base on it will already be in itself causally adequate. This is because the objective meaning-context of the act with which I start itself discloses the typical subjective meaning-context which corresponds to the act or, more strictly speaking, *can* correspond to it. Therefore, if I am going to construct a personal ideal type in a scientifically correct manner, it is not enough that the action in question probably take place. Rather, what is required in addition to this is that the action be *repeatable* and that the postulate of its repeatability not be inconsistent with the whole body of our scientific knowledge. This is a good time to repeat our previous observation that Weber starts out with an external action and seeks to connect with it an intended meaning without accounting for the fact that even the concept of the unity of the action presupposes a subjective foundation once we ask what the intended meaning is. However, this error turns out to be harmless if we follow his further train of thought. Causal adequacy is for him above all a category of the *social sciences*; hence, only sociological and historical understanding is bound by it. However, such understanding takes place via the construction of personal ideal types derived from a course of external behaviour that has been isolated arbitrarily by the social scientist. If we set it down as a requirement that such constructs be derived only from acts occurring with a certain known frequency, then what we really have here is a heuristic principle based on the economy of thought. It means simply that a construct is appropriate and to be recommended only if it derives from acts that are not isolated but have a certain probability of repetition or frequency. If the postulate of causal adequacy is conceived in this way, then

---

[3] A critique of this concept, for which we do not have the space here, would show that its universal validity is quite doubtful. Cf., with respect to its usefulness in criminal law, Felix Kaufmann, *Die philosophischen Grundprobleme der Lehre von der Strafrechtsschuld*, Leipzig and Vienna, 1929, pp. 78ff.

it is by no means a principle essential to all the social sciences. It would be binding upon sociology only and not upon history, since it derives from the basic approach of the sociologist toward his problems. But this would then leave everyone at liberty to decide whether he wanted to carry on the scientific study of the social world *qua* sociologist or *qua* historian.

But Weber's postulate of causal adequacy means something more than this. For reasons we have yet to discuss, the sociologist prefers the interpretive scheme of the *rational* action (specifically, either that of the action oriented to an ordinary purpose, or the action oriented to an absolute value)[4] to all other interpretive schemes. Every ordinary purposive action takes place within the means-end relationship. Establishing the pattern of such an action simply means seeking out how typical ends and typical means are related. In other words, the actor's choice of goals, his in-order-to projects, is determined via ideal-typical construction. Once this is done—that is, once the actor's goal is defined—it is only a matter of selecting those means for him that experience has shown to be appropriate. We can now interpret Weber's postulate of causal adequacy in the following way: in a type construct of ordinary purposive action, the means must be, in the light of our past experience, appropriate to the goal. Later, when we discuss rational action and rational method, we shall explain in detail what we mean by this second concept of causal adequacy.

An ideal-typical construct is said to be causally adequate when it turns out to predict what actually happens, in accord with all the rules of frequency. But this does not mean that what it predicts must always happen. Weber himself gives as an example the probability of a typical error in calculation. Let us suppose that we wish to multiply a given number by a two-digit number. Then, instead of placing the second partial product one point to the left of the first, we place it one point to the right. It would be causally adequate to conclude that we are going to come out with the wrong answer. But this conclusion would not be correct for all cases in which the above procedure was employed; for instance, if the two digits of the multiplier are the same, it does not matter whether the second partial product is moved to the left or to the right of the first. Here, as a matter of fact, we have Weber's ideal case of numerically assignable probability, for, out of ten such operations, nine will be incorrect and one correct. However, if we look more closely, we shall see that causal adequacy, or agreement with past experience, is based on typically comprehended meaning-adequate relations, in this case the laws of arithmetic and number theory as applied to the operation of multiplication. We can even go further and

---

[4] [See *Wirtschaft und Gesellschaft*, p. 12; E.T., p. 115.]

make the general statement that all causal adequacy which pertains to human action is based on principles of meaning-adequacy of some kind or other. For such causal adequacy means the consistency of the type construct of a human action with the total context of our past experience. Furthermore, we can come to know a human action only by ordering it within a meaning-context, whether objective or subjective. Causal adequacy, then, in so far as it is a concept applying to human behaviour, is only a special case of meaning-adequacy.[5]

Our position on this point will immediately become more intelligible as we proceed to our analysis of the nature of meaning-adequacy.

2. MEANING-ADEQUACY

According to Weber, a continuous course of behaviour is meaning-adequate, or adequate on the level of meaning, to the degree that the relation of its constituent parts is affirmed by us as a typical meaning-context in accordance with average habits of thought and feeling. Here again we encounter the paradox that dominates Weber's whole philosophy of social science. He postulates as the task of social science the discovery of intended meaning—indeed, the intended meaning of the actor. But this 'intended meaning' turns out to be a meaning which is given to the observer and not to the actor. In our terminology, Weber is saying that an action is meaning-adequate when it can be ordered under an objective context of meaning. We have already shown that such objective interpretation is quite a different thing from discovering what the actor himself has in mind. Our next question must therefore be whether meaning-adequacy is attained through objective interpretation or whether we have to go further and show without contradiction how the actor could himself have subjectively intended a certain meaning. We shall have to decide in favour of the second alternative, as we shall see.[6]

This distinction is by no means irrelevant for Weber's theory of meaning-adequacy. For him, behaviour is meaning-adequate if it is in accord with '*average* habits of thought and feeling'. What he means by this afterthought is not at all clear. For average habits of thought and feeling are a matter of causally adequate, not meaning-adequate interpretation. It seems contradictory to set up the sociologist as judge of what is meaning-adequate,

---

[5] But not, of course, in the case of the natural sciences. The phenomena of nature are in principle beyond interpretive understanding and have no 'meaning', since they fall outside man's consciousness and belong to an objective spatiotemporal order. This is not the place to investigate more deeply the distinction between the natural and the cultural sciences.

[6] Since only a conscious experience can be meaningful (*sinnhaft*), we need not, in speaking of meaning-adequacy, distinguish between its application to cultural and its application to natural objects, as we did in the case of causal adequacy.

unless we mean by 'knowledge of average habits of thought and feeling' the knowledge the social sciences have of all conceivable subjective experiences whatsoever. It is enough for the meaningful interpretation of another's behaviour that I assume that my ideal construct stands in a context of meaning *for him*. This suffices even if such a meaning-context clashes with my own knowledge. For instance, I can regard the totemistic interpretation of the behaviour of a primitive tribe as meaning-adequate even though the whole totemistic way of thinking is foreign to the 'average habits of thought and feeling' of our culture, or at least of the sociologists of our culture. But that is not at all what Max Weber means. For he is very conscious of the fact that these 'average habits of thought and feeling' refer back to given personal ideal types. He knows also that it is a matter of our experience, that is, of the experience of the social sciences, whether certain meaning-contexts can be ordered under a definite personal ideal type in a way that is typically adequate rather than type-transcendent. And so our attempt to discover a criterion for what is meaning-adequate has come down to this: we are back once again at the subjective meaning-context and the personal ideal type, which in turn have to be constructed in terms of the postulate of causal adequacy.

On the other hand, we can regard an ideal-typical construct as adequate for a given action if the corresponding subjective meaning-context can can really be ascribed to the actor in question without contradicting what else we know about him. Of course this person whose subjective experiences we are interpreting may appear to us as more or less determinate depending on how well we know him. Thus understood, the problem of meaning-adequacy pertains only to the interpretation of a concrete action via already constituted ideal types. On the other hand, the sociologist would have a completely free hand in the construction of a personal ideal type, because he so equips the latter's ideal consciousness that it is quite capable of having the subjective experiences appropriate to the typical behaviour in question.

Our analysis has thus shown that, so far as Max Weber is concerned, the two concepts of causal adequacy and meaning-adequacy are convertible. Any interpretation which is meaning-adequate must also be causally adequate, and vice versa. The two postulates really require that there be no contradiction to previous experience. As soon as one assumes that there is a definite stock of such experience at hand—in other words, as soon as only one person is making that interpretation, and from only one point of view—then either both of the postulates will be fulfilled or neither of them will. If it appears otherwise, that is only because a number of interpreters are introduced or because a number of temporal vantage points are assumed, in which, for instance, one interpretation already meaning-adequate in itself conflicts causally with another, later one.

For even where a given instance of behaviour seems incomprehensible to the observer, for instance, behaviour which is on the one hand causally adequate but on the other seems lacking in meaning-adequacy, meaning-adequacy may well exist, even in such cases from the point of view of the actor himself. Suppose, for instance, that an observer who is quite ignorant of the linguistic statistics in historical research comes on a man counting the frequency of certain words in the works of Plato. In terms of 'average habits of thought and feeling' he will simply not know what to make of such behaviour. He will begin to make sense out of the man's actions only when it is explained to him that in different periods of his life a person shows a preference for certain words and that, therefore, by studying the frequency of given words in his writings one will have made a start toward establishing a chronology for them. What was merely causally adequate then becomes meaning-adequate as well and therefore fully intelligible. We shall presently see how Weber's concept of meaning-adequacy really derives from the in-order-to motive of rational action and how his concept of intelligibility (*Verstehbarkeit*) is closely bound up with his notion of an action oriented to an ordinary purpose.

At this point we must add a remark on the situation underlying the distinction between causal adequacy and meaning-adequacy. The postulate that an ideal-typical construct must be both causally adequate and adequate on the level of meaning implies that it must be formulated as a *pure* construct without any admixture of type-transcending behaviour.[7] Furthermore, it must be compatible with our experience of the world in general and therefore with our experience of other people in general and of the particular person in general whose acts we are seeking to understand by means of the construct. Another demand of the postulate is that the construct be based only on repeatable behaviour. So much for the demands of the postulate of adequacy in so far as it deals with the *formation* of ideal-typical constructs. What are its requirements so far as the application of these types to concrete acts is concerned? Here the postulate of adequacy states that the type must *be sufficient to explain the action without contradicting previous experience*. But an action is sufficiently explained via an ideal type only when its motives are understood as typical ones; the explanation must, therefore, be meaning-adequate. To say that the motives must be causally adequate means merely that the motives could

---

[7] With respect to this concept, see above, p. 191. (Not reprinted here. Schutz points out that a man's behaviour in a role not covered by a particular ideal type cannot be predicted on the basis of that ideal type. Ed.)

have brought about this action and, more strictly, that they probably did so.

3. INTERPRETIVE SOCIOLOGY'S PREFERENCE FOR RATIONAL ACTION TYPES

Let us recall once again our definition of action. Action is behaviour based on an antecedent project. Since every project has an 'in-order-to' or 'for-the-sake-of-which' structure, it follows that every action is rational. Without such a project, one does not 'act'; one merely 'behaves' or 'has experiences'. Every action can, in its turn, be placed in a higher context of meaning, within which it is merely a means to a further end. Now, this end or higher goal may be clearly pictured, while the action leading up to it is carried out in a confused and uncertain manner. Or conversely, the goal may be vaguely conceived, while the action leading to it is well thought out. An example of the first situation would be a direction like 'The post office is that way', in contrast to 'Take your first right, then after two blocks a left.' An example of the second situation would be a chemist carrying out careful experiments on a newly discovered substance whose nature is as yet unknown. Both of these situations are alien to the kind of ideal type that is constructed in the social sciences and, as a matter of fact, in all indirect knowledge of social reality. The ideal type proper to such indirect social experience is one in which both ends and means are clearly conceived. For, since within these types the in-order-to motive is fixed and invariant, the corresponding ends and means must be assumed to have a maximum of meaning-adequacy and the action itself a maximum chance of being carried out. An action type of this kind is, according to Weber, a *rational* action.[8] It does not matter whether the rational action is oriented to an ordinary purpose or to an absolute value. This latter distinction really pertains to the genuine because-motive which can be co-ordinated to the typical in-order-to motive. Whether an act is oriented to an ordinary purpose or to an absolute value depends upon the interest of the actor; the same may be said for the problems he sets up for himself and the experiences he selects as relevant to their solution.[9]

This means-end relation can be thought of in an objective context of meaning and its objective probability estimated. With a suitable choice

[8] For an analysis of the concept of rational action see Hermann J. Grab's valuable monograph *Der Begriff des Rationalen in der Soziologie Max Webers*, Karlsruhe, 1927. Needless to say, my agreement with Grab can only be partial, since he presupposes Scheler's concept of objective values.

[9] For the derivation of the two types of action in question see Mises, 'Soziologie und Geschichte', *Archiv für Sozialwissenschaft und Sozialpolitik*, lxi (1929), 479.

of type, the objective meaning-context of the means-end relation can be treated as a subjective meaning-context and the objective probability as a subjective probability. This will be true the more universal are the problem situations which are the genuine because-motives corresponding to the typical in-order-to motives in question. For this reason interpretive sociology—but in this it is by no means alone—prefers rational action types. Irrational action (namely, action whose ends or means are confused or uncertain) is interpreted as a variant function of rational action. This is done by postulating a rational action type and then making certain changes in its in-order-to motives; the result is a deviant type. We must keep in mind the fact that sociology is concerned primarily with social interactions and that the latter involve reciprocal orientations in which the calculation of means and ends plays a large role. It is precisely because of the centrality of this calculation that rational action is such an important concept for interpretive sociology. But this does not by any means imply that interpretive sociology neglects irrational action. Weber has again and again stressed that the latter is part of the subject-matter of sociology. His works on the sociology of religion, for instance, make exemplary use of categories of irrational, emotional, and traditional action.

This preference for rational action types we must very sharply distinguish from the so-called 'rational method' of interpretive sociology. Sociology can claim no monopoly on rational method. The methodologies of all true sciences are rational, involving, as they do, the use of formal logic and interpretive schemes. All true sciences demand the maximum of clarity and distinctness for all their propositions. There is no such thing as an irrational science. We must never cease reiterating that the method of Weber's sociology is a rational one and that the position of interpretive sociology should in no way be confused with that of Dilthey, who opposes to rational science another, so-called 'interpretive' science based on metaphysical presuppositions and incorrigible 'intuition'.

It is true that the postulate of such an interpretive science arose historically from the necessity of breaking through the barriers that were erected between the rational special sciences and the understanding of living human experience. But it was forgotten by those proposing this new approach that life and thought are two different things and that science remains a matter of thought even when its subject-matter is life. It cannot, therefore, base itself on some vague and confused empathy or on value presuppositions or on descriptions lacking in intellectual rigour. It was this point and nothing else that lay at the centre of Weber's insistence on the objectivity of the knowledge attained in the social sciences. And it was Weber who first raised interpretive sociology to the rank of a science.

4. OBJECTIVE AND SUBJECTIVE MEANING IN THE SOCIAL SCIENCES

Having completed our analysis of the most important basic concepts of interpretive sociology, we must now try to answer the questions we formulated in section 43* concerning the relationship between the meaning-endowing acts of everyday life and their interpretation by the social sciences. Our answer is this: *All social sciences are objective meaning-contexts of subjective meaning-contexts.* We shall now try to clarify what we mean by this statement.

All scientific knowledge of the social world is indirect. It is knowledge of the world of contemporaries and the world of predecessors, never of the world of immediate social reality. Accordingly, the social sciences can understand man in his everyday social life not as a living individual person with a unique consciousness, but only as a personal ideal type without duration or spontaneity. They can understand him only as existing within an impersonal and anonymous objective time which no one ever has, or ever can experience. To this ideal type are assigned only such conscious experiences as are required to accompany motives already formally postulated. We have already outlined the methodology involved in this postulation. We have seen that it must take place in a manner that is both meaning-adequate and causally adequate. This means that there must be constant recourse to pregiven knowledge of the social world and of the world in general. It means that the motives postulated must not be incompatible with those of the observer's previously constructed ideal types.

Since the social sciences *qua* social sciences never actually encounter real people but deal only in personal ideal types, it can hardly be their function to understand the subjective meaning of human action in the sense that one person understands another's meaning when he is directly interacting with him. However, we saw that the nature of subjective meaning itself changes with the transition from direct to indirect social experience. In the process of ideal-typical construction, subjective meaning-contexts that can be directly experienced are successively replaced by a series of objective meaning-contexts. These are constructed gradually, each one upon its predecessor, and they interpenetrate one another in Chinese-box fashion, so that it is difficult to say where one leaves off and the other begins. However, it is precisely this process of construction which makes it possible for the social scientist, or indeed for any observer, to understand what the actor means; for it is this process alone which gives a dimension

---

* Not reprinted here. Schutz is again concerned with the gap between the individual's first-hand, subjective experience of the social world and the social scientist's impersonal explanation of that world in causal terms (Ed.).

of objectivity to his meaning. Of course, this process of constitution can only be disclosed to the interpreter by means of his own typifying method. What he will thus come to know is only a conceptual model, not a real person.

We have already seen that there can be personal ideal types of all degrees of anonymity or concreteness. By studying a given cultural product we can gain some insight into what its creator had in mind, regardless of the anonymity of the ideal type we are employing. Accordingly, the different social sciences deal with subject-matter of very different degrees of anonymity and concreteness. This should be obvious enough when we consider that the social sciences include, according to our own concept, such widely separated disciplines as individual biography, jurisprudence, and pure economics. And here we should add that not all the social sciences have as their goal the interpretation of the subjective meaning of products by means of personal ideal types. Some of them are concerned with what we have called course-of-action types. Examples of such social sciences are the history of law, the history of art, and political science. This latter group of disciplines simply takes for granted the lower stages of meaning-establishment and pays no attention to them. Their scientific goal is not to study the process of meaning-establishment but rather the cultural products which are the result of that meaning-establishment. These products are then regarded as meaningful in themselves (*als sinnhafte Erzeugnisse*) and are classified into course-of-action types.

At this point an obvious objection will be raised. It will be pointed out that the existence of the so-called law-constructing (or nomothetic) social sciences contradicts our assertion that all social sciences are type-constructing in nature. These law-constructing social sciences, it will be said, are able to provide us with universally valid knowledge prior to all experience. Let us look closely at these sciences and their attitude toward the subjective and objective meaning of the social world, using as our example pure economics.

The Austrian marginal utility school, the Anglo-American scholars working along similar lines, and the mathematical economists as well all claim to have an exact theoretical science, the principles of which are universally valid for all situations in which economic activity occurs. Among the more recent writers of this orientation, Mises can be regarded as the most significant advocate of the pure *a priori* character of economics. In his treatise 'Soziologie und Geschichte', which we have already quoted repeatedly, he takes up a position opposed to that of Weber on the problem of the contrast between theoretical and historical social science. For Mises economics is only a part of sociology, though, to be sure, the most highly developed part. In his polemic against Weber, Mises asks 'whether the concepts of economics actually have the logical character of ideal types'. His conclusion is:

This question must be answered quite flatly in the negative. In fact, our theoretical concepts 'can be empirically discovered nowhere in reality in their pure conceptual form'. Concepts can never be encountered in reality; they belong not to the realm of reality, but to that of thought. They are the intellectual means with which we seek to grasp reality on the level of thought. But one cannot say of these economic concepts that they are formed 'by the one-sided accentuation of one or more points of view and by the synthesis of a great many diffuse, discrete, more or less present and occasionally absent *concrete individual* phenomena, which are arranged according to those one-sidedly emphasized viewpoints into a unified *analytical* construct (*Gedankenbild*).[10] Rather, they are acquired by means of abstraction, which aims at selecting for conceptualization certain aspects of each of the individual phenomena under consideration.[11]

Max Weber's basic error lies in his misunderstanding of what is meant by saying that the sociological principle is universally valid. The economic principle, the fundamental laws of the formation of rates of exchange, the law of profit, the law of population and all other such propositions are valid always and everywhere when the conditions presupposed by them are present.[12]

No doubt Mises's criticism is valid against Weber's earliest formulations of the concept of ideal type, and it is these to which Mises is here referring. According to this earliest view of Weber's, the ideal types would in principle be applicable only to historical data. They would stand in contrast to the concepts of theoretical sociology derived by abstraction from aspects of *each* of the individual phenomena under consideration. However, the theory of ideal types which I have set forth in the present work—a method which is, in my opinion, already foreshadowed in Weber's later works[13] —is an entirely different one, so far as its deduction is concerned. According to our view, ideal types are constructed by postulating certain motives

[10] Quoted from Weber's 'Die Objektivität sozialwissenschaftlicher und sozial-politischer Erkenntnis', *Gesammelte Aufsätze zur Wissenschaftslehre* (1904), p. 191. [Cf. *Max Weber on the Methodology of the Social Sciences*, trans. and ed. by Edward A. Shils and Henry A. Finch, Glencoe, Ill., 1949, p. 90, from which our translation of the above quotation is taken.]

[11] Mises, 'Soziologie und Geschichte', p. 474.

[12] Ibid., p. 480.

[13] Max Weber's well-known formulation of the concept of ideal type, made in 1904, which he himself calls "sketchy and therefore perhaps partially incorrect' is indeed fragmentary because it has in mind chiefly the ideal type of his theory of history. It must be strongly emphasized that once Weber's thought makes the transition to sociology, the conception of the ideal type itself undergoes a thorough change. Unfortunately, this fact is only hinted at in a few statements in *Wirtschaft und Gesellschaft*, e.g. on p. 10 [E.T., p. 110]. Cf. Walther, 'Max Weber als Soziologe', *Jahrbuch für Soziologie*, ii. 1–65.

as fixed and invariant within the range of variation of the actual self-interpretation in which the Ego interprets its own action as it acts. To be sure, this postulation of certain motives as invariant does refer back to previous 'experience' (*Erfahrung*). But this is not the 'experience' of shallow empiricism. It is rather the immediate prepredicative encounter which we have with any direct object of intuition.[14] The ideal type may, therefore, be derived from many kinds of 'experiences' and by means of more than one kind of constituting process. Both 'empirical' and eidetic ideal types may be constructed. By empirical we mean 'derived from the senses', and by eidetic we mean 'derived from essential insight'.[15] The manner of construction may be abstraction, generalization, or formalization, the principle of meaning-adequacy always, of course, being observed. Our own theory of ideal types, therefore, covers the concepts and propositions of the theoretical social sciences, including those of pure economics. For even the examples cited by Mises—the economic principle, the basic laws of price formation, and so forth—are in our sense ideal types. Of course these principles must be based upon a thoroughgoing formalization and generalization of material that has already been postulated as fixed and invariant. It is this formalization and generalization which give the ideal types universal validity.[16] Such ideal types do not refer to any individual or spatio-temporal collection of individuals. They are statements about anyone's action, about action or behaviour considered as occurring in complete anonymity and without any specification of time or place. They are precisely for that reason lacking in concreteness.[17] Mises[18] is right when he criticizes Weber for interpreting the marginal utility theory in too narrow a fashion, so that it appears to describe an economy run entirely according to the calculations of entrepreneurs. He justly remarks that Weber is here confusing the marginal utility model with that of classical political economy. The latter, he points out, has in mind a more concrete and less anonymous concept of 'economic man'. Modern theoretical economics,[19] on the other hand, starts not from the behaviour

[14] [See the first chapter of Husserl's *Ideas*, tr. W. Boyce Gibson (London: Allen and Unwin, 1931).]

[15] [See ibid., esp. § 3 (E.T., p. 54).]

[16] These two points are merely expressed in a slightly different way by Mises when he says that the theoretical propositions are universally valid *under the stipulated conditions*.

[17] In the sense of our discussion in sect. 39; see above, p. 195. (Not reprinted here. Schutz contrasts the anonymity of the ideal type with the concreteness of the actual individuals with whom we are in interaction. Ed.)

[18] Op. cit., p. 486.

[19] [The reference here is to the marginal utility school emanating from Jevons, Menger, and Bohm-Bawerk.]

of the businessman but from that of the consumer, in other words, from
the behaviour of anyone and everyone. Such behaviour, of course, can
serve as the basis of an ideal type of a higher degree of anonymity. It is
because of this, in turn, that the principles of catallactics possess a higher
degree of generality. Here, as Mises repeatedly emphasizes, is to be found
the basis of the objectivism and objectivity of the propositions of catallactics.[20] But this 'objectivity' of Mises is, therefore, the same as the concept of objectivity we ourselves put forward in our discussion of the objective and subjective contexts of meaning. The law of marginal utility,
then, turns out to be a stipulation that merely marks out the fixed boundaries of the only area within which economic acts can by definition
take place.[21]

In our view, pure economics is a perfect example of an objective meaning-
complex about subjective meaning-complexes, in other words, of an
objective meaning-configuration stipulating the typical and invariant subjective experiences of anyone who acts within an economic framework.
Of course the word 'typical' takes on a special meaning here, as Mises
comes to admit when he emphasizes that an action running contrary to the
'principle of marginal utility' (and therefore in our sense 'atypical') is
inconceivable. But that holds true only so long as one conceives the principle of marginal utility as a definition of the purely formal action as such.
Excluded from such a scheme would have to be any consideration of the
uses to which the 'goods' are to be put after they are acquired.[22] But once
we do turn our attention to the subjective meaning of a real individual person, leaving the anonymous 'anyone' behind, then of course it makes sense
to speak of behaviour that is atypical—atypical in relation to standardized
economic goals. To be sure, such behaviour is irrelevant from the point of
view of economics, and it is in this sense that economic principles are, in
Mises's words, 'not a statement of what usually happens, but of what
necessarily must happen'.[23]

Mises's criticism therefore does not rule out the applicability of ideal
types as such to economic activity. For how could ideal types be excluded
from this area, since all scientific knowledge is essentially ideal-typical in
character? On the contrary, Mises's argument really turns out to be a
defence against the intrusion of ideal types of too great concreteness and

[20] Op. cit., pp. 482, 486.

[21] Cf. Felix Kaufmann, 'Logik und Wirtschaftswissenschaft', *Archiv für Sozial-
wissenschaften*, liv (1925), 614–56, esp. 650.

[22] We need not here pursue the problem of the reduction of the concept 'economic
good' to less anonymous and more concrete psychological concepts. Cf. Mises, op. cit.,
p. 476; also Kaufmann, 'Logik und Wirtschaftswissenschaft', p. 628.

[23] Mises, op. cit., p. 484.

too little anonymity into economics. And with this we must agree. At the same time, we must state that the very objectivity of economic knowledge consists in the ordering of subjective meaning-contexts (such as subjective valuations) into the objective meaning-context of scientific knowledge.

Let us now see how the contrast between objective and subjective meaning exhibits itself in a science that is methodologically of a quite different character, namely, the 'pure jurisprudence' of Hans Kelsen. Here we find our problem cropping up in the following way:

> Is a constitution republican, for instance, merely because it announces itself as such? Is a state federal merely because its constitution calls it such? Since legal acts usually have a verbal form, they can say something about their own meaning. This fact alone betrays an important difference between the subject-matter of jurisprudence, indeed of the *social sciences* as such, and the subject-matter of the natural sicences. We need not fear, for instance, that a stone will ever announce itself to be an animal. On the other hand, one cannot take the declared legal meaning of certain human acts at their face value; to do so is simply to beg the question of whether such declared meaning is really the objective legal meaning. For whether these acts are really legal acts at all, if they are, what their place is in the legal system, what significance they have for other legal acts—all these considerations will depend on the *basic norm* by means of which the scheme that interprets them is produced.[24]

> Jurisprudence must pronounce that certain acts standing at the outer boundary of the legal system are, contrary to their own claim, *invalid acts*. The root of the problem is that the human acts which are the subject-matter of jurisprudence have their own immanent subjective meaning which may or may not coincide with the objective meaning that accrues to them in the legal system to which they belong, *and by the basic norm postulated by the theory governing the system.*[25]

It would be hard to find a more penetrating formulation of the true relation of the social sciences to their subject-matter, which we have defined as the ordering of subjective meaning-contexts within an objective meaning-context. According to Kelsen, the subjective meaning which the individual legal acts have for those enacting or performing them must be ordered within an objective meaning-context by means of what *we* should call ideal-typical constructions on the part of the interpreting science in jurisprudence. The ideal-typical construction that we find in jurisprudence is carried out through formalization and generalization, just as in pure economics. In pure economics the principle of marginal utility is the defining principle of the whole field and presents a highest interpretive scheme which alone makes possible the scientific systematization of the subjective meaning-contexts of individual economic

---

[24] Kelsen, *Allgemeine Staatslehre*, Berlin, 1925, p. 129; italics ours.
[25] Ibid., p. 278.

acts. Correspondingly, in the realm of pure jurisprudence, as Kelsen him-self clearly recognizes, application of a pre-supposed basic norm determines the area of invariance for all those subjective meaning-contexts of legal acts which are relevant for jurisprudence or which, to use technical terminology, bear the mark of positivity.²⁶ In another work Kelsen formu-lates this thought in the following way:

> While positivism means that only that is law which has been created by constitutional procedure, it does not mean that everything which has been thus created is acceptable as law, or that it is acceptable as law in the sense which it attributes to itself. The assumption of a basic norm which establishes a supreme authority for the purpose of law-making is the ultimate presup-position which enables us to consider as 'law' only those materials which have been fashioned by a certain method. The above described interpretation of legal material has actually long been in use by legal science. If it is correct, and if this imputation of an objective meaning is possible (without which there can be no legal science), then it must be the basic norm itself which gives the significance of law to material produced by a certain procedure. It must, moreover, be possible to ascertain from this basic norm which part of the material is valid 'law', and also the objective meaning of the legal material, which actually may conflict with its own subjective meaning. The hypothesis of the basic norm simply expresses the assumptions necessary for legal cognition.²⁷

There is nothing to add to these ideas from the standpoint of the theory being advocated here. Kelsen quite clearly indicates that his basic norm is the principle by which are constructed those ideal-typical schemes which make it possible to interpret subjective meaning-contexts as objective meaning-contexts of law.

In these two examples we have shown how the two most advanced 'theoretical' social sciences—pure economics and jurisprudence—make use of ideal-typical constructs (in our sense) in order to delimit their sub-ject areas and establish an objective context of meaning. What is true for the 'theoretical' social sciences is generally true for all the social sciences.²⁸

²⁶ [Cf. Kelsen, *General Theory of Law and State*, Cambridge, Mass., 1945, pp. 114ff.: 'Law is always positive law and its positivity lies in the fact that it is created and an-nulled by acts of human beings, thus being independent of morality and similar norm systems' (E.T., Anders Wedberg).]
  For a discussion of the concept of 'basic norm' see Felix Kaufmann, 'Juristischer und soziologischer Rechtsbegriff', in the anniversary volume for Hans Kelsen, *Gesellschaft, Staat und Recht: Untersuchungen zur reinen Rechtslehre*, Vienna, 1931, pp. 14–41, esp. pp. 19ff. and 30f.
  ²⁷ Kelsen, 'Die philosophischen Grundlagen der Naturrechtslehre und des Rechtspositivismus', *Philosophische Vorträge der Kantgesellschaft*, Charlottenburg, 1928, pp. 24f. [E.T., 'Natural Law Doctrine and Legal Positivism', by Wolfgang Kraus in Kelsen, *General Theory of Law and the State*.]
  ²⁸ Cf. the discussion in sect. 28. (Not reprinted here. Schutz contrasts 'pure' economic theory with economic history, for instance. Ed.)

Subjective meaning-contexts are comprehended by means of a process in which that which is scientifically relevant in them is separated from that which is irrelevant. This process is made possible by an antecedently given highest interpretive scheme which defines once and for all the nature of the constructs which may be used.

It would require a treatise in itself to define the specific problems of each social science—especially the historical disciplines—and the methods peculiar to each of them and then, on the basis of these determinations, to attempt a classification of the sciences in question. As the principle of classification we should, first of all, put forward the degree of anonymity of the ideal constructs used in each social science, in other words, the fundamental attitude of each science to the subjective meaning-context with which it deals. Furthermore, the social sciences fall into two classes. First, they can be *pure theories of the form* of the social world, which deal with the constitution of social relationships and social patterns, the act-objectives and artifacts in the conscious processes of individuals who live in the social world, meanwhile comprehending all these things by a purely descriptive method. However, the social sciences can also take as their subject-matter the *real-ontological content* of the social world as already constituted and study the relationships and patterns in themselves— the already given historical or social acts and the artifacts as objects independent of the subjective experiences in which they were constituted.

There is still a word to be said about the field and method of interpretive sociology. The primary task of this science is to describe the processes of meaning-establishment and meaning-interpretation as these are carried out by individuals living in the social world. This description can be empirical or eidetic; it can take as its subject-matter the individual or the typical; it can be performed in concrete situations of everyday life or with a high degree of generality. But, over and above this, interpretive sociology approaches such cultural objects and seeks to understand their meaning by applying to them the interpretive schemes thus obtained.

NOTES ON THE CONTRIBUTORS

Alasdair MacIntyre was until recently Professor of Social Philosophy at the University of Essex and is now Professor of the History of Ideas at Brandeis. His publications include *A Short History of Ethics* (1967) and *Against the Self-Images of the Age* (1971).

Martin Hollis is a member of the Department of Philosophy at the University of East Anglia.

George Homans is at Harvard, and was President of the American Sociological Association in 1964. His publications include *The Human Group* (1950), *Social Behaviour* (1961), and *The Nature of Social Science* (1967).

R. P. Dore is Professor of Sociology in the Institute of Development Studies, University of Sussex. Among his publications is *City Life in Japan* (1953).

J. W. N. Watkins is a Professor in the Philosophy Department of the London School of Economics. His *Hobbes's System of Ideas* was published in 1965.

Maurice Mandelbaum is a Professor at Johns Hopkins University, Baltimore, Among his many publications are *The Problem of Historical Knowledge* (1938). and *Philosophy, Science, and Sense Perception* (1964).

Steven Lukes is a Fellow and Tutor in Politics at Balliol College, Oxford.

Ernest Nagel was until recently John Dewey Professor of Philosophy at Columbia University in New York. His major publications are *An Introduction to Logic and Scientific Method* (with M. R. Cohen, 1934), *Principles of the Theory of Probability* (1939), *Logic without Metaphysics* (1956), and *The Structure of Science* (1961).

Charles Taylor is a Professor in the Department of Political Science at McGill University, and a former Fellow of All Souls College, Oxford. His *The Explanation of Behaviour* was published in 1964.

W. G. Runciman is a Fellow of Trinity College, Cambridge. Among his publications are *Social Science and Political Theory* (1963), and *A Critique of Max Weber's Philosophy of Science* (1972).

Alfred Schutz, who died in 1959, was born in Vienna. From 1943 he was Professor of Philosophy and Sociology at the Graduate Faculty of the New School for Social Research in New York. His *The Phenomenology of the Social World* was published in 1967.

BIBLIOGRAPHY

This bibliography makes no attempt to be comprehensive; the best bibliography known to me is in Brodbeck below. Books with useful bibliographies are marked thus *. Generally, I have not listed articles which appear in the anthologies cited below; the *International Encyclopedia of the Social Sciences* (New York: Macmillan, 1968) and the *Encyclopedia of Philosophy* (New York: Macmillan, 1967) contain useful bibliographies with every entry.

Classics

J. S. Mill: *A System of Logic* (London: Longmans, 1961).

E. Durkheim: *The Rules of Sociological Method* (Glencoe, Ill.: The Free Press, 1965).

M. Weber: *The Methodology of the Social Sciences* (New York: Macmillan, 1950).

Anthologies

M. Black (ed.): *The Social Theories of Talcott Parsons* (Englewood Cliffs, N.J.: Prentice-Hall, 1961).

D. Braybrooke (ed.): *Philosophical Problems of Social Science* (New York: Macmillan, 1965) (London: Collier-Macmillan, 1965).

M. Brodbeck (ed.): *Readings in the Philosophy of the Social Sciences** (New York: Macmillan, 1968).

N. Demerath and N. Peterson (eds.): *System, Change and Conflict* (New York: Macmillan, 1967).

W. Dray (ed.): *Philosophical Analysis and History* (New York: Harper and Row, 1966).

D. Emmet and A. MacIntyre (eds.) *Sociological Theory and Philosophical Analysis* (London: Macmillan, 1970).

P. Gardiner (ed.): *Theories of History* (London: Allen and Unwin, 1960).

A. Giddens (ed.): *Sociology and Philosophy* (London: Heinemann, 1973).

I. Lakatos and A. Musgrave (eds.): *Criticism and the Growth of Knowledge* (Cambridge: Cambridge University Press, 1970).

M. Lane (ed.): *Structuralism: A Reader** (London: Jonathan Cape, 1970).

P. Laslett *et al.* (eds.): *Philosophy, Politics and Society*, Series I–IV (Oxford: Blackwell, 1956–72).

M. Natanson (ed.): *Philosophy of the Social Sciences:* A Reader* (New York: Random House, 1953).

P. Nidditch (ed.): *Philosophy of Science** (Oxford: The Clarendon Press, 1968).

J. O'Neill (ed.): *Modes of Individualism and Collectivism** (London: Heinemann, 1973).

B. Wilson (ed.): *Rationality* (Oxford: Blackwell, 1970).

Books

G. Boudon: *The Uses of Structuralism* (London: Heinemann, 1971).

R. Brown: *Explanation in Social Science* (London: Routledge, 1963).

N. Chomsky: *Language and Mind* (New York: Harcourt, Brace & World, 1968).

P. Cohen: *Modern Social Theory* (London: Heinemann, 1968).

R. Collingwood: *The Idea of History* (Oxford: Clarendon Press, 1946).

R. Dahrendorf: *Essays in the Theory of Society* (London: Routledge, 1968).

W. Dray: *Laws and Explanation in History* (Oxford: Clarendon Press, 1957).

D. Easton: *The Political System* (New York: Knopf, 1953).

M. Friedman: *Essays in Positive Economics* (Chicago: Chicago University Press, n.e. 1966).

B. Gallie: *Philosophy and Historical Understanding* (London: Chatto and Windus 1964).

P. Gardiner: *The Nature of Historical Explanation* (Oxford: Clarendon Press, 1952).

E. Gellner: *Thought and Change* (London: Weidenfeld, 1965).

Q. Gibson: *The Logic of Social Enquiry* (London: Routledge, 1960).

L. Goldmann: *The Human Sciences and Philosophy* (London: Jonathan Cape, 1967).

J. Habermas: *Knowledge and Interest* (London: Heinemann, 1972).

R. Harré and P. Secord: *The Explanation of Social Behaviour* (Oxford: Blackwell, 1972).

A. von Hayek: *The Counter Revolution of Science* (Glencoe, Ill.: The Free Press, 1964).

C. Hempel: *Philosophy of Natural Science* (Englewood Cliffs, N.J.: Prentice-Hall, 1966).

——: *Aspects of Scientific Explanation* (Glencoe, Ill.: The Free Press, 1965).

G. Homans: *The Nature of Social Science* (New York: Harcourt, Brace & World, 1967).

W. Isajiw: *Causation and Functionalism in Sociology** (London: Routledge, 1968).

I. Jarvie: *Concepts and Society* (London: Routledge, 1972).

A. Kaplan: *The Conduct of Inquiry*.

T. Koopmans: *Three Essays on the State of Economic Science* (New York: McGraw-Hill, 1957).

T. Kuhn: *The Structure of Scientific Revolutions* (Chicago: Chicago University Press, 2nd ed. 1970).

A. Louch: *Explanation and Human Action* (Blackwell: Oxford, 1967).

A. MacIntyre: *Against the Self-Images of the Age* (New York: Schocken Books; London: Duckworth, 1971).

K. Mannheim: *Ideology and Utopia* (London: Routledge, 1966).

M. Merleau-Ponty: *The Primary of Perception* (Evanston, Ill.: Northwestern University Press, 1964).

S. Nadel: *The Theory of Social Structure* (London: Routledge, 1957).

E. Nagel: *Logic Without Metaphysics* (Glencoe, Ill. The Free Press, 1956)

——: *The Structure of Science* (London: Routledge, 1961).

J. Piaget: *Structuralism* (London: Routledge, 1971).

K. Popper: *The Open Society and Its Enemies* (London: Routledge, n.e. 1962).

——: *The Poverty of Historicism* (London: Routledge, 1960).

J. Rex: *Key Problems of Sociological Theory* (London: Routledge, 1963).

L. Robbins: *An Essay on the Nature and Significance of Economic Science* (London: Macmillan, 1936).

R. Rudner: *Philosophy of Social Science* (Englewood Cliffs, N.J.: Prentice-Hall, 1966).

W. Runciman: *Social Science and Political Theory* (Cambridge: Cambridge University Press, 1969).
——: *Sociology in its Place* (Cambridge: Cambridge University Press, 1970).
A. Ryan: *The Philosophy of the Social Sciences* (London: Macmillan, 1970).
A. Schutz: *Collected Papers*, vols. i–iii (The Hague: Martinus Nidjhoff, 1962–6).
——: *The Phenomenology of the Social World* (Evanston, Ill.: Northwestern University Press; London: Heinemann, 1972).
H. Stretton: *The Political Sciences* (London: Routledge, 1969).
C. Taylor: *The Explanation of Behaviour* (London: Routledge, 1964).
P. Winch: *The Idea of a Social Science* (London: Routledge, 1958).
G. von Wright: *Explanation and Understanding* (London: Routledge, 1971).

Articles
V. Aubert: 'Predictability in Life and in Science', *Inquiry*, v (1961), 131–47.
P. Bourdieu: 'Structuralism and the Theory of Sociological Knowledge', *Social Research*, xxxv (1968), 681–706.
M. Brodbeck, A. Gewirth, R. Rudner: 'Symposium on the Philosophy of the Social Sciences', *Philosophy of Science*, xxi (1954), 140–68.
C. G. Bryant: 'In Defence of Sociology', *British Journal of Sociology*, xxi (1970), 95–107.
P. Diesing: 'Objectivism and Subjectivism in the Social Sciences', *Philosophy of Science*, xxxiii (1966), 124–33.
J. Galtung: 'Notes on the Difference between Social and Physical Science', *Inquiry*, i (1958), 7–34.
E. Gellner: 'Nature and Society in Social Anthropology', *Philosophy of Science* xxx (1963), 236–51.
R. Gruner: 'Understanding in the Social Sciences and in History', *Inquiry*, x (1967), 151–63.
M. Hollis, S. Lukes, J. Torrance: 'Symposium on Rationality', *European Journal of Sociology*, viii (1967), 247–81.
D. Horowitz: 'Social Science or Ideology', *Berkeley Journal of Sociology*, xv (1970), 95–107.
I. C. Jarvie: 'On Theories of Fieldwork and the Scientific Character of Social Anthropology', *Philosophy of Science*, xxxiv (1967), 223–42.
M. Lessnoff: 'Functionalism and Explanation in Social Science', *Sociological Review*, xvii (1969), 323–40.
R. Lichtman: 'Indeterminacy in the Social Sciences', *Inquiry*, x (1967), 139–50.
A. R. Louch: 'The Very Idea of a Social Science', *Inquiry*, vi (1963), 273–86.
R. W. Marris: 'The Logical Adequacy of Homans' Social Theory', *American Sociological Review*, xxxv (1970), 1069–81.
M. Natanson: 'Alfred Schutz on Social Reality and Social Science', *Social Research*, xxxv (1968), 217–44.
M. Natanson: 'Phenomenology and Typification', *Social Research*, xxxvii (1970), 1–22.
J. D. Y. Peel: 'Understanding Alien Belief Systems', *British Journal of Sociology*, xx (1969), 69–84.
C. E. Schutz: 'Significance and Action in Social Science', *Ethics*, lxxiii (1965), 233–46.
S. Silvers: 'On our Knowledge of the Social World', *Inquiry*, x (1967), 96–7.

N. Smart: 'Social Anthropology and the Philosophy of Religion', *Inquiry*, vi (1963), 287–99.

P. G. Winch: 'Understanding a Primitive Society', *American Philosophical Quarterly*, i (1964), 307–24.

INDEX OF NAMES

(not including authors mentioned only in the Bibliography)